Discourse in educational and social research

Conducting Educational Research

Series Editor: Harry Torrance, University of Sussex

This series is aimed at research students in education and those under-taking related professional, vocational and social research. It takes current methodological debates seriously and offers well-informed advice to students on how to respond to such debates. Books in the series review and engage with current methodological issues, while relating such issues to the sorts of decisions that research students have to make when designing, conducting and writing up research. Thus the series both contributes to methodological debate and has a practical orientation by providing students with advice on how to engage with such debate and use particular methods in their work. Series authors are experienced researchers and supervisors. Each book provides students with insights into a different form of educational research, while also providing them with the critical tools and knowledge necessary to make informed judgements about the strengths and weaknesses of different approaches.

Current titles:
Tony Brown and Liz Jones: *Action Research and Postmodernism*
Maggie MacLure: *Discourse in Educational and Social Research*
John Schostak: *Understanding, Designing and Conducting Qualitative Research in Education*
John Schostak: *Interviewing and Representation in Qualitative Research Projects*
Gary Thomas: *Education and Theory – Strangers in Paradigms*
Lyn Yates: *What is Good Educational Research?*

Discourse in educational and social research

Maggie MacLure

Open University Press
Buckingham · Philadelphia

Open University Press
Celtic Court
22 Ballmoor
Buckingham
MK18 1XW

email: enquiries@openup.co.uk
world wide web: www.openup.co.uk

and
325 Chestnut Street
Philadelphia, PA 19106, USA

First Published 2003

A catalogue record of this book is available from the British Library

ISBN   0 335 20190 3 (pb)   0 335 20191 1 (hb)

Library of Congress Cataloging-in-Publication Data

MacLure, Margaret.
     Discourse in educational and social research / Maggie MacLure.
       p. cm. — (Conducting educational research)
     Includes bibliographical references and index.
     ISBN 0–335–20191–1 — ISBN 0–335–20190–3 (pbk.)
        1. Education—Research—Methodology. 2. Social sciences—Research—Methodology. 3. Discourse analysis. I. Title. II. Series.

 LB1028 .M262 2003
 370'.7'2—dc21   2002035474

Typeset by Graphicraft Limited, Hong Kong
Printed in Great Britain by Biddles Ltd, Guildford and King's Lynn

For Martha

Would that it would, would that it could, come clean, this true real. I so badly want that wink of recognition, that complicity with the nature of nature. But the more I want it, the more I realize it's not for me. Nor for you either . . . which leaves us in this silly and often desperate place wanting the impossible so badly that while we believe it's our rightful destiny and so act as accomplices of the real, we also know in our heart of hearts that the way we picture and talk is bound to a dense set of representational gimmicks which, to coin a phrase, have but an arbitrary relationship to the slippery referent easing its way out of graspable sight.

(Michael Taussig 1993: xviii)

Contents

Preface   viii
Acknowledgements   x

 1 Introducing discourse and educational research   1
 2 The discourse of disgust: press engagements in the
    'war' over standard English   22
 3 Interrogating the discourse of home–school relations:
    the case of 'parents' evenings' *(with Barbara Walker)*   48
 4 Taking a text apart: a discourse analysis of a polemical
    article   69
 5 The fabrication of research   80
 6 The threat of writing   105
 7 Fabricating the self: metaphors of method in life-history
    interviews   119
 8 The repulsion of theory: women writing research   133
 9 The sudden laugh from nowhere: mimesis and illusion
    in art and research   149
10 Conclusion: deconstruction and educational research   163

Appendices
 1 Definitions of discourse: a sketchy overview   174
 2 Standard English: chronology of policy events   192
 3 Anatomy of a blaming sequence   193

Notes   195
References   213
Index   226

Preface

Reading instructions

The notion of text is central to this book. The chapters engage with many different kinds of text, often in some detail – newspaper articles, parent–teacher consultations, policy documents, life-history interviews, ethnographic studies, research reports, a child's letter. By picking apart the fabric of these texts, the book tries to show how big and familiar issues of curriculum, opportunity, authority, policy, history, power and point of view are woven into the most mundane fragments of talk and writing. Although the main focus of the book is on educational texts and educational research, the methodological dilemmas and issues that it pursues are of relevance to social science research in general.

It will be clear from the outset that this is not a recipe book. It does not set out to present discourse analysis as a method or a model, with rules and principles that can be 'applied' to educational phenomena, although it provides plenty of examples of what such analysis could look like. It is more concerned with helping readers to grasp, or glimpse, something that is quite elusive – namely, the discursive nature of educational and other social realities. It is very hard to grasp the discursive texture of educational, or any other, worlds. Our usual habits of thought and ways of seeing – as researchers and as 'lay' people – inexorably lead us to look through or past the discourse 'fabric' of events, as if the bigger truths or the harder facts lay somewhere behind. This book tries to interrupt those customary ways of seeing and reading educational phenomena, by insistently focusing on their *textual* status. Sometimes this involves examples from fields that seem very distant from education, such as TV shows, paintings and novels. And although the book is written mainly in a relatively straightforward academic style (or so I hope), there is an element of 'playfulness' that might disconcert readers expecting a more earnest exposition. The first chapter, for instance, plunges straight into a fragment from a short story, rather than doing the more familiar ground-clearing work that introductions usually provide. The rationale for adopting this playful stance is discussed extensively throughout the book; but it is worth stating here that the main reason is to draw attention to research itself as *writing*. For readers who would still prefer a more secure foothold on the approaches to discourse on which the book draws, I provide a summary overview of perspectives and definitions in Appendix 1.

Acknowledgements

I am grateful to the students, teachers and parents who helped to weave the fabric of the research texts that form the material of this book. I also want to thank my friends and colleagues in the Centre for Applied Research in Education at the University of East Anglia for continuing to provide the kind of critical friendship that supports the tricky business of researching and writing. CARE is a 'research community' in the fullest sense, as well as a place to have fun. It would be unreasonable to single out individual people for special mention, with two exceptions: Barbara Walker and May Pettigrew were centrally involved in two of the research projects on which this book draws, and their critical and creative insights are woven into the text. Several of the chapters first came to life in seminars with staff and research students in the School of Education and Professional Development, and as presentations to the CARE Summer Conferences in Applied Social Research, and they have benefited from the lively engagement of the participants. The Social and Economic Research Council provided support for the research on media discourses and on parents' evenings. I am grateful to *The New Statesman* for permission to reproduce the article that forms the topic of Chapter 4. Special thanks are due to Graham Caveney, undisputed champion of the parlour game of 'Spot the Binaries', for all the good discussions, the laughs, the crime fiction and the education in American literature. I hardly know where to begin to thank Harry Torrance, editor *extraordinaire*, for his advice, helpful references and materials, patience (well, mostly) and critical engagement with the ideas that I have struggled with in this book. More than any of that, though, I have to thank Harry for his friendship and companionship, not just on the trips to Amsterdam and Naples, which had a direct influence on Chapter 9, but in life's other avenues and detours. Lastly, I want to express my debt to my family: to my dad, Jimmy Wood, and especially to those remarkable women from three generations who have left their mark on me – my mother, the late Helen Wood, my sister Jan Sturrock, and my daughter Martha MacLure. Martha's lessons in philosophy, parenting, love and research methods are most evident in Chapter 10, but are woven throughout this book, and this life. Thank you, lovely girl.

Introducing discourse and
educational research

> Never does one open the discussion by coming right to the heart of
> the matter. For the heart of the matter is always somewhere else
> than where it is supposed to be.
>
> (Trinh, T. Minh-Ha 1989: 1)

Bear with me...

In one of his comic Creation stories, 'All at One Point', Italo Calvino tells
how the universe was created in a single utterance. His narrator, Qfwfq,
recalls the time before time, when all matter was concentrated in a single
point, and so too were Qfwfq and his neighbours. There was only one
good thing about dwelling in this overcrowded, spaceless point, and that
was the embrace of the motherly Mrs. Ph(i)Nk$_o$. Since everyone inhabited the same single point, they also inhabited one another. This was a
phenomenal embrace.

It all came to an end suddenly, when the affectionate Mrs. Ph(i)Nk$_o$
was moved to speech. This is what she said: 'Oh, if I only had some
room, how I'd like to make some noodles for you boys!' Here's what
happened next:

> And in that moment we all thought of the space that her round
> arms would occupy, moving backward and forward with the rolling
> pin over the dough, her bosom leaning over the great mound of
> flour and eggs which cluttered the wide board while her arms
> kneaded and kneaded, white and shiny with oil up to the elbows;
> we thought of the space that the flour would occupy, and the wheat
> for the flour, and the fields to raise the wheat, and the mountains
> from which the water would flow to irrigate the fields, and the
> grazing lands for the herds of calves that would give their meat for
> the sauce; of the space it would take for the sun to arrive with its
> rays, to ripen the wheat; of the space for the sun to condense from

the clouds of stellar gases and burn; of the quantities of stars and galaxies and galactic masses in flight through space which would be needed to hold suspended every galaxy, every nebula, every sun, every planet, and at the same time we thought of it, this space was inevitably being formed, at the same time that Mrs. Ph(i)Nk$_0$ was uttering those words: '. . . ah, what noodles, boys!' the point that contained her and all of us was expanding in a halo of distance in light-years and light-centuries and billions of light-millennia, and we were being hurled to the four corners of the universe[. . .], and she, dissolved into I don't know what kind of energy-light-heat, she, Mrs. Ph(i)Nk$_0$, she who in the midst of our closed, petty world had been capable of a generous impulse. 'Boys, the noodles I would make for you!', a true outburst of general love, initiating at the same moment the concept of space and, properly speaking, space itself, and time, and universal gravitation, and the gravitating universe, making possible billions and billions of suns, and of planets, and fields of wheat, and Mrs. Ph(i)Nk$_0$, scattered through the continents of the planets, kneading with floury, oil-shiny, generous arms, and she lost at that very moment, and we, mourning her loss.

(Calvino 1994: 46–7)

It's a paradox of course. The 'point' inhabited by Qfwfq and the rest was *already* seething with the seedy vitality of an Italian tenement, in Calvino's description, prior to the Utterance from which the universe issued. There was a cleaning woman, and even some much maligned 'immigrants', even though, as Qfwfq points out, 'neither before nor after existed, nor any place to immigrate from'. Mrs. Ph(i)Nk$_0$ was already emphatically corporeal (she wore an orange dressing gown), well before she spoke the words that invoked her own bodily splendours. And it's hard to imagine the word 'noodles' spoken, before there were things 'out there', or the idea of them, entitled to receive the name. Yet it's equally weird to think of things, later-to-be-called-noodles, existing prior to language – in advance of the complex, verbal cultures within which, and from which, they take their meanings. Most marvellous of all is the economy with which Mrs. Ph(i)Nk$_0$'s magic exclamation itself implies, in so few words, an entire implied relationship – maternal, domestic, sexual, sensual – between her and her adult 'boys'. But then again, how could one utterance ('Boys, the noodles I would make for you!') do this kind of work – of invoking relationship, identity, sensation and belonging – if it did not emerge out of a society that had *already* created those gendered 'subject positions', in Althusser's phrase, for people to occupy, and from which to recognize and desire (and punish and condemn) one another?

This probably appears a long way from the ostensible topic of a book on discourse and educational research. But Calvino's story opens up a space – or so I hope – for engaging with some notions that are going to be central to this book. One of the most important of these is the paradoxical nature of the relationship between language and reality, words and things, in which the prospect of knowing which 'came first', or even of wholly disentangling one from the other, is endlessly frustrated. Another is the peculiar significance of the *space* that language opens. Mrs. Ph(i)Nk$_o$'s utterance puts a distance between her and her boys. Or perhaps it is their mutual desire, rather than Mrs. P's words, that forces the space from which the universe issues.[1] But either way (both ways), the space that opens up is also a space that inexorably *divides* them from one another. Qfwfq's story ends on a note of loss and nostalgia – for that original embrace in which Mrs. P and her boys, self and other, were completely indivisible and wholly present in each other.

Calvino's story tells how the space opened by language is an ambivalent one. It is both productive and disabling. Without distance – or, to use the term coined by Jacques Derrida, without *différance* – there would be no gap across which desire might spark. We would not be able to imagine others as distinct from ourselves or, indeed, to conceive of a unique and individual self. Without that gap, there would be no meaning either – no intervening difference that would allow one word to signify another. Without the spacing that language interposes, it would be impossible to grasp an 'outer' reality of material objects (planets, tables, noodles, floury arms) insulated from our 'inner' subjective world of feelings, imaginings and delusions. No subjects and objects indeed. But this means that difference, distance, absence and separation lie 'at the heart' of meaning, being and reality. We are driven, like Qfwfq, to desire that which we can never wholly attain and, indeed, never existed in a pure and unmediated form. Derrida called this the desire of *presence* – this longing for unmediated access to fundamental things. He noted how it is set in motion by *différance*:

> Without the possibility of différance, the desire of presence as such would not find its breathing-space. That means by the same token that this desire carries in itself the destiny of its nonsatisfaction. Différance produces what it forbids, making possible the very thing that it makes impossible.
>
> (Derrida 1976: 143)

The chapters that follow are, in direct and implicit ways, concerned with these strange but essential spaces and gaps in the foundations of qualitative research. This is not, I hope, as fanciful as it might seem. Many familiar methodological questions, looked at slightly differently, are precisely scenes of worrying away at problematic gaps and spaces – between self and other, theory and practice, rhetoric and reality. Consider, for instance, the pervasive concern in contemporary research about how to represent participants without 'Othering' them – that is, without reinforcing their marginal status and their difference from 'Us'. This concern is intimately connected with anxiety about the space between self and other, researcher and researched, and the desire to dissolve, or at least ethically regulate it (see, for example, Fine 1994). Similarly, the search for self-knowledge or self-realization that animates some forms of action research can be seen as an attempt to recover the 'presence' of the self that lies at the heart of practice. Then there is the gap between language and reality itself, a live methodological issue at a time when politicians and their advisers are castigating researchers for dealing in rhetoric rather than classroom realities, or for failing to write in a 'plain language' that would translate those realities without distortion. The phantasm of a direct engagement with reality haunts research and policy. It stalks all the chapters of this book too.

We are in a very different world, then, from that proposed by common sense or scientific reason, where language merely reflects, or corresponds to, a pre-existing reality. This new(ish) world, which is not one but many, is the product of a 'linguistic turn'[2] that has spread like a virus through the disciplines of the social sciences and the humanities, eating away at the boundaries between them, and unsettling old, humanistic narratives of truth, progress and emancipation. The linguistic turn has insisted that truths are textual; that the way we see the world is 'always already' infected by language.[3] Some speak of a 'crisis of representation'. But whatever you call it, it is aptly summarized in Patti Lather's (1991) comment: 'Whatever "the real" is, it is discursive' (p. 25).

I want this book to show how educational research can engage with the unavoidably discursive nature of educational realities, including those realities that are created by educational research itself. We may be sceptical about the notion of the world being created by a word for pasta. But there are numerous occasions when the constitutive force of language – its power to create that which it seems simply to describe – is there for all to see. Think of how recently minted words such as 'road rage' or 'date rape' conjure acts and sensations that formerly were not speakable.[4] Coming closer to home, or rather to school, we might ask whether the 'Key Stage 1 Child' existed before her naming in the UK National Curriculum framework. Or to take an example from educational research: it could be said that Bernstein's (1971) identification of a 'restricted code' named, and therefore instituted, a new linguistic disability for working-class children to suffer from, in classrooms across Britain in the 1970s and 1980s (see Edwards and Furlong 1978).

As Derek Edwards (1996) puts it, words 'map onto, carve up, bring into being [. . .] categorize and explain the things they describe' (p. 51). It is not surprising, then, that words are routinely disputed, defended, claimed, challenged and dreaded – and not just in law courts, where reality wars are waged over whether an act shall be called murder rather than manslaughter; shoplifting as opposed to absentmindedness. Children learn this at an early age, like the small daughter of a colleague who, when told not to 'torment' a ladybird, replied that she was 'only teasing'.

This book argues the educational importance of getting to grips with the ways in which language is entangled with reality. As Allan Luke (1995) points out, life in the twenty-first century is, if anything, even more of a 'text-saturated' condition than ever. It is worth quoting his remarks at some length, as they help to open up further the 'space' that this book will occupy.

> The 21ˢᵗ century citizen will work in media-, text-, and symbol-saturated environments. For the unemployed, under-employed, and employed alike, a great deal of service and information-based work, consumption, and leisure depends on their capacities to construct, control and manipulate texts and symbols. It should not be surprising, then, that many of the new social conflicts are about representation and subjectivity. In terms of representation, they involve the production and consumption of texts, access to and legal control over texts, and the rights to name, to construe, to depict and to describe. In terms of subjectivity, they involve how one is being named, positioned, desired and described and in which language, texts and terms of reference. These are battles of contracts and billboards, 'infotainment' and cable TV rights, pornographic software and racist slurs, rap lyrics and textbooks, battles over what we call each other and how we present ourselves in face-to-face and electronic encounters, whether in courts of law and legislatures, classrooms and staffrooms, on the internet or on the streets. Fighting words indeed: texts and identities, work and cultures.
>
> (Luke 1995: 5–6)

Discursive literacy

The discursive nature of reality is pretty much an open secret these days, across a broad spectrum of cultural production. From cartoons and TV ads to political commentaries and sociological treatises, one can spot a kind of 'discursive literacy' at work – an understanding of the rhetorical fabric out of which institutions are built. It can be found in *The Simpsons* cartoon series, for instance, where almost every episode contains a parody of some American institution or lifestyle – the family, the law, the shopping mall, schooling, religion. *The Simpsons* also displays a knowingness about its *own* discursive construction. The characters make ironic allusions to the conventions governing their cartoon realities, and watch their own TV cartoon series.

You can also see this kind of discursive flair in press journalism. Consider the following extract from a report of a speech by Tony Blair, leader of the opposition Labour Party, at the time when 'New Labour' was being presented to the British public. Headlined 'New Labour. New nouns. Real words. No verbs', the article included these remarks:

> As so often in a Blair speech, as it progressed, it began to shed verbs. Sentences were reduced to a cluster. Nouns and pronouns. Sentences, verbless.
>
> 'Fairness at work. Practical proposals. In crime, tough on crime, tough on the causes of crime. In Europe, leadership not isolation . . .
>
> [. . .] Smaller classes. Shorter waiting lists. A turning point in British politics. New Labour. New life for Britain'.
>
> For too long the party's energy wasted. On verbs. For the British people, now, no more verbs. Tough on verbs. Tough on the causes of verbs. New Labour. New nouns, adjectives. Real words. Words for a new Britain.
>
> There is a purpose to this. Verbless sentences sound as if they are firm promises [. . .] Yet nothing concrete has been proposed.
>
> (Simon Hoggart, *The Guardian*, 5 July 1996, p. 2)

This is a piece of discourse analysis. The writer has tuned in to the way language is used (in this case, its grammatical and rhetorical structures) to invoke political and moral virtues, and parodied them to comic effect. Or, as Clifford Geertz (1988) puts it more economically, he recognizes that 'the way of saying is the what of saying' (p. 68).

As suggested above, everybody knows this in some sense, on some occasions. We know that one person's freedom fighter is someone else's terrorist. We can spot the spin in politicians' messages, and appreciate or deplore the 'intertextuality' of advertisements that parody one another or mimic the conventions of more 'serious' cultural forms – such as the infamous Benetton clothing ads that played off photo-realist images of famine and disease, or the lager commercial that passes, until its very last moment, as a documentary film about aboriginal bush life. But such complicity between texts and realities is generally held to be some kind of deviation from a more innocent and pure relation between word and world, something practised by politicians, journalists, novelists or script writers, for venal, frivolous or aesthetic purposes, but not to be indulged by more serious or virtuous people. Simon Hoggart's lampoon of Blair's verbless manifesto was provoked precisely by a sense that something had gone *wrong* with the proper relationships between words and deeds, that New Labour's language had become (intentionally) detached from its moorings in reality.

There is still a widespread conviction that serious enterprises such as education, research, science and scholarship are, or should be, free from this kind of entanglement with rhetoric. Research, in the view of many methodologists, should *keep its distance* from those other activities, such as political journalism, literature, cultural studies or advertising, even though it shares a number of rather similar practices. Consider these remarks from Martyn Hammersley, arguing the need to preserve the structural integrity of the 'boat' of ethnography and qualitative research in general:

> There is not just one boat on the high seas but many, and we need to *keep our distance from the others* if we are to avoid collisions. Of course, there is nothing wrong with the humanities, political jour- nalism or imaginative literature and poetry; indeed, we can learn a great deal from them. But they are different from social science.
>
> (Hammersley 1999: 580; my emphasis)

Hammersley is taking issue with arguments, often associated with postmodernism, for a 'blurring of the genres' across the academic dis- ciplines, and between scholarship and more popular forms of cultural production. Hammersley is one among many researchers who are uneasy about any such blurring of genres, and especially of any suggestion that it might be practised rather than policed (for a discussion of the anxiety provoked by postmodernism, see Stronach and MacLure 1997).

I want to show in this book how those boundaries that would keep the 'serious' disciplines, including education and research, at a safe dis- tance from the textual 'play' of polemic or aesthetics, are always open to breaches and incursions. In fact, Hammersley's own plea for 'distance' *exemplifies* the very collision with other genres that he wants to avoid. The figure of the boat is, after all, a familiar metaphor, and seems equally to belong to literature, poetry and polemic. As Derrida (1987) remarked, 'Boats are never far away when one is handling figures of rhetoric' (p. 54).

The discursive and the real, I shall suggest, are always *entangled*.[5] Sometimes, this entanglement is fairly obvious. Education policy makers, for example, often display an ambivalent commitment to reality. Some- times they want reality taken 'straight' – no entanglements with style or artifice as, for instance, when they criticize educational research for its 'jargon' or 'cleverness' (see below). Other times, they show considerable interest in playing with the discursive nature of reality. For instance, the Department for Education and Skills publishes a journal called *Teachers*, which apes the format of popular magazines. The first issue had a *Cosmo-* style cover with a full-page head-shot of an attractive young woman and side-bar headlines (' "I WAS A TEENAGE TRUANT" . . . New strategies for tackling trouble'). There was a letters page entitled 'Dear David' (i.e. Blunkett – then Education Secretary) and a problem page headed 'See Me After Class' (DfEE 1999).[6]

One might question whether this strategy of impersonating popular culture will necessarily succeed in its aim – whether this is to sell education policy to teachers or, as the editorial states, to give them a 'platform' in the policy-making process. Such explicit pastiches are likely to call attention to themselves as impostures and attract derision, rather than cashing in on the allure and vitality of the imitated form.[7] But my point here is that those who most loudly profess their allegiance to the real world also freely deploy their considerable discursive resources for manifestly rhetorical purposes. They have no problems with blurring the boundaries between high and low culture, solemn and serious texts, when it suits them.

Why, then, should educational researchers feel the need to check in their discursive literacy at the door? That is what is often recommended in textbooks or implied in tacit assumptions about good practice. Qualitative research methodology, I will suggest in this book, offers all sorts of incitements *not* to see the texture, the textuality of educational situations and practices. Yet the 'real world with real teachers in real schools' is a violently contested discursive milieu, invested with power, privilege and point of view, as a few examples to be discussed below will begin to demonstrate. Research method generally tries to render down that complexity. Analysis, for instance, often involves looking for the themes or categories that underlie the surface linguistic disorder of the 'data'. Interview technique invites the real person to emerge from behind the false fronts. 'Triangulation' is used to eliminate ambiguity or resolve conflicting meanings. And research writing is expected to keep its distance, as already noted, from the taint of deliberate technique, literary pretension or journalistic leanings.

This book puts the case for (re)mobilizing discursive literacy in educational research. Partly, this is a matter of learning, or choosing, to 'read' educational events and situations as *texts*. As Luke (1995) pointed out (above), life is 'text-saturated': 'every waking moment is caught up in engagement with text of some kind: from children's story to political speech, from television sitcom to casual conversation, from classroom lesson to memorandum' (p. 13). He describes how identities are woven by, and woven into, texts:

> For human subjects, texts are not just something that they, as 'child', 'student', 'teacher', and 'parent', use as part of a stabilized or fixed role or identity; these texts are the actual media and instances through which their socially constructed and contested identity, or subjectivity, is made and remade [. . .] It is through these texts that one learns how to recognize, represent, and 'be', for instance, a 'rapper', a 'learning disabled', a 'loyal American', or, for that matter, a member of 'Generation X'. *Decolonization*
>
> (Luke 1995: 14)

For Luke (1995: 20), one of the main tasks of discourse analysis is to 'disarticulate' the texts of everyday life as a way of 'disrupting common sense' about the naturalness or inevitability of identities, values and concepts, thus showing the workings of power and material interests in the most seemingly innocent of texts. This book shares that view of the disruptive, or interruptive, project of discourse analysis. A discourse-based educational research would set itself the work of taking that which offers itself as common-sensical, obvious, natural, given or unquestionable, and trying to unravel it a bit – to *open it up* to further questioning.

'Us' and 'them': the binary structure of discursive realities

[handwritten margin note: language is not innocent it is value laden]

I want to turn now to some brief examples of what it might mean to unravel, or 'disarticulate', the texts of education and of everyday life. In order to disarticulate, it is necessary of course to be able to spot the ways in which texts are 'articulated' – that is, joined or stitched together. One of the most general and commonplace ways in which this articulation is done is through the setting up of binary oppositions. Some of these oppositions are very deep-seated and enduring in Western culture, and this book will return many times to them: for example, nature/culture; language/reality; mind/body. But there are also familiar, everyday examples. Think, for instance, of the well-known example of the 'freedom fighter' versus the 'terrorist'.[8] Each of these words locates the person it describes within a particular moral universe, and invests them with a particular identity – heroic or villainous. Both might even describe, in different contexts, the 'same' person. The choice of one word rather than the other also invests the speaker or writer with moral or political allegiances. If, in a particular political context, I call a group of people 'freedom fighters', I do not just 'describe' that population; I also display my own political allegiances and identity (i.e. as 'sympathizer').

A press article at the time of the Gulf War satirized this phenomenon in a list of terms used by the British press to describe British and Iraqi soldiers:

Our boys are . . .	Theirs are . . .
Professional	Brainwashed
Lion-hearts	Paper tigers
Cautious	Cowardly
Confident	Desperate
Heroes	Cornered
Dare-devils	Cannon-fodder
Young knights of the skies	Bastards of Baghdad

Loyal	Blindly obedient
Desert rats	Mad dogs
Resolute	Ruthless
Brave	Fanatical

[*The Guardian* (unattributed), 23 January 1991]

This is another example of journalistic discourse analysis. The writer who drew up the list has identified the rhetorical construction, and population, of a moral battlefield. She or he has also grasped the *oppositional* structure on which the alleged moral superiority of the British soldiers is built. Each 'virtue' on the left-hand side is mirrored by a bad opposite on the right. Such 'binary' structures – unfair pairs, we might call them – are a pervasive feature of argumentation and of the making of identity claims. They are everywhere to be found in educational research. Consider this statement from an interview with an educational researcher who is aligning herself and her colleagues with a group of researchers in another university (the 'Wessex' group):

> I mean we have differences with Wessex in terms of methodology, but [there] is a big similarity in that we very much believe in going into schools. It's because we're educators, we're not psychologists. We're not sociologists. Who have a perfectly good methodology but it's not ours. And we are concerned with what's happening in schools.

The researcher sets up an opposition between 'her' group (the 'educators') on the one hand, and the 'psychologists' and the 'sociologists' of education on the other. The educators are distinguished from the others in terms of their commitment to 'what's happening in schools' – a distinction that tacitly charges those others with *not* sharing that concern, and thus carries some moral weight.

Such binary oppositions are one of the key ways in which meaning and knowledge are produced – 'carved out and carved up', as Edwards put it. One 'side' achieves definition – comes to meaning – through its *difference* with respect to a (constructed) 'other' which is always lacking, lesser or derivative in some respect. According to Derrida (1998), this oppositional logic reflects a form of 'metaphysical' thinking that has been practised by Western philosophy from Plato onwards, and which he called 'logocentrism'. Some core principle or concept is established as the superior term – the first, last, deepest, universal, central, purest or most fundamental of all – in a 'violent hierarchy' of meaning: '. . . good before evil, the positive before the negative, the pure before the impure, the simple before the complex, the essential before the accidental, the imitated before the imitation, etc.' (p. 93).

Relations of difference and opposition, and the epistemic 'violence' that they effect, can be found everywhere – from the minutiae of in-group academic skirmishes and the xenophobia of the British press, as noted above, to the fundamentals of philosophy. They are, of course, everywhere to be found in the discourses of education. The next section outlines the workings of this kind of binary logic in the discursive representation of 'the teacher', 'the classroom' and 'the child'.

'The teacher'

Teachers have often found themselves on the 'wrong' side of one discursive opposition or another, in policy and media discourses. From the mid-1970s until the mid-1990s, they were often portrayed, generically, as a constituency who were opposed to the interests of other social groups, and were held up to ridicule in what Ball (1990b) called a 'discourse of derision'. Teachers of English, for instance, were commonly represented as the alien 'Other' with respect to the voices of reason, consensus or common sense, who reputedly wanted children to be taught 'correct' English, which the teachers reputedly did not (see MacLure and Pettigrew 1996: ch. 2). Parents were the group most frequently and passionately depicted as the moral opponents of the teachers.[9]

But there are many different discourses of education, and individuals and groups may end up on different 'sides' in the moral economy of opposition, in different discourses. So, while parents may crudely be said to have been portrayed as the 'goodies' in the policy discourse sketched above, they might find themselves – some of them at least – on the other side of the binary when the discourse shifts to that of parental *responsibility* (for example, for monitoring children's behaviour and making sure they do their homework). And when the discourses of education intersect with those of law and order, parents may even find themselves responsible for crime rates, through their 'failure' to prevent truancy.[10]

Teachers have also, latterly, been implicated in a discursive contrast with educational researchers – generally a constituency of low public visibility, not to mention interest – in an oppositional discourse concerning *relevance*. UK policy makers and their advisers have been much exercised by the claimed failure of educational research to engage with issues of direct relevance to teaching and learning, and thus by its failure to support the work and interests of teachers. Teachers are, therefore, placed on the moral high ground in this particular opposition, with researchers occupying the place of the bad 'Other'. Here, for example, is Chris Woodhead, then Chief Inspector of Schools, writing in the *New Statesman*:

I used to try to read these [academic] journals. Life is too short. There is too much to do in the real world with real teachers in real schools to worry about methodological quarrels or to waste time decoding unintelligible, jargon-ridden prose to reach (if one is lucky) a conclusion that is often so transparently partisan as to be worthless.

(Woodhead 1998: 5)

The Chief Inspector's appeal to the real is a common tactic in the construction of binary arguments about *relevance*, an issue that has a long pedigree as a boundary that constructs educational heroes and villains. The 'discourse of derision' referred to above drew much of its force from the claimed irrelevance of teachers' outmoded views and values. Thus teachers have been constructed as both the enemies and the defenders of relevance.[11]

My point in assembling the oppositions sketched above is not to refute or endorse them, nor even really to engage with them right now.[12] I summon them here to point to the kind of *work* that they do in producing versions of reality. If I were to define a discourse-based approach to educational research (a problematic task, as we will see later), one of the more general things I might say is that you have to *suspend your belief in the innocence of words and the transparency of language as a window on an objectively graspable reality*. We have just seen how 'the teacher' is a site of multiple meanings and differences. And there are many more, contradictory and fragmented, teacher identities that could be mentioned, some of which originate or circulate in the discourses of educational research. For instance, there is the discerning, 'reflective practitioner' of action research (e.g. McKernan 1991) and the nurturing, mothering figure identified by several researchers (e.g. Casey 1990). In stark contrast to these constructions, there is the teacher as drone or technician, implicitly addressed in the training programme for Labour's 'National Literacy Strategy', who must absorb the details of a highly structured programme, delivered by trainers, who, in turn, speak from prepared scripts that instruct them on what to say and when to display the next overhead transparency. Then there are the local, internal differences that teachers make among themselves in forcing a space for the self to inhabit – the dedicated classroom teacher versus the career professional; the scientist versus the arts specialist (Sikes *et al.* 1985); the townie versus the village dweller.

A discourse-oriented educational research would attend to the multiplicity of meanings that attach to (and divide) the people, spaces, objects and furniture that comprise its focus – the teachers, children, classrooms, textbooks, policy documents – and to the passion and the politics that are inevitably woven into those meanings. It would not try to distinguish the 'real' teacher from the rhetorical ones. But it would be immensely interested in how appeals to 'real teachers' and 'real worlds' *work* as rhetorical power-plays that try to install some version of reality by disqualifying others.

'The classroom'

Let's sidle closer to definitions of what a discourse orientation could look like through a few more examples. Take 'the classroom'. Again, common sense or the dictionary may tell us that it has a basic meaning – something like a place where teaching gets done, or a room where classes are held. But just as Mrs. Ph(i)Nk$_0$'s noodles far exceeded their dictionary meaning ('a ribbon-like strip of pasta'), so 'the classroom' may assume a whole range of other meanings for different people in different contexts. For some teachers, it may represent a kind of sacred space or even a sort of home – the locus of their values and the place where they feel most fully 'themselves'. For this teaching head of a first school, the classroom stands in opposition to (and as a rebuke to) 'the office' where he does his administrative work: '. . . because the kids come first. And the – the whole of my ethos, if you like, for running the school is that, er, I don't give a monkey's what goes on in here [i.e. the office] really [. . .] the classroom is the priority, always' (Stronach and MacLure 1997: 43). The classroom, where the kids are, is the warm centre in Jack's account of his professional life (at least at this point, in this version of his life). It gains its pre-eminence – its 'presence', to use Derrida's term – from its opposition to the cold world of 'the office', where Jack feels himself prey to the excessive bureaucratic demands of the local education authority and the policy makers. It is a place of enclosure, to be defended against an alien 'outside' world. For other teachers, however, 'the classroom' could mean a place of enclosure in a negative rather than a positive sense – a site of intellectual stasis, poor promotion prospects, or restricted opportunities to influence educational decision making (see Stronach and MacLure 1997: ch. 7).

The UK Teacher Training Agency (TTA) also represents the classroom as the warm space of teaching, as Figure 1 shows. An early version of the homepage of its internet web-site, aimed at potential recruits to the profession, shows a smiling young woman pointing to a chalkboard while looking down over her shoulder, at what we assume to be her class, although only one 'student' partially intrudes into the frame. This is a very familiar scene. Indeed, it is because its elements and their disposition are so culturally familiar – the standing figure, the chalk handwriting, the spectator – that it is possible effortlessly to 'read' the picture *as* a representation of a teacher in a classroom. Look at the formal similarities between the TTA picture and the pared-down graphic representation of Figure 2, taken from the library of 'Clip Art' signs and symbols provided with a popular home computing software package.

The classroom has a deeply iconic status in popular culture, therefore. Indeed, this traditional configuration of teacher-at-the-front, students massed before her, is not only immediately 'readable', but is also an

Figure 1 Teacher Training Agency (TTA) homepage.

Figure 2 'Teachers & Pupils (BW)', from Clarisworks 'Clip Art'.

enduring symbol of social control and order. The image of the traditional classroom is so powerfully lodged in popular conceptions, and so strongly associated with discipline, authority and learning, that alternative arrangements for teaching and learning often present themselves as alien or threatening (see Ball 1993).

In Bill Green's (1998) words, the 'traditional' classroom is thus a key element in 'the discursive production of the scene of teaching' (p. 175). And it is this image that the TTA chooses for its recruitment web-site. There is a certain irony in the contrast between the chalky nostalgia of the blackboard writing and the sophisticated electronic media that will have led the potential recruit to the homepage. And those two worlds are, in fact, combined in the simulated chalk words, since these conceal/reveal the electronic links to the other pages at the site. In fact, you go 'through' the blackboard in order to get started on your new career.

There is more that could be said about the TTA picture. But I want to get 'back to the classroom', a phrase with some resonance, as we will see shortly. For *parents*, in contrast to the sense of belonging felt by some teachers, and invoked by the TTA, the classroom might mean a place of exclusion: a space which, like prisons or nuclear power stations, they are not supposed to enter except on open nights or guided tours. It might be a prison for children too, though it could work for some as a social club or as a place of refuge from an unsafe home. It could be a place of boredom or, for the lucky ones, a place where interesting or satisfying things are done. The classroom has a special significance within the discourses of progressive education, according to Walkerdine (1988: 272), as the 'environment' that nourishes the developing child.

Inside/outside

These different meanings of 'the classroom' connect to some very general and pervasive dualities that are used to build and defend versions of reality – inside/outside, public/private, core/perhiperal, and so on. But the valency of the terms can flip over as we have seen – the 'inside-ness' of the classroom can be (made to be) positive in one discourse, negative in another. 'Inside/outside' arguments run through the discourses of educational research as well, with the classroom again standing as the 'interior' to be defended or, alternatively, denigrated in relation to the Outside.[13] Here is an academic arguing the strengths of action research as opposed to other kinds of educational research:

> Experience of 'action research' over the last ten years has indicated that teachers make excellent co-researchers, bringing to the research activity a sensitivity of classrooms and of children's development. What is more such practitioners are also able to communicate the outcomes of research to peers in ways which help the community at large feel a sense of ownership of the outcomes. Research outcomes will then not be imposed by clever, out-of-touch outsiders but negotiable with members of their own close community.
>
> (Lewis 1992: 1)

The classroom is the inside – the ground of teachers' 'own close community', a place to which the 'outsiders' do not have full access. This paragraph is read more closely in Chapter 4.

'The classroom' is a curious and amorphous discursive space, therefore – expanding and contracting under the pressures of different discourses that police its boundaries and construct its interiority in disparate ways. Warm, womb-like, nurturing. Overheated, insular, stifling. Or the no-nonsense heartland of education, where (real) teachers teach, children learn and researchers ought to, but don't, research. Moreover, these different discourses of policy, research and practice overlap and infect one another. Like the tortoise and the hedgehog in Kipling's story,[14] they borrow one another's coloration and habits, the better to hide from and prey on one another, ending up as intertextual armadillos and other hybrid creatures, whose messages and meanings are far from clear-cut.

For example, when policy makers, heads of quangos and journalists echo the voices of action researchers and other educationists, urging researchers to focus more on classroom practice and demanding greater involvement of teachers in research, are they all 'saying the same thing'? In some mouths, the exhortation to researchers to get 'back to the classroom' sounds a little like back to the kitchen. Back into the domestic interior where researchers will not presume to question the policy decisions of the big Outside. But then again, it could be argued there has indeed been an evacuation of the classroom by educational research in the UK, especially the (relatively) expensive research that is funded by the research councils; and that it is legitimate to call for a return. Or it could be argued that educational researchers who object to policies that promote the involvement of classroom teachers are defending an outmoded and elitist binary opposition between 'proper' research and practitioner inquiry. The point, here, is that words accumulate different resonances according to the institutions and discourses from which they emanate, and the institutional and social location of those who are making or critiquing them. As Bakhtin (1981) put it, in a much-quoted passage: 'All words have the "taste" of a profession, a genre, a tendency, a party, a particular work, a particular person, a generation, an age group, the day and hour. Each word tastes of the context and contexts in which it has lived its socially charged life' (pp. 293–4). Or, in Janet Maybin's (2001) paraphrase, taken from the mouth of Dennis Potter: ' "The trouble with words is that you don't know whose mouths they have been in" ' (p. 68).

In any event, spaces and places are never 'merely' objective locations, waiting passive and self-contained to be occupied by people and furniture, and scrutinized dispassionately by researchers. They shrink or swell; blow hot and cold. Some places expand hugely, as the result of a malign or disastrous event, to take on an incalculable discursive weight. Dunblane. Lockerbie. Chernobyl. The grassy knoll. The Twin Towers. Hiroshima. Waco. Bhopal. And again, there is a politics in the naming of places.

Michael Shapiro (2001) points out, for instance, that when people refer to 'Latin America', they do not just point to a place on the globe, but 'help reproduce an institutionalized form of dominance, one in which the minority, Hispanic part of populations in the region control the original, indigenous groups' (p. 321). Names of nations and states, writes Shapiro, often 'license a forgetting' of the history of conflict out of which they emerged. This is why territorial resistance often includes repudiation of the name under which people have been obliged to live. Contemporary struggles over the naming of Derry/Londonderry in Northern Ireland, or the reclamation of the Maori name of Aotearoa/New Zealand, testify to the importance of the name in resistance to the officially sanctioned 'forgetting' of history.

As Mrs. Ph(i)Nk$_0$'s tale instructs us, space is implicated in desire, power and identity. Places both express and constrain people's hopes and fears. We can never come to them fresh, see them 'objectively', as they are 'in themselves'. As Derrida (1996) says, 'to relate to an object *as such* means to relate to it as if you were dead' (p. 216). This applies to researchers as much as anyone else. We cannot relate to things as if we were dead. We bring our own hopes, fears and expectations to the places and objects of our research.

'The child'

One of the most significant aspects of the 'linguistic turn' across the disciplines has been the challenge to the idea of an inner or authentic self that exists outside of discourse, or 'prior to language'. When we speak, we may think we are producing meaning – that language is coming out of us, as it were. This is the legacy of the humanistic or Enlightenment worldview that places the rational, thinking subject ('man') at the centre of its narratives of progress and emancipation. But we are also 'born into language', to use Lacan's (1977: 103) phrase. It is through their entry into language that children get their sense of what it is to be a person, of the possibilities of self-hood. And as anthropologists have shown, notions of individuality and of the nature of the self are by no means constant across cultures.

The possibilities for selfhood differ within as well as across cultures. One of the dimensions on which identity is most obviously differentially 'available' is that of gender. Poststructural writers call this phenomenon 'positioning': girls and boys, men and women, are called into differing 'subject positions' within language. The linguist Deborah Cameron (1992) gives a neat example (which I suspect may be apocryphal) concerning a hospital nursery in which the cribs of the newborn babies bore a label reading either 'I'm a boy!' or 'It's a girl!' Thus, she writes, boys were

Thinking   object

unproblematically 'hailed' by the culture as active, 'speaking subjects', while girls were not (pp. 161–2).

The constitution of identities, or subjectivities, is obviously vastly more complex than this example suggests. Our 'identity papers', to borrow Allan Luke's (1995: 22) phrase, are assembled, and continuously updated through talk and text, as part of the mundane business of daily interaction. One of the examples Luke discusses is a mother chatting with her 2-year-old in a restaurant queue: 'We're in a long line, Jason. Aren't we? There are lots of people lined up here, waiting for a drink. Look [pointing] they're carrying a Christmas tree with lots of things on it. They're moving it. Do we have a Christmas tree like that?' (p. 21).

In this unremarkable little monologue, Jason's mother conjures a bit of the world for him. She names it and peoples it; invests actions with purpose and reason; establishes what is normal (including the fact that parents do this kind of naming work and ask questions to which they already know the answer). She invites Jason to consider his place within this world, while also showing him that he can stand 'outside' it to observe and comment on it. Through interactions such as these Jason learns what the world will be for him, and what will be the identity, scope for action and obligations of a person in such a world. His identity papers, says Luke, are 'watermarked' in and through texts like these. The watermark will vary, of course, according to the cultural logic and habits of a child's milieu. Jason's is oriented, writes Luke, 'toward family, toward property, and toward who "does" what kinds of social practices and who owns particular economic commodities. Jason's subjectivity and discursive resources as a young, male Anglo-Australian are being established and negotiated' (Luke 1995: 22).

The formation of the child's identity is not just the 'business' of the family of course. Education is another primary scene for shaping up what it means to be a child. Think of that daily event in nursery and infant classrooms called 'news time' or 'carpet time', when the children sit on the floor at the teacher's feet, while individual students talk about themselves and their recent doings. What does being a 5-year old involve in these encounters? What kinds of experiences is it legitimate, or even possible, to 'have'? The child that is 'hailed' in these events is one who has birthdays, new baby sisters, new clothes, toys, pets, holidays, minor accidents. She also knows how to 'discipline' herself and manage her body – where to sit, when to listen, how to look attentive or surprised. She knows how to be part of a collective under the leadership of the teacher, while still being an individual. The child that is hailed in these events is *not* one who was bored all weekend, got smacked for bad behaviour, is jealous of her baby sister, scared of her dad, doesn't like the way her grandmother smells, wets the bed, likes picking her scabs, gets sad without really knowing why, hates coming to school, and so on. These would not be valid experiences and feelings for this sort of educational scene, though they might be relevant in other settings – talking to the educational psychologist, for instance, or writing a fictional story, or confiding in a friend.

By taking part in regular events such as news-time, as well as curriculum activities such as painting and writing, children learn how to scan their lives and sift out bits that can be produced and recognized as 'experiences'. Experience is not, therefore, something that is natural and self-evident: it is *produced* through discursive practices that constitute children as 'the child' of progressive pedagogy and developmental psychology. As Valerie Walkerdine (1988) writes, '[t]he truth of children is produced in classrooms' (p. 204).

This does not mean that identities are singular, within or outside the classroom. Children and adults are 'subjected' to a variety of different, often conflicting, discourses, with differing criteria of authenticity and truth. The inquisitive, self-actualizing child summoned by progressive pedagogy may not be recognizable in the compliant, dependent learner addressed in textbooks, tests and National Curriculum documents. And neither of these may 'fit' with the identities that children negotiate in their peer groups. Identity is complex, confusing and, above all, an ongoing struggle. Although subjectivities are formed within discourses, people are not simply passive recipients of their 'identity papers'. On the contrary, identity is a constant process of becoming – an endlessly revised accomplishment that depends on very subtle interactional judgements, and is always risky. Children have to do considerable discursive 'work' – even 5-year-olds at news-time – to respond *competently* to the summons to speak 'as' a child. And throughout their school careers, in the classroom and the playground, they will have to negotiate the rapids of the desirable and undesirable identities that can befall children as they are summoned by the different discourses of gender, education, adolescence, sexuality – high achiever, slow reader, Key Stage 3 student, bully, victim, disaffected, disruptive, attention-seeking, common, working class, bottom set, wimp, slag, teacher's pet, cry-baby.

Like 'the teacher' and 'the classroom', 'the child' is a site of discursive power and contestation therefore. A discursive educational research would be attentive to the multiplicity of meanings invested in the child, and would resist reading children as 'natural'. The chapters that follow will continue to interrogate the objects, practices, principles and identities that pass as 'natural' or beyond question in various discourses that connect with education – policy, media, curriculum, and so on. The later chapters will be especially concerned with the discourses of educational research, and with taking apart the assumptions and practices that inform qualitative methodology.

The multiple meanings of 'discourse'

Definitions of discourse are difficult, because the word has very different meanings within different disciplines. *And yet*, there seems to be something that holds across these diverse disciplinary spaces. Not a common core of meaning, to be sure; but a trace, a scent of a notion. Still, as Terry Threadgold (2000) observes, the 'field' of discourse studies is a particularly contested terrain – not so much a field, in fact, as 'a global space of migration and hybridisation' (p. 41).[15] Threadgold sketches the perplexing geography and history of discourse, as it has moved back and forward across the globe over the past century, between Russia, Prague, Paris and the USA, circulating in the names of Saussure, Jakobson, Levi-Strauss, Volosinov, Bakhtin, Kristeva, Foucault. She notes also that, despite this panoply of great names, the field is also marked by 'uncertain authorship and delayed transmission' of ideas (p. 40). It is still not certain, for example, whether Bakhtin and Volosinov were the same person; or, indeed, whether Saussure is the 'same' person for linguists as he is for literary theorists, who find very different, and even incompatible, truths 'in' his writings.[16]

Notions of discourse have now disseminated so widely across the arts and social sciences that they can be found 'inside' almost every discipline, under hybrid names that do not always explicitly advertise their discursive orientation. Fields of inquiry that include a discursive 'grasp' on affairs would include: conversation analysis, ethnomethodology, critical discourse analysis, critical literacy, the ethnography of communication, discursive psychology, pragmatics, deconstruction, interaction sociology, social semiotics, queer theory, critical race theory, postcolonialism, experimental ethnography, poststructuralist feminism, among many others. Threadgold (2000) concludes that what is needed is a 'new kind of geography and a different sort of map' of the field of discourse (p. 41). This book cannot aspire to provide a map; but it will trace a path of sorts, wandering among different theories and approaches in the search for ways of grasping the texture of education, and of educational research, as discourse.

I have refrained here from giving summaries of approaches and paradigms, preferring to sidle up to definitions by way of examples, metaphors and pictures. But for readers who prefer more secure footholds, or a more considered discussion of the intellectual background out of which the book emerges, I include in Appendix 1 a sketch of some possible contours of the contested ground of discourse studies. The approach to discourse adopted in this book is intentionally 'impure'. It moves back and forwards among the foci and priorities of differing discourse traditions, sometimes homing in on the details of specific texts, at other times adopting the more grandiose view that tries to glimpse the movements of culture and history that are insinuated in those texts. The chapters draw promiscuously on insights from conversation analysis, Foucault, critical discourse analysis and various other discourse approaches, although the book is most animated by deconstruction and poststructuralism. The chapters to come also draw on a wide range of disciplines and fields – anthropology, literary theory, art history, surrealist thought. It hardly needs to be said that they fail to do justice to any one of these approaches or fields in terms that would be acceptable to their proponents. The value of such an impure method can only really be judged by reading on, and seeing whether the book succeeds in generating some moments of 'profane illumination', in Walter Benjamin's (1978) memorable phrase, where analysis produces a spark or flash that momentarily disrupts the smooth contours of habit and allows a different kind of engagement with education and with research.

The discourse of disgust: press engagements in the 'war' over standard English

Preamble

> Today, not to understand the structure of a sentence is an overwhelming obstacle in the way of most gainful employment.

Thus wrote Simon Jenkins, a columnist with the *Sunday Times*, in 1988. He was arguing for the teaching of 'standard English' in UK schools – that is, for teaching the 'prestige dialect' associated with educated, middle-class speakers. Standard English was not just essential for getting jobs, Jenkins continued. Shifting from economic futures to glorious pasts, he reminded his readers that standard English (or 'grammar' – the terms were often used interchangeably in the press) was also the key to 'the castle of literature'. He went on to quote Churchill's appreciation of 'the normal structure of the British sentence'. These remarks convey something of the power of standard English to evoke weighty matters: nationhood, social order, literary value, economic prosperity. Such intense appreciation of standard English is often accompanied, as its obverse, by an intense revulsion towards non-standard dialects. Later, I will look at some journalistic expressions of this revulsion. For the moment, I wish simply to point to the huge discursive fuss that the topic of standard English often generates.

This chapter looks at representations in the British press of the standard English issue, as this unfolded as part of the National Curriculum reforms in the UK from the late 1980s to the mid-1990s. The New Curriculum framework specified that all children should be taught to write and speak standard English. This was a controversial proposal, especially as far as the spoken language was concerned, since the long-standing view among teachers of English, and academics, had been one of equal recognition of all dialects. Such tolerance of dialectical diversity, and the refusal to grant superiority to standard English, came under repeated attack by politicians and journalists over the period under study, who dismissed it as one of many aberrations of 'trendy', 'liberal' or 'progressive' thinking. The papers (and the government ministers whose remarks they reported) frequently cast the issue as a *war* – against 'sloppy language', recalcitrant teachers, 'woolly liberals', and so on.[1]

This was a turbulent period in the recent history of education in the UK, and it is important to understand that standard English was one item on a much broader political agenda of reform, at all levels of the education system. The press treatment of the standard English question was in one sense, therefore, part of a specific policy struggle, which took place at a particular time. Yet standard English also *transcends* the specificity of particular times and policy trends. Its hold upon people's imaginations – as a sacred vessel of national identity, an engine of economic expansion, or a kind of societal super-glue – goes back a long way in national and colonial history, as we will see below. The demand for 'proper' English also connects, I argue below, with deeper psychic anxieties about the threat of 'Others'. Standard English is, in other words, a topic with a densely tangled history, in which politics, curriculum, subject knowledge, class, power, race, professional expertise, media interests and psychic investments intertwine. In this chapter, I attempt to unravel a few of these threads. I hope that the effort will be of interest in its own right, as a way of opening up the sclerotic debate about standard English to some new questions, which might, in turn, interrupt the recirculation of prejudice and glib educational 'solutions' that the 'debate' inevitably produces. On a methodological level, I hope to show how analysis of discourse needs to do two, virtually incompatible things. First, it needs to stick close to the details of particular texts (here, newspaper columns), worrying away at the word-y fabric out of which arguments are woven. But, secondly, analysis is also a matter of moving *away* from the details of the specific text – of moving back and forwards through other texts, of other times, to try to glimpse the vastly bigger fabric of intertextual associations within which each particular text is suspended.

The policy context: a summary

The chapter takes a close look at several articles on standard English that appeared in the British press between 1988 and 1995. The first of these dates marks the publication of the first 'Cox Report', which became, in its essentials, the first version of the National Curriculum for English.

The second date marks the publication of the new statutory Order for English, offering a 'slimmed down' curriculum. Between those two dates, various other reviews and versions of the English curriculum were produced. A chronology of the significant policy events is provided in Appendix 2. The analysis concentrates on articles by the star columnists on the papers, since their status as eminent non-specialists helped to 'carry' educational debate to a wide general readership.[2]

Standard English in the 'Cox Report' and its successors

The National Curriculum Working Group on English, chaired by Brian Cox, was set up by Conservative Education Secretary Kenneth Baker in April 1988. Its first report, on primary English, was published in November of that year (DES 1988), and its second, covering the whole of compulsory schooling 5–16, in mid-1989 (DES 1989). The 1988 Report put standard English firmly on the agenda of a National Curriculum, recommending that pupils should be taught to understand and use written standard English. But it was less prescriptive about the spoken form, referring rather vaguely to 'entitlement', 'access' and the need for older pupils to be 'helped to move towards' the spoken standard. Contrary to expectations from some quarters, the report did not prescribe a return to traditional grammar teaching, and it continued to endorse the linguistic/educational orthodoxy which emphasized language diversity.

In the ensuing years, those original pronouncements on standard English were 'tightened', 'sharpened' and 'strengthened' – to use the policy keywords of the times – through the interventions of the politicians (i.e. Baker himself and the four Tory education secretaries who succeeded him), none of whom were ever satisfied that the requirements relating to standard English went far enough.[3] By the time the new English Order appeared in 1995, standard English, both written *and* spoken, figured prominently in the English curriculum. It had also ceased to be an issue of much press interest – but that is an issue to be pursued later.

It is hardly surprising that standard English should have figured on a Conservative education agenda. It has been associated with appeals to tradition, social order and 'cultural nationalism' for several centuries (Crowley 1989, 1996). The press study on which this chapter is based found that standard English was used to invoke both glorious pasts and bright futures, accommodating both neo-conservative appeals to national pride and social order and – as the 'lingua franca' of global commerce – neo-liberal interests in markets, employment and economic competitiveness (see Ball 1990b; MacLure and Pettigrew 1996). Simon Jenkins' remarks above contain traces of both of these appeals.

The issue was also consistently represented, as already noted, as a struggle against the hegemony of a generation of progressive educators and teachers who had made it illegitimate to speak of non-standard dialects as incorrect, socially disadvantageous or intellectually inferior. Educationists were accused of silencing dissent from a supposed majority of parents, employers and the public at large, who purportedly wanted children to be taught to write and speak 'correct' – in other words, 'standard' – English. The debate was thus part of that much wider critique of 'progressive' education referred to in Chapter 1. Standard English became another discursive wedge to force a space between the education professionals on the one hand, and the voices of reason, consensus and common sense on the other. Standard English was thereafter available as a rallying point for opinion on the liberal left as well as the right. While liberal educational opinion had, as noted, tended to emphasize linguistic diversity and respect for children's dialects, and to view the imposition of standard English as a form of cultural imperialism, a new quasi-liberal consensus was forged around notions such as 'equity' and 'entitlement', keywords that were central to the discourses of the 'New Right' from the mid-1980s to the mid-1990s (Ball 1990: 45; Fairclough 1995: ch. 10). Teachers who did not want to teach standard English were characterized as depriving children, often wilfully so, of their cultural and intellectual entitlements.[4]

Press responses: some examples

Press opinion on standard English did not divide along party lines in a clear-cut manner. In fact, there was probably more commonality than difference across the papers over the standard English question, at least among the opinion sections – that is, the leaders and the columnists. The following statements, culled from leaders and columns over the period, suggest the general tenor of the response. It would be difficult, I suggest, to match the excerpts with the papers in which they appeared (the 'answers' are given at the end of the list):

(a) Hence, the traditional indifference (now obscured by educational theorists' cant) to the need to give children the uniquely essential means for social liberation: an ability to speak and write their own language correctly.

(b) The Prince of Wales has the happy knack of articulating the concerns of ordinary people [. . .] This week, Prince Charles directed his passion against standards of written English. He himself had to correct all the letters sent from his office, he said, because English was taught 'so bloody badly'.

(c) And while the ideological arguments rage, common sense will get short shrift. If the need for spoken standard English is not self-evident to – of all people – an English teacher, then is s/he really in the right job?

(d) There is correct English and there is bad English [...] Some educationists may regret that examiners and employers mind about grammar and spelling. They may see such concern as mere pedantry. But bad grammar is a sign of carelessness in the use of language, which denotes a lack of mental discipline in other areas.

(e) Children can be given no finer passport to opportunity than the ability to use the Queen's English correctly.

(f) Standard English is an international language and therefore a passport to a wider world. Those who are not conversant with it will be denied a huge range of opportunities in life.

(g) That is why schools which until recently permitted sloppy and undisciplined speech did their pupils no service [...] The ability to use standard English when appropriate remains a passport to a wider world.

Key: (a) Janet Daley, *Independent*, 4 October 1989; (b) Melanie Phillips, *Guardian*, 30 June 1989; (c) Susan Elkin, *Independent*, 17 October 1994; (d) Leader, *Times*, 22 April 1992; (e) Leader, *Daily Telegraph*, 24 June 1989; (f) Leader, *Daily Mail*, 23 June 1989; (g) Leader, *Independent*, 9 April 1992.[5]

These excerpts contain themes which recurred throughout the opinion sections of the papers over the period: the discrediting of teachers and educationists; the accusation that they had withheld 'opportunity' from children by denying them the chance to learn standard English; the assertion of the superiority and correctness of standard English; the association of non-standard speech with negative moral qualities (indiscipline, carelessness, mental frailty); the lack of reference (or deference) to the counter-arguments of linguistic 'experts'; the use of recurring metaphors (*passport*; *sloppy speech*); the association of 'good' English with the speech habits of the royal family.[6]

The columnists' entry into the policy debate

Let us go back to the publication of the first Cox Report at the end of 1988. Although the columnists approved of the new importance given to standard English, they were, as already noted, hostile to the continued endorsement of language diversity, and the characterization of standard English as a 'prestige dialect' whose grammatical structures were no more correct, proper, pure or good than those of other dialects. This view was roundly dismissed by the columnists, who asserted the correctness, purity and superiority of standard English. Janet Daley called for a return to 'universal correct English', 'correct standards of grammar', 'proper English' and 'real grammar'. She pronounced the teaching of grammar to be a 'force for equality' and rebuked the 'progressives' of the education fraternity for their 'simple failure to understand the sense in which learning grammar is "intellectually broadening"'. Simon Jenkins, in the piece referred to above, referred to standard English as 'complete English'.

The dismissal of dialect

Reciprocally, non-standard English was emphatically condemned as inferior, ungrammatical, slack, sloppy, impenetrable and impoverished. Alan Coren at *The Times* described Cox's examples of non-standard English, such as 'we was' and 'he ain't done it', as 'Standard non-English', and dropped the humorous tone that prevailed through most of his column to confess himself 'unable to see how a child can be taught to appreciate what comes off the page if he is that insensitive to what comes off the tongue'. Some columnists invented their own examples of 'mockney' and cod-dialect. Valerie Grove opened her interview with Brian Cox in the *Sunday Times* with 'Who'd of thunk it?' Melanie Phillips in *The Guardian* embarked on a more extended flight of derisory dialect, imagining the response of the 'dialect-speaking child' to the Report: 'This 'ere standard English what I ain't never learnt's a waste of time because the geezer what sez it's better than what I sez is historically inaccurate and conceptually confused'.

Repeatedly in the coverage of Cox and the subsequent policy documents, journalists quoted or invented examples of dialect to ridicule it. Simply putting it on the page often seemed to be considered enough to demonstrate its insufficiency – as a vehicle for thought, a medium of communication, a bearer of democratic value, a cultural aesthetic or a mode of self-expression. At best, dialect was approved as exotic or quaint. Quoting dialect in this way works as a kind of 'Othering'. It lines the reader up with the writer as spectators of the alien difference of those who are placed on the other side of the boundary that separates the linguistically virtuous from their opposites. Dialect stands for what is deviant, irrational, incomplete, immature, incomprehensible, ridiculous, against the Standard of normality, rationality, stability, clarity, completeness, universality, solemnity.

'I didn't get where I am today . . .'

At the same time, several of the columnists who slurred the speech of non-standard speakers also claimed to have been former members of such disadvantaged constituencies. Coren alluded to his (and Baker's) childhood and the bracing effects of 'a clip round the ear' in correcting dialect errors. Owning up to a dialect-speaking ancestry was one way in which the columnists played the *equality/entitlement* 'card'. It allowed them to claim to speak authentically for the linguistically 'deprived'. Melanie Phillips wrote: 'Those of us whose parents or grandparents were trapped by their dialects, their patois, who mourned the way they were ground down by their inability to use the language to gain some power over their lives, react with bewildered fury to the misguided idealism which insists that dialects and patois are as good as standard English'. Exercising her heightened rhetoric on behalf of 'those of us' whose families spoke dialect and patois, Phillips claims a bond with her readers, and almost manages to insinuate a black as well as a working-class ancestry. Janet Daley used a similar strategy, lining herself up with the huddled mass of American immigrants, without actually claiming to be of recent immigrant stock: 'Much more rigid language teaching' was, she asserts, one of the ways of effecting the 'forceful assimilation' of immigrants into an 'egalitarian society'. 'My own primary schooling in Boston in the 1950s', she wrote, 'was dominated by its strictures on sentence structure and punctuation'. In presenting themselves as former dialect speakers who 'made good', the columnists used themselves as evidence of the emancipatory power of 'correct' English.[7]

Metaphors of linguistic deprivation: prisons and poverty

Recurring metaphors are a handy indicator of the terms on which a debate is being conducted and constructed. *Poverty* and *prisons* were favourite figures of speech in the columnists' arguments about the deprivations of dialect, and the emancipatory power of standard English. Sometimes the two metaphors were linked, as in the headline to Janet Daley's (1989) *Independent* article: 'Locked into Poverty by Poor Language'. An earlier article by Daley in the *Sunday Times*, on the first Cox Report, had also used the prison metaphor: 'The failure to teach proper English reinforces the class system, locking children from uneducated homes into a narrow, self-defeating social prison'. Melanie Phillips wrote in similar vein on the same occasion: 'The anti-elitist passion, translated into a refusal to teach children that there is a correct way to write or speak English, has helped to imprison children inside the ghetto'. The notions of prison and poverty are combined in the figure of the *ghetto*, together with an inflection of racial difference. The ghetto cropped up again in Susan Crosland's piece in the *Sunday Times*: 'Often, the anti-grammarians have also been anti-elitists, so it is sadly ironic that their idealism has in fact pinioned many underprivileged children [. . .] This handicap is not confined to what is usually meant when the British speak of ghettos in this land'. Other verbs of incarceration such as 'locking' and 'condemning' performed similar metaphorical work, as in Valerie Grove's identification of a 'lexical bar' that 'condemns sub-literate children to incomprehension of their lives and emotions'. Janet Daley described a young girl with a provincial accent as 'locked into the social and economic limitations of the milieu in which she was born'.

Impoverished was a word that recurred in connection with non-standard speech (and speakers), as in Valerie Grove's statement that many children's vocabulary was 'dismally impoverished'. One of the subtleties of the use of the word 'impoverished' is that it allows for casual, yet tacitly causal, associations to be made between different _kinds_ of poverty, especially when combined with one of its recurring lexical partners – 'intellectually' or 'culturally'. Thus Daley, in the article that invoked the American 'immigrants', went on to attack 'middle-class guilt' for its reluctance to 'make the hurtful suggestion that working-class life is _intellectually impoverished_' (my emphasis). In this way, a link is established between economic, linguistic and intellectual poverty. A year later, Daley concluded an _Independent_ article with an almost identical rhetorical turn. Substituting 'culturally' for 'intellectually', she castigated the 'muddled patronising reluctance to admit that working-class life was culturally impoverished'. Towards the end of the period, we find Education Secretary Gillian Shephard invoking the impoverishment metaphor at the 1994 Tory Party conference: 'For too long we have been too slack in our treatment of English and we have impoverished our children in the process' (_The Times_, 14 October 1994).

The prison/poverty metaphor was put to work, then, to support a kind of 'tough love' rationale for imposing unpalatable policy decisions. It can be seen as one instance of a much more pervasive rhetorical strategy for effecting 'cultural governance', as Norman Fairclough (2000) suggests, by targeting 'the claimed cultural deficiencies of socially excluded people' (p. 61).[8] Baynham (1995) describes a similar discursive strategy, which he labels 'deficit thinking' – a discourse which inexorably 'colonizes other social domains' (pp. 14–15). This is what we observe here, as the metaphor of 'impoverishment' insinuates itself into economic, cultural and intellectual domains.

The jailers in this rhetoric of prisons and poverty were the deluded 'anti-elitists' of the 1960s: the teachers, 'progressives' and 'woolly liberals', a phrase that ricocheted through press and political discourse at the time (see MacLure and Pettigrew 1996). The prison/poverty metaphor was used to effect a rhetorical _reversal_, therefore, in which the anti-elitists were themselves unmasked as elitists. But the columnists were not alone – or the first – in construing dialect as a prison and the progressives as jailers. The notion had been around from the early 1980s, as reflected in the title of John Honey's (1983) pamphlet, *The Language Trap*. Honey's pamphlet, published by a right-wing educational pressure group, attracted enormous press and policy attention.[9] His virulent attack on linguists and educationists for imposing an 'orthodoxy' of tolerance of language diversity became a key text in the controversy over standard English.

Language for jobs

Prominent among the forms of poverty to which the anti-elitists had condemned children, in the opinion of the columnists, was economic poverty as a result of unemployment. Simon Jenkins, whose remarks opened this chapter, continued his ruminations by wondering 'how many children were reduced to unemployment by not being able to craft a simple sentence'. Janet Daley provided a more extended argument on the theme of exclusion from employment, prompted, she wrote, by a TV documentary on hostels for young homeless people. Slipping into the language of the Victorian anthropologists of the urban poor, Daley notes the 'sparse but well-kept lodgings' in which a 'well-groomed girl' called Jane was filmed doing the washing up. Daley was suspicious about Jane's seeming unemployability:

> Why should this presentable, able-bodied girl who seemed so willing and meticulous in carrying out her chores, find herself in such a hopeless position? Surely London employers were suffering from a desperate shortage of school-leavers? Even without paper qualifications, a well-motivated young girl should be able to find work as a shop assistant, a waitress, an office junior. There had to be some missing piece to Jane's story.
>
> Then she was interviewed. Out of the mouth of this serious, pretty girl came an impenetrable, sub-literate provincial dialect. As it happens, it was Geordie in origin but it might equally well have been Liverpool or Sheffield.
>
> Jane was not without either self-respect or sincerity. She was not even inarticulate in the sense that she could express her own feelings convincingly. She was just very nearly unintelligible and her speech was full of that idiomatic ungrammaticalness which characterises the true dialect speaker. Her 12 years of compulsory schooling had left her exactly where they had found her – locked into the social and economic limitations of the milieu in which she was born.
>
> Who was responsible for this pleasant girl being effectively unemployable? Educational dogmatists who insist that middle class values (and hence speech) must not be foisted on working class children; a society which has never had any real commitment to the idea of education as a key to social mobility; guilt-ridden liberal sentimentality about working class cultural identity.

In these remarks there is the familiar fingering of the educationists as the cause of unemployment, through their failure to help working-class children to escape from the prison of their language. Equally interesting, here, is the mixture of concern and fastidious distaste with which Daley depicts the object of her gaze. She might be describing an orphan in a nineteenth-century charitable institution. Jane is clearly to be considered one of the virtuous, as opposed to the feckless, poor. Her exclusion from the late-twentieth-century equivalent of domestic service is not the result of personal shortcomings, but of her speech. The problem, writes Daley, is that 'out of the mouth of this serious, pretty girl came an impenetrable, sub-literate provincial dialect'. This is a very interesting sentence, coming as it does after three paragraphs of prose that have built up a picture of Jane's moral and physical virtue. In describing the impenetrable dialect as issuing *out of the mouth* of the 'serious, pretty girl', there is a strong implication that the dialect is ugly and disfiguring. Indeed, if asked to complete the sentence 'Out of the mouth of this serious, pretty girl came . . .', we might, given the contextual build-up, have predicted alternatives such as 'a string of obscenities' or even 'a stream of ectoplasm'.

The threat of urban dialects

Daley's article testifies to the fear of others that often lies behind, or alongside, arguments for incorporating them into civil society and making them just like Us. This mixture of fear and philanthropy towards the working classes is an old one, as is the displacement of their threat onto their language and their cultural habits. Tony Crowley (1996) describes the revulsion towards dialects prompted by the rapid rise of an industrial working class, and the resurgence of interest in imposing a standard language. As Crowley notes, the hostility of nineteenth-century reformers and educators was directed specifically at *urban* dialects: 'Urban space was the location of linguistic degradation, particularly amongst the working class' (p. 168). Rural dialects, by contrast, were not stigmatized. Indeed, as Crowley shows, rural speech was often cherished as the repository of the values of a quickly vanishing 'real England'. It is not at all surprising, therefore, to find that Janet Daley's exemplars of 'impenetrable' dialect are those of the big industrial cities: 'Geordie', Liverpool and Sheffield.[10]

Another expression of disgust yoked to philanthropic zeal came from Susan Elkin in the *Independent* in 1994. Elkin's piece was prompted, or licensed, by a speech to the Conservative Party Conference by the Education Secretary Gillian Shephard, attacking 'communication by grunt' and announcing a 'crusade' for better English. The headline positioned Elkin's article firmly within the 'prison' imagery (mixed with the familiar metaphor of 'war'): 'Prisoners of incomprehensible English: Susan Elkin hails the war on sloppy speech, arguing that to succeed one must be understood'. Again, I want to quote at some length from the opening paragraphs.

The grunters, whose mode of speech Mrs Shephard so roundly condemns, swarm noisily past my windows between 11 and half past on Fridays and Saturdays after an evening in the nearby pub. They shout, gurgle and gobble in a largely consonant-free stream of noisy and incomprehensible diphthongs, among which the only recognisable – and oft-repeated – word invariably begins with the letter 'f'.

I suppose that, at some basic transactional level, they understand each other. But what happens when these young people try to communicate beyond their own narrow circle? The usual greeting is 'aw-ia?' That is a corruption of that somewhat banal and inadequate greeting, 'All right?' 'Ssoi-ih' and 'nu'ih, with an upward inflection on the second syllable, are vernacular Kent-speak for 'something' and 'nothing'. And so it goes on.

Last summer I interviewed some young Liverpudlians at an outdoor education centre. One boy told me about his school, or so I thought, but I was understanding very little. I would probably have fared better with a French child, yet this lad and I were meant to be speakers of the same language. Thank goodness for the listening youth leader. He spoke standard English (enhanced by a soft and attractive Cumbrian accent). Realising that I was getting the wrong end of the stick he tactfully interjected: 'Tell Susan where you found the sheep's skull'. It was a nice illustration of the essential value of standard English and why all children need it. Interestingly, my young interviewee seemed to have no difficulty in following me. Our misunderstandings were all one-way. He hears my own brand of neutral standard English quite often on television. Some would argue that his 'version' is as valuable as mine – and in a way they are right. His English, however, is only spoken by a smallish pocket of people in the North-west of England. Mine, like it or not, has a historical and cultural universality.

My standard English is much more than the limited fashionable or liberal view – 'just another dialect' – admits. It enables me to communicate effectively with people all over the world. What a dreadful thing if that boy grows up trapped, locked into his own narrow background, all choice lost to him. In this shrinking cosmopolitan world, that is what will happen to those who can only communicate with their immediate neighbours. They are, and will remain, the prisoners of the cultural and linguistic insularity in which their misguided teachers strand them.

Elkin's article has many of the characteristics that have already been discussed: the claim that standard English is neutral and universal, and dialect slack and sloppy; the attack on liberalism; the prison metaphor, with the 'misguided teachers' as jailers. Like Daley, her target is urban dialect (Liverpool this time). Elkin also displays the romantic appreciation of rural speech noted by Crowley among the nineteenth-century reformers: she approves the 'soft and attractive Cumbrian accent' of the youth leader.

Elkin's article is particularly striking, though, for its mixed messages of concern for working-class youth and fear and loathing of their language. The loathing is more explicit than Daley's. Taking her cue from Education Secretary Shephard's attack on 'communication by grunt', Elkin characterizes the behaviour – linguistic and non-linguistic – of the 'grunters'. The insinuation that dialect speakers are almost sub-human is fairly explicit in the word 'grunters' itself, and is further built up in 'shout, gurgle and gobble'. But in the second paragraph, Elkin's grunters become 'these young people'. This is a shift in 'wording' – that is, the use of a different word with a seemingly similar meaning. Wording is significant because, as we saw in Chapter 1, it is one of the ways in which realities are configured from within particular cultural or discursive perspectives (see Fairclough 1992: 191).[11] It is interesting to trace the wording of young people as it runs through the article. When Elkin replaces 'grunters' with 'these young people', a discourse of social concern starts to seep into the discourse of disgust. Additionally, there is a claim to *scientific* authority, in the attempt to transcribe the sounds of the young people's speech, using a sort of do-it-yourself phonetics or 'journo-linguistics'. The wording changes again in the next paragraph when Elkin describes her encounter with the linguistically poor of Liverpool. Here we get 'boy', 'lad' and 'my young interviewee'. These words seem to invoke a rather 'warmer' posture of authority: perhaps that of a parent, or a 'sentimental sociologist', or a friendly youth worker like the one who translates the lad's dialect into standard English.[12] This paragraph is reminiscent of Daley's stance towards her 'well-groomed girl': the lad is well-intentioned. Lastly, there is the generic 'children' of educational pronouncement. These shifts in wording stitch together the threads of disgust and concern that run through Elkin's article.

The 'economy of exclusion'

Elkin's article, like Daley's, organizes what Crowley (1989: 216) calls an 'economy of exclusion', in which those who are judged to be alien, marginal, 'primitive' or inimical to civil society are also excluded from *language*. Elkin's young interviewee is unequivocally cast as a linguistic alien. Less comprehensible than a French child, he is not really British. Trapped in his narrow background, he is not really a member of the global community either. Most striking of all is the insinuation, already noted, of exclusion from humanity itself, in the description of the noises made by the 'grunters'. Compare Elkin's description of the grunters with this description of an inarticulate urban mob, written in 1902: 'They drifted through the streets hoarsely cheering, breaking into fatuous irritating laughter, singing quaint militant melodies [. . .] Later the drink got into them, and they reeled and struck, and swore, walking and leaping and blaspheming God' (Masterman 1902, quoted in Crowley 1989: 217).

The working-class 'barbarians', Masterman also wrote, 'never reach that level of ordered articulate utterance; never attain a language that the world beyond can hear'. Note the similarity with Elkin's observations: the drunkenness, the swearing, the noise, the disorderly movement through the street. And above all the assertion that the working class have no recognizable language. This, says Crowley (1996), was a 'key trope' at that time. Using Bakhtin's concepts, Crowley relates the dehumanizing of working-class speech to the 'centripetalizing' tendencies of society, which seek to maintain social order and unity through the imposition of a unitary language ('monologism') on the unruly 'heteroglossia' (i.e. multivoicedness) of speech. Crowley identifies an 'organisation of discourse' in accounts such as Masterman's in which working-class is always found to be inarticulate:

> [. . .] they speak, but not in a language which is socially acceptable, or understood. They are not so much silent as silenced. The forces of monologism in the social order, which take standard spoken English, the language of the educated, to be 'proper English', have the effect of silencing the working class in this particular historical context.
>
> (Crowley 1996: 176)

As Crowley notes, the silencing effects of monoglossia are also everywhere evident in the history and experience of colonialism, where the language of the colonized subjects is routinely deemed inarticulate, primitive or sub-human by the colonialists. Jill Lepore (2001) discusses one particular example: the 'grim tale of linguistic racism' perpetrated upon the North American Indians over the centuries, in colonialist descriptions of their speech. She describes seventeenth-century colonial observers, for instance, as 'almost universally disdainful of Indian speech', considering it to be 'barbaric, gutteral, grating, ridiculous, impossible to learn, and possibly satanic' (p. 98). The columnists who betrayed such revulsion towards working-class dialects in the early 1990s were deploying very old tropes of linguistic exclusion for their particular contemporary purposes.

A discourse of disgust

One final example shows particularly clearly how revulsion towards the language of urban dialect speakers is ultimately indistinguishable from revulsion towards the speakers themselves. It comes from another article by Simon Jenkins, which appeared 2 days after Gillian Shephard's 'grunt' speech to the Tory Party conference (and 2 days before Elkin's article). Jenkins does not mention Shephard, but the target of his revulsion was also the first-mentioned target of Shephard's 'crusade': the novelist James Kelman, who had just won the Booker prize for his novel, *How Late It Was, How Late* (1995), about a drunken low-lifer in Glasgow, written in dialect. Jenkins declared war: 'If it comes to war my English will win as long as Mr Kelman and the Booker judges are in the enemy camp'. His attack on Kelman's book begins with a reminiscence about an encounter with a 'real' Glaswegian:

> I once found myself alone in a no-smoking compartment of a corridor train to Glasgow. An ambassador for that city lurched into the compartment and crashed down opposite me. He took out a bottle of cider, rolled himself a cigarette, leant across to me and belched, 'Ye git a light, Jimmy'? For almost an hour I humoured him, chided him, remonstrated with him, fearful for the safety of the Indian conductor who I knew was coming down the train (and who wisely passed us by). My reeking companion demanded attention like a two-year old. He told me his so-called life story, requested money with menaces, swore and eventually relieved himself into the seat. Reading Mr Kelman's book was a similar experience.[13]
>
> (*The Times*, 12 October 1994)

Like Elkin's grunters, Jenkins' Glaswegian is unwelcome, drunk, noisy and profane. Jenkins goes on to deride the expletive-ridden first-person narrative of Kelman's fictional hero, Sammy, and then imagines the Booker judges 'tittering in the corner' of his railway carriage in admiration of Kelman as he 'gobs on the floor'. Jenkins thus unites Kelman's fictional hero, the putatively real Glaswegian, the Booker judges and Kelman himself as objects of linguistic derision and physical revulsion.

The articles discussed above reflect and promote a view of non-standard speakers as so deeply 'Other' that they are, at best, exotic; and, at worst, barely human.[14] One characteristic which they all share – perhaps so obvious as to be in danger of being overlooked – is their concentration on the *sound* of non-standard speech. It is difficult to avoid the suspicion that a particular offence of non-standard English is the way it sounds. As we have seen, the columnists often attempted their own phonetic transcriptions to convey the alien sound of dialect – sometimes even suggesting phonetic deviance where none exists. Melanie

Phillips' invented response of the dialect-speaking child to the Cox Report, quoted above, transcribes 'says' as 'sez'. This is a rough approximation to the way that many speakers, standard or not, would pronounce the word; but the unorthodox spelling makes it *look* deviant. This is the 'Li'l Abner Syndrome', used by novelists and journalists for comic effect. Deborah Cameron (2001) notes that those who are mocked are 'usually working class and/or provincial' (p. 41).

Then there is the association of the sound of non-standard speech with *noise* – that is, with sound that is non-linguistic and, by extension, less than human. The threat that dialect speakers represent – whether to law and order, cultural heritage or economic recovery – is *embodied* in the physicality and materiality of the noises they purportedly make. Daley recoiled from the 'sub-literate' dialect which came 'out of the mouth' of the serious, pretty girl. Elkins wrote of grunting, gurgling and gobbling – words which might describe the noises of animals or base bodily functions. Jenkins' language is similarly visceral: his Glaswegian reeks, urinates, gobs and belches. Indeed, he belches in (or even as) the act of uttering. Urban speech is apprehended by these columnists in terms of the meaningless noises of animals, or the involuntary rumblings and gross emissions of internal organs. This is the 'economy of exclusion' at its most extreme. It replays the denial of humanity to 'foreign' enemies that has been a feature of colonial aggression over the centuries.[15]

Accentuating accent

In their concentration on the sound of non-standard dialects, the columnists (and at least one education secretary) were foregrounding an aspect of language that had been downplayed in the Cox Reports and the succeeding English curriculum documents: namely, *accent*. Accent has always been, and to some extent remains, the forbidden issue for late-twentieth-century language reformers. The Cox Report insisted that standard English was a matter of syntax and vocabulary and could be spoken with any accent: to criticize accent would be an assault on cultural and class sensibilities. This 'line' held throughout the succeeding curriculum revisions. In ventilating their disgusted concern about accent, the columnists were therefore pushing at the limits of what was 'sayable' within the discourses of education.

It might appear that this is a clear instance of the press attempting to intervene in the English curriculum against the better judgement of the educational 'experts' on the working parties.[16] And it is certainly clear that the press and the politicians were often united against that perceived orthodoxy – that is, that accent was beyond the remit of curriculum reform. But the issue is not clear-cut. The curriculum documents themselves betray a certain ambivalence. Alongside the routine exemption of accent from the ambit of policy, it is possible to glimpse a covert assault, in the recurrent strictures about *clarity, diction* and *intonation* that have been a feature of the standard English specifications from Cox onwards. The 1993 review, for instance, stated: 'Spoken standard English can be expressed in a variety of regional and social accents. The requirement to speak standard English does not undermine the integrity of either regional accents or dialects although *clear diction* is important to enhance communication' (DfE 1993: 9; my emphasis). In the Dearing proposals of the following year, the emphasis on clarity and diction was rather more blunt: 'Pupils may speak in different accents, but they should be taught to speak with clear diction and pronunciation and appropriate intonation' (SCAA 1994: 3). This inexorable demand for 'clear diction' seems tacitly to encompass accent, if not to be a euphemism for it. In both of the quoted documents, the yoking together of accent and 'clear diction' in a single sentence strongly insinuates that there are problems of comprehensibility associated with non-standard accents.

The rage for 'clarity' is never an innocent or neutral matter, as the history of colonialism shows, with its imposition of European languages in the interest of administrative, economic and cultural transparency. The demand that the less powerful, or the less favoured, render themselves intelligible in the language of the dominant culture is always an exercise of power (see Scheurich 2000; Chapter 5). The columnists' demand for clarity may have been expressed in decidedly more visceral terms than those of the curriculum designers. But it could be argued that the columnists were exploiting a view that was already 'there', in some sense, in the curriculum documents. Some critics of the English curriculum reforms detected an ambivalence towards non-standard speech right from the start. Norman Fairclough (1995), for instance, detected residual traces of 'a tradition of prescriptive bigotry towards non-standard varieties' in the Cox Report, in a comment to the effect that these might be more widely '*tolerated*' in the spoken form (p. 237).

The voices of the press, politicians and curriculum writers were more intricately entangled on the issue of spoken dialect, therefore, than the two-sided metaphor of war against the 'progressives' allows. In fact, the denial of language to certain groups has a history within expert and academic discourses of education. For instance, the conviction that children from working-class homes start school 'without any language' has often been expressed by early years school teachers. An educationally legitimized version of that conviction circulated widely during the 1970s, when Basil Bernstein's (1971) class-based analysis of language in terms of 'restricted' and 'elaborated' codes was appropriated as evidence of the impoverishment of working-class speech (see Edwards and

Furlong 1978). Empirical research such as that of Joan Tough (1977), which seemed to show class-based differences in children's language and cognitive development, had a marked impact on teacher education programmes. It matters very little that Bernstein distanced himself from such 'deficit' views of working-class language, or that the training college lecturers and researchers who reported class-based language differences never actually articulated the extreme view that working-class children had 'no language'. What is important is that the academic and professional debate over class-based language difference was available as another *resource* in the recurring controversy over varieties of language.

Standard English in the context of the 'New Right' critique of education

The pungent mixture of concern and revulsion displayed by the newspaper columnists towards non-standard speech is one manifestation therefore of a pervasive and persistent discursive economy of exclusion. Each manifestation of this economy of exclusion carries, and reactivates, complex histories of fear (of social change) and desire (for social order). But each manifestation is also triggered by the specifics of its particular time and place of occurrence. In the case of the language 'wars' with which we have been concerned – that is, the English curriculum reforms of the mid-1980s to 1990s – the context was one of sustained critique of the so-called 'progressive' educational values of the 1960s. Standard English was only one of a number of controversial topics within the English curriculum. Other topics, or targets, included the teaching of 'grammar', the restoration of 'phonics' in reading instruction and the reassertion of a literary 'canon' of exemplary texts. The attack on the English curriculum was, according to many commentators, one element of an even broader critique by the 'New Right' of comprehensive education and the post-war education settlement. Seen from this viewpoint, the English curriculum was only one theatre of war on a very broad educational front. Other arenas included student-centred learning, with its associated pedagogies of group work and student-led participation; 'mixed-ability' teaching; the history curriculum; the alleged 'political motivation' of teachers (almost always urban teachers); the denial of 'choice' to parents; and the power (allegedly excessive or malign) of local government.[17]

The particular significance of English as a subject, within this wider New Right critique, was, according to Bill Green (1998), linked to a loss of faith in the symbolic figure of the Teacher as the embodiment of authority and social stability. The progressive reforms of the 'always mythic 1960s', in Green's words, may have been relatively short-lived and seldom fully embraced. But they were widely feared to have corroded the bonds of discipline and respect that held together classrooms and, prospectively, society as a whole. English teaching, above all other subjects, is liable to bear this special symbolic freight, according to Green, because of its direct link to the emergence of mass compulsory education from the nineteenth-century onwards. Green, like Crowley (1996), stresses the association of English teaching with the emergence of *urban* schooling, especially in literacy, for a newly industrialized society (see also Goodson and Medway 1990). English teaching, therefore, has always been linked in special ways to the development of capitalism and is always likely to be a site of special interest for state intervention and public apprehension.[18]

As Green notes, English teachers have not only been held responsible for the safe management of urban culture: they are repeatedly found to have *failed*. Green suggests that the failure of English teachers is a 'necessary' failure, which, 'paradoxically, induces a more extensive examination of the need for urban schooling' (D. Jones, quoted in Green 1998: 197). English teachers are always liable to be found in need of 'disciplining'; and the debate about literacy is 'always renewable' (p. 197). The state of English teaching – not just in Britain but globally – is thus permanently available for a 'crisis' reading (p. 173). Viewed from this angle, concern about English teaching is one among many resources that statist or centralizing discourses may mobilize to discipline teachers. English teaching provides, likewise, one arena among many for governments to parade their vigilance about 'standards', economic competitiveness or social order. Ian Stronach (1999) suggests that the contemporary mode in which educational policy discourses are conducted is that of the global *spectacle*, a kind of Olympic Games in which nations enact 'a fantasy of educational and economic efficiency' (p. 184). Stronach argues that these Olympic spectacles work to install the idea of competition itself as 'morally unassailable', in the interests of the 'underlying game' of global capitalism.

So the argument about school English is not, and never was, just 'about' English. And it is never just the business of educational or linguistic professionals. Each time a skirmish breaks out, there is always more at stake than the local victory of one particular theory, educational ethos, or set of prejudices, over another. To understand what might have been at stake in the interventions of the columnists in the standard English debates of the 1980s and early 1990s, it has been necessary to read back and forwards in time and space, trying to unravel (or to connect, which is the same thing) the threads that tie the specifics of each article to other historical, political and educational domains. It has also been necessary to grasp the symbolic significance of standard English within wider discourses of nationhood or global economic competition.

Bodily eruptions

Still, after all these detours through the dry terrain of curriculum, politics and history, I am still fascinated by the wet patches, where the columnists' disgust at non-standard speech seeped or spurted out in metaphors of bodily emissions. I want to return to the visceral nature of their repulsion – their apprehension of dialect speech in terms of vile stuff that comes out of bodily orifices. In this language of intestinal revulsion, sub-literate dialect shocks as it issues 'out of the mouth', incomprehensible diphthongs discharge in a 'stream', and speech is figured as the sound of the internal organs processing their waste – as grunt, gobble, gurgle or belch. Or even as the waste itself – as piss, reek, gob.

I want to suggest that the columnists, in their fascination with the gross physicality of dialect speech, are registering something that has largely been overlooked (or repressed) by linguists, liberal educators and theorists of culture alike. Namely, the materiality of speech, and its intimate and fraught relation to the *body*. Speech does actually come from our 'insides', after all. It has an intimate, if problematic, link to our fleshy bodies. Zali Gurevitch (1999) reminds us of the double meaning of *tongue*, as both a part of the body and a word for language itself. The tongue is the place where the impossible reconciliation between 'dumb matter' and the symbolic order (i.e. language) is played out, and it is no wonder, says Gurevitch, that the tongue sometimes stumbles, stutters and reveals its inability to measure up to this task.

But linguistics, and the other social sciences that deal with language and culture, have tended to ignore the fleshy connections of language and the untidy, one-off contingencies of 'performance'. Cate Poynton notes that mainstream linguistics has always operated with a disembodied and idealist notion of speech. The spoken language that is analysed (and therefore produced) by linguists is a stablized, idealized, written-down kind of speech.[19] Fixed in transcriptions which lend it 'an illusory completeness and finality', speech is dislocated from the materiality and specificity of performance, and stripped of 'its rhythms, its tunes, its vocality, its timbres, its voice qualities' (Poynton 2000: 25). The suppression of the material aspects of language is not only done by theorists. It is also evident in the liberal educational position on standard English, which says, in effect, 'pay attention to the incorporeal aspects of dialect – the grammar and the vocabulary – and ignore accent'. But the long history of linguistic vilification that I have sketched in this chapter suggests that the physical and bodily impacts of accents are not easily set aside. The columnists' disgust, and the more fastidious distaste congealed in the policy-speak of 'clarity' and 'diction', are only late manifestations of a widespread hostility to the speech habits of others.

An unfamiliar dialect has the power to disturb because it directs attention to something about language that speakers usually manage to forget (just like the linguists and the liberal educators): that this strange flow of noise and breath, stirred up by the tongue's moist and meaty tissue, is the frail lodging for meaning and truth. Gurevitch notes that there are occasions when words become emptied of their meaning, and we become hyper-aware of the weird noises and gestures in themselves. This is disconcerting.

> [T]he performing aspect [of speech] . . . 'monkeys' us, brings us back to the tongue, the wagging tail/tale, the talking hands, the grimaces of the face, the 'primitive' postures of the dance. For a moment, the balloons that flower or burst from the mouths of comic figures are seen not for what's written in them (even bodily noises as grunting, snoring, hissing, etc.) but for their own blown figures – the blowing of speech.
>
> (Gurevitch 1999: 535)[20]

One reading, therefore, of the columnists' repulsion would be as a displacement onto others of the distressing recognition that speech has its animalistic, bodily dimension, and that this unreliable, disgusting flesh is the carrier of those incorporeal fundamentals cherished by Enlightenment thought – ideas, values, concepts, and so on.

Abject bodies

The displacement is not random or innocent, though. As we have seen, it is directed to particular kinds of others and is, therefore, hegemonic – that is, it proclaims the beliefs and, indeed, the subjectivity of a dominant group as the only true or valid ones, precisely by excluding certain others as beyond reason or humanity. Judith Butler has argued that such 'exclusionary' practices are central to the ways in which bodies are 'materialized', and subjects produced, in discourse. Focusing on the production and regulation of sexuality, Butler (1993) argues that (heterosexual) subjects are produced through the creation of 'abject beings, those who are not yet "subjects", but who form the constitutive outside to the domain of the subject' (p. 3). The 'abject', says Butler, designates an 'uninhabitable zone' of social life, populated by those whose bodies are perceived to be lacking or deficient. She describes the abject as 'that site of dreaded identification against which – and by virtue of which – the domain of the subject will circumscribe its own claim to autonomy and to life' (ibid.). This is how 'bodies that matter' (the title of Butler's book) are material-ized.

It is not hard to read dialect as just such a 'site of dreaded identification', where the subjectivity of the columnists (their 'claim to autonomy and to life') is maintained at the expense of the abjected, brutish 'sub-literates', whose deficient bodies and speech form the 'constitutive outside'. Simon Jenkins rather neatly, if unintentionally, summed up the oppositional dynamic by which his own subjectivity (presumably cerebral, urbane, continent, coherent) *depended* on that of Kelman's incontinent, incoherent Scotsman: 'If it comes to war my English will win as long as Mr Kelman and the Booker judges are in the enemy camp'. As Vicky Kirby (1997) argues, in her extended discussion of the entanglements of language and bodies, 'word and flesh are utterly implicated' (p. 127). The failure to acknowledge, and find some way to deal with, that bodily implication (folded-in-ness) of speech sustains homophobia, racism, sexism and class antagonism.

Julia Kristeva's (1982) treatment of abjection has, perhaps, even more resonance than Butler's in helping to understand the peculiarly nauseous character of the columnists' response to dialect, since for Kristeva, abjection is directly and intimately associated with bodily waste and defilement. Kristeva, like Butler, understands abjection as a mechanism for maintaining 'proper' subjectivity in the face of the threat of disorder, dissolution or ambiguity, by violently expelling to the 'outside' that which cannot be assimilated. Kristeva draws on Mary Douglas' (1970) anthropological work on purification rites as devices for patrolling the boundaries of the social. Abjection, says Kristeva (1982), is a 'demarcating imperative' (p. 68) activated by our need to separate clean from unclean, inside from outside, in order to maintain the integrity of 'the self's clean and proper body' (p. 72). Kristeva quotes Douglas' lucid description of the significance of bodily filth as 'marginal stuff': 'Matter issuing from them [the orifices of the body] is marginal stuff of the most obvious kind. Spittle, blood, milk, urine, faeces or tears by simply issuing forth have traversed the boundary of the body' (Kristeva 1982: 69).

Bodily waste distresses because it blurs the boundary between inside and outside that keeps the self intact. For Kristeva (1982), the primary scene of abjection is psychoanalytic. It is lodged within the 'deep psycho-symbolic economy' of the speaking subject and is, therefore, universal, although it assumes particular socio-historical manifestations in different times and places (p. 68). Filth ultimately threatens the 'symbolic order', which for Kristeva is that 'device of discriminations, of differences' (p. 69) that organizes life at both the individual and social levels. The symbolic order holds chaos at bay through its disciplinary machinery of hierarchies, categories and recurrence. Language is pre-eminently the vehicle of the symbolic order, with its structures, levels and taxonomies, and is associated in psychoanalytic theorizing with the masculine principle of the Law – 'the legal, phallic, linguistic symbolic establishment', as Kristeva puts it (p. 72). But she argues that, in addition to the paternal authority imposed on the child through language, there is also *maternal* authority – the 'frustrations and prohibitions' imposed on the child in the mother's mapping of his or her body as 'a *territory* having areas, orifices, points and lines, surfaces and hollows, where the archaic power of mastery and neglect, of the differentiation of proper-clean and improper-dirty, possible and impossible is impressed and exerted' (p. 72; original emphasis).

'Maternal authority', writes Kristeva (1982), 'is the trustee of that mapping of the self's clean and proper body' (p. 72). Corporeal waste, in its endlessly repeated separation from the body, signifies the state of 'permanent loss' that is the price of maintaining a clean and proper body (p. 108). In short, bodily waste stands for that which lies outside the symbolic order and frustrates (yet facilitates) its restless policing of the boundary between inside and outside. Non-standard dialect, as stuff that issues from the entrails, performs a similar function for the columnists – shoring up their self-certainty as custodians of the language of order and civilization.

Abjection is a site where the social and the psychic are folded together – that is, implicated. Boundary-maintaining practices that operate at a 'big', societal level – such as the imposition of a standard language – link 'back' to traumatic events in the formation of individual subjects. The 'deep psycho-symbolic economy' of abjection helps to explain, then, why defence of the social boundaries patrolled by standard language often takes such a gut-wrenching character. And, above all, why the discourse of disgust at the speech habits of marginalized groups *recurs*.

Ending

What can we make of all this? Looking back over the chapter, the main methodological point that I hope will have emerged is that analysing texts involves much more than attending to whatever is 'in' those texts. I have tried to challenge the idea of the text as something with clear boundaries that safely contain the meaning that lies 'inside'. In fact, it becomes rather unclear 'where' (or when) a text's meaning is located. It might be more helpful to envisage analysis as a process of constant shuttling back and forth *between* different domains: between specific dates and longer historical stretches; between close focus on the words on the page and other social and cultural texts; between different theoretical vantage points. The point, then, is not to get the text to lay bare its meanings (or its prejudices), but to trace some of the threads that connect that text to others. Analysis, in this sense, is simultaneously a kind of unravelling of densely knotted threads and a new weaving of further threads, since a new text is created too. Derrida points out that the words 'text' and 'textile' have the same derivation, and he cautions against delusions of mastery in textual criticism:

> There is always a surprise in store for the anatomy or physiology of any criticism that might think it had mastered the game, surveyed all the threads at once, deluding itself, too, in wanting to look at the text without touching it, without laying a hand on the 'object', without risking – which is the only chance of entering into the game, by getting a few fingers caught – the addition of some new thread.
>
> (Derrida 1981: 63)

In order to criticize/analyse, which for Derrida is ultimately the same thing as to *read*, you need to get your fingers caught in the threads of the ceaselessly weaving and unravelling text.[21]

This chapter has been caught up in several different threads, therefore, in unravelling the implications of the standard English issue in the curriculum reforms of the mid-1980s to early 1990s: the political and educational landscape of that period, and its entanglements with the print media; the history of English as a curriculum subject, and its special place in the emergence of mass compulsory education; the disciplinary force of standard languages as a device for managing subject populations and forging a sense of nationhood; and the psychic fear of otherness that often spills out as disgust at language itself. The complex nature of these entanglements means that standard English will not necessarily be foregrounded as an *educational* issue at all times – or not explicitly so at any rate. At the time of writing this book, for instance, around the turn of the millennium, standard English was not a hot item on the public educational agenda in the UK. Press and policy attention were concentrated on the Labour government's 'National Literacy Strategy', a massive reform of curriculum and pedagogy that refocused priorities and resources around the written word, the rhetoric of 'basics' and the (always renewable) panic about 'standards'.[22] Standard English is, however, still written into the National Curriculum; and an exception is still made of accent, while 'clarity' is still pursued.[23]

But at this moment of writing, there is no heat in the topic. The odd bush fire of linguistic revulsion has broken out in the press – as, for instance, when the novelist Beryl Bainbridge reviled the accents of her native Liverpool – but these have not, in recent years, ignited into concern at policy levels. It could be argued, of course, that this is because the 'battle' over standard English in the curriculum has been won by the forces of monoglossia. That may be so for the moment. But – for the reasons unravelled in this chapter – there is no reason to think that standard English has made its last appearance as a controversial curriculum issue.

In any case, linguistic revulsion does not need the official sanction of educational policy to keep it in circulation. How, then, might schooling *interrupt* the recirculation of disgust? Educators, linguists and students may need to find ways of engaging directly the unpleasantness that tends to erupt when non-standard speech becomes a matter of public attention. The tacit consensus *not* to recognize accent as an educational issue leaves educators with nothing to say when linguistic revulsion breaks out. Acknowledging the disgust that dialect speech often provokes is, of course, a risky strategy, which may in itself make students feel vulnerable. As Judith Butler (1997) notes in her examination of the politics of racist and homophobic 'hate speech', the discussion of linguistic abuse always risks repeating the terms of that abuse, since examples must be 'cited' one more time. 'There is no way to invoke examples of racist speech', she writes, 'for instance in a classroom, without invoking the sensibility of racism, the trauma and, for some, the excitement (p. 37). But she argues that the risk of repetition needs to be taken, precisely to interrupt and disrupt the terms on which the repetition of hate speech is usually done. The key question, then, says Butler, is 'what best use is to be made of repetition' (p. 37).

Butler (1997) argues the need to find workable strategies of 'reverse citation', in which hate speech is productively 'cited against itself'. For instance, the seizure of a hate-word such as 'queer' as a positive term of identity is a reassertion of agency by those who have been marginalized by language. Kristeva (1982) argues in a similar manner that the abject has the potential to confound and destabilize the forces of order, precisely because abjection works at and on the margins – that is, the boundaries that protect subjectivity, social order and discipline. Postcolonial writers have, for instance, seized the colonialist discourses of disgust that portrayed the colonial subject as 'filthy native' in contrast to the clean bodies of the colonizers. Esty (1999) shows how 'excremental language' is used 'counter-discursively' by post-independence West African writers such as Wole Soyinka and Ayi Kwei Armah, as well as those 'celebrated scatologists' of Irish anti-colonialism, James Joyce and Samuel Beckett. In their re-direction of the excremental language of colonial disgust, these writers reassert the power of the native as 'a living threat to the hygienic symbolic order of empire'; yet at the same time they *also* challenge the utopian fictions promoted by the post-independent neocolonial elites (Esty 1999: 29).

These literary uses of the abject suggest that one strategy for engaging with the discourse of disgust around non-standard English would be to exploit, rather than ignore, its capacity to *unsettle* the linguistic and social status quo. Zali Gurevitch argues that this is precisely what is brought off in the various forms of 'hip-hop culture'. Hip-hop, says Gurevitch, acknowledges the 'verbal violence' exerted upon, and in turn practised by, black youths, in a 'playful spirit' that aestheticizes the contorted relationship between body and language, and the implications (folded-in-ness) of all this with the experience of racial oppression.

This African American and African Caribbean youth culture [i.e. hip hop] features different ways of the 'tongue' in talk (speaking-singing rap), body (break dancing), and writing (graffiti), combining funk rhythm, biting criticisms, and in-your-face rhetoric that sticks it tongue out with scornful fire, rage, screeching guitar riffs and scratching turntables. The aesthetics of these various performance styles is founded on breaks and ruptures that are not merely a style but employed as strategies and forces in cultural-political discourse.

(Gurevitch 1999: 533–4)

Gurevitch's appreciation of the 'tongue's break-dance' in hip-hop culture does not dwell on the further ambivalences that rap has provoked, such as the imputations of misogyny and homophobia which have brought feminist and racist discourses into highly problematic proximity (see Butler 1997). Nor does he consider whether rap has lost its unsettling force in its transmutation into a 'world-wide style'. Still, the example of rap's unsettling idiom, and its emphasis on the body and on performance, gives some idea of the kind of 'play' that could be involved in a politics of language that took seriously (that is, playfully) the disruptive potential of non-standard speech and speakers.

One final example.

Listen Mr Oxford Don
John Agard (1985)

Me not no Oxford don
me a simple immigrant
from Clapham Common
I didn't graduate
I immigrate
But listen Mr Oxford don
I'm a man on de run
and a man on de run
is a dangerous one
I ent have no gun
I ent have no knife
but mugging de Queen's English
is the story of my life
I don't need no axe
to split/ up you syntax
I don't need no hammer
to mash up yu grammar
I warning you Mr Oxford don
I'm a wanted man
and a wanted man

is a dangerous one
Dem accuse me of assault
on de Oxford dictionary/
imagine a concise peaceful man like me/
dem want me serve time
for inciting rhyme to riot
but I tekking it quiet

I'm not a violent man Mr Oxford don
I only armed wit mih human breath
but human breath
is a dangerous weapon
So mek dem send one big word after me
I ent serving no jail sentence
I slashing suffix in self-defence
I bashing future wit present tense
and if necessary
I making de Queen's English accessory/to my offence
            (from *Mangoes and Bullets: Selected and New Poems, 1972–84*)

Interrogating the discourse of home–school relations: the case of 'parents' evenings' (with Barbara Walker)

Preamble

Parents' evenings are familiar events in the secondary school calendar. On their allotted evening, the parents of students in a particular year-group are invited to school for a series of brief consultations with their children's teachers. This chapter takes a look at parents' evenings and, in particular, at the parent–teacher consultations themselves. It draws on a study of five schools jointly carried out with Barbara Walker.[1]

As well as being worthy of study in their own right, parent–teacher consultations are also of interest as concrete manifestations of 'home–school relations' – that 'important and pervasive abstraction', as Baker and Keogh (1995: 265) call it. As these authors point out, the notion of home–school relations is invested with enormous educational significance and political aspiration, but very little attention has been paid to how these relations actually play out in practice. Towards the end of the chapter, I consider how an understanding of parent–teacher consultations might connect with the 'bigger' policy and public discourses that surround the notion of home–school relations.

The main focus in this chapter is on *spoken* discourse. The orientation is strongly influenced by the approach known as conversation analysis, itself an off-shoot of ethnomethodology. Conversation analysis, notable for its extremely fine-grained analysis of transcriptions of speech, is concerned with the ways in which speakers produce order, meaning and coherence in and through their interactions. The chapter is especially influenced by the studies of 'institutional talk' that have emerged as a major strand of conversational analysts' work in recent years (e.g. Drew and Heritage 1992). Through their close attention to the details of interaction in settings such as courtrooms, surgeries, boardrooms and newsrooms, conversation analysts have illuminated the ways in which participants 'talk an institution into being' (Heritage 1984: 290).

Parent–teacher consultations are doubly interesting, perhaps because the participants are generally talking not one but *two* institutions into being. Or trying to. These are 'threshold' events – encounters that construct a brief 'opening' between those two institutions that loom large in children's lives: the family and the school. As we will see below, this partly accounts for the tensions that people often report, since the two institutions do not necessarily carry the same definitions of expertise, responsibility and moral conduct. For instance, parent and teacher may find themselves at odds over what is in the student's 'best interests', who has the right to decide on this, and who is to blame if those interests are seen not to be served.

Parents' evenings are very much concerned with identity, with the making of *subjects*. As Jayne Keogh (1992) found in her study, the participants in these brief encounters are intensely preoccupied with establishing and defending their identities as 'good' parents, teachers and students. Definitions of what it means to be a teacher, a parent, a learner, an adolescent, a son, a daughter, an expert, are tacitly invoked in these consultations. As we shall see below, the participants hold one another accountable for conducting themselves 'properly' in these various personae.

Parents' evenings are suffused with *power*, therefore, in Foucault's sense of a mechanism that works in and through institutions to produce particular kinds of subjects, knowledge and truth (e.g. Foucault 1979, 1980). For Foucault, power is not a force wielded by one group or sovereign figure against others, but a more sinuous and insinuating mechanism that works its way in a 'capillary' fashion into the 'very grain' of individuals, inhabiting their bodies, their beliefs and their self-hood, and binding them together as institutional subjects (Foucault 1980: 39). Power, in this sense, is both coercive and enabling. It is not imposed from 'outside' or 'above', but circulates within institutions and social bodies, producing subjects who exert a 'mutual "hold"' on one another. Foucault called it, memorably, 'a mutual and indefinite "blackmail"', which binds superiors and subordinates in 'a relationship of mutual support and conditioning' (p. 159). The consultations described below offer telling examples of this kind of power at work in the interactions of parents and teachers.

The overall organization of parents' evenings

Parents' evenings are typically rather fraught and noisy affairs. Teachers sit at small tables set out around the school hall or other spaces, seeing a long succession of parents for pre-arranged, five-minute consultations. Queues form as appointments back up. Parents mill around looking for their next teacher. Students are not always expected or invited to attend; and those who do turn up may find there is no seat at the table for them (see Walker 1998). One commentator described these events as 'a cross between a social security office, a doctor's surgery and King's Cross station' (Nias 1981). Another ranked them 'close to a visit to the dentist in terms of discomfiture' (B. Limerick, quoted in Baker and Keogh 1995: 264).

The comparison with consultations in other professions such as medicine, dentistry and social services is apt, since there are contextual similarities. The 'professionals' (here, the teachers) control the location, scheduling, duration and general agenda of each encounter; and they have access to specialist knowledge or resources that are not available to 'the clients'.[2] The talk tends to be 'asymmetrical' in terms of its organiza-tion and structure; that is, the 'expert' participant exerts more control over the direction and content of the talk than the other(s) (see, for example, Ten Have 1991; Drew and Heritage 1992).[3] Institutional talk exhibits such 'standard patterns', according to Drew and Heritage, partly because of the inevitable routinization involved in repeated professional encounters. However, they also note that this is perhaps one of the most poignant sources of interactional 'asymmetry', since what is routine for the professional is emphatically not so for the 'client' (Drew and Herit-age 1992: 50–1).

The absent student

But parents' evenings also have features that make them rather different from other professional–client encounters. For a start, they are *three-cornered* interactions involving parent(s), teacher and student. This is no less the case in those consultations where the student is absent (about half in the study we conducted). Indeed, there is a powerful paradox concerning the presence or absence of students, which produces byzantine complexities of power, blame and accountability in these encounters. Common sense might predict that students would have more of a 'voice' in discussions of their schooling if they were allowed to attend the consultations. But our study found that this made very little difference to their power to intervene. In terms of active participation, students were effectively absent even when they were physically present. On the other hand, the (absent) student is the person around whom the whole dynamic of the consultation revolves. It is not just that the discussion is 'about' the student, but also that he or she is the figure that sets justifica-tion, gratification, blame and self-regard in motion. The reputations of teacher and parent are intimately tied to that of the student as this is elaborated during the consultation itself, and they fluctuate according to whose 'version' of the student prevails, as we shall see below. You could say that the figure of the student haunts the consultation, to a point where even those students who are physically present are rather ghostly apparitions – animating the interaction between parent and teacher, yet unable to make a direct impact upon it, and obliged to wait and see what the others 'make' of them.

Parent–teacher consultations are always 'triangular' therefore, even when only two people face one another across the table in the school hall, and this distinguishes them in some respects from professional–client encounters in other settings.[4] Another critical difference relates to the contested status of *expertise* in these educational consultations. Because the main concern is with the student's behaviour and disposition – including, crucially, what he or she does *at home* – the teacher's status as the 'expert' in these encounters is always potentially challengeable by counter-claims from parents to the effect that they know their child better. So the maintenance and management of expertise is an ever-present issue for the participants.

The organization of parent–teacher consultations

Let us now turn to some of the details of the consultations, as found in the study conducted with Barbara Walker. The consultations were strikingly similar across different schools and participants, in terms of their turn-taking patterns and episodic structure. Most of them began, after brief greetings and preambles, with an unbroken stretch of talk from the teacher, which we termed the *diagnosis*, during which the teacher would report on the student's current state of academic 'health' – her achievements, difficulties or progress – and often on her personal qualities and behaviour (enthusiastic, chatty, lively, quiet, etc.). The diagnosis was usually followed by a *dialogic* episode involving alternating turns by teacher and parent(s), devoted to the pursuit of issues arising from the diagnosis or from additional concerns raised by parents. The consultation ended with a *closing* episode. Students, if present, usually said very little, beyond responding when addressed directly.[5]

In terms of turn-taking patterns, the dominant form of the consultations can be thought of as a tadpole: the (largely uninterrupted) teacher diagnosis forming the head and the string of alternating turns of the dialogue and closing sequence as the tail. The length of the 'tail' varied considerably, from a few desultory turns followed by thanks and farewells, as in the example below, to extended and occasionally heated interchanges lasting up to ten minutes. The dominant episodic structure looked like this:

1 **PREAMBLE**   [greetings; orientations: finding coursework, etc.]
2 **DIAGNOSIS**   [teacher talking; parent(s) acknowledging]
3 **DIALOGUE**   [alternating turns]
4 **CLOSING**   [thanks; farewells, etc.]

The following is an example ['T' = Teacher, 'M' = Mother, 'S' = Student; '__' (underlining) = overlapping turns]

Example 1

T Right, very good. Annabel, you
are doing well. You're working
hard and I'm thrilled to bits with
your work, your notebook's good,
and erm you ask good questions,
you try to answer the questions,
you've passed both tests. You got
66% for the first test, which was
to do with the plant nutrition,
you know, with all the ecology,
all of that early work, yeah? And
the respiration test you got 56%,
you went down a bit, but it's a
harder test, you know, the marks
generally are harder on that, are
lower on that one, because it's a
harder test. Erm, I think that
you're learning a lot of science.
I'm happy with the way you're
working. I think your notebook
is good, and you do seem to
understand what's going on,
most of the time. I can only
say you could improve on one
thing and that is don't get
sucked into the other group
of too much gossip. Yeah? And
I think I've done something
about that, 'cause I've done
some splitting up [M laughs]
– all to help

M Good

T But you're a great girl and I'm
very impressed

DIAGNOSIS
[*T addresses diagnosis to S*]

[*Summarizing: bringing
diagnosis episode to a close*]

M	– Oh that's good, I'm really pleased, well, erm . . . the GCSEs with science [T: Yes], they obviously have to take science?	[*M acknowledging 'juncture'*] **DIALOGUE** [*M 'opens up' the dialogue*]
T	Yeah	
S	– double science	
M	double science	
S	Is there double science?	
T	Double science, yes, that's what we would . . . you would do, double GCSE science. So you get ten hours a fortnight next year, OK? That will be covering elements of physics, chemistry and biology, so you'd do double science, it would count as double. Two out of ten. Is that all right?	
M	That's fine, I'm very pleased	[*signalling closure*]
T	Is there anything else you wanted to ask?	**CLOSINGS**
M	No, not really, I'm quite happy	
T	Well you could double her pocket money on the basis of science	
M	[laughs] Well I won't tell her dad then! Well that's lovely, yes, thank you very much. I'm very pleased	
T	OK, we are, I am as well	
M	Oh good	
T	Mr Cheshire as well [other science teacher]	
M	Lovely	
T	Keep it up	
M	Thanks very much	
T	OK?	
M	Thank you	
T	Bye now, nice to meet you as well	
M	Thank you	
T	Bye Annabel	
S	Bye	

This is one of the briefer consultations, but it is characteristic in its outline structure. It exemplifies the 'tadpole' shape, with a monologue from the teacher, followed by a 'tail' of alternating turns initiated by the teacher, who 'hands over the floor' to the parent with a summary comment. The student, Annabel, takes very little part in the proceedings. Note that, even though the teacher addresses his remarks to her (which happened relatively rarely), it is her *mother* who responds.

'Membership categorization': sketches of identity

The opening diagnosis sets some crucial parameters for the rest of the consultation. Most importantly, it starts to elaborate who the participants 'are', and what sort of behaviour and responsibilities are expected of them. Carolyn Baker, who found virtually identical monologues in her study in Queensland, Australia, describes their 'categorization work' in these terms:

> [The teacher's opening statement] can be treated as an initial sketch, a proposal, for who the participants relevantly are in this interactional event [. . .] what they do and should do [. . .] and how these categories and activities (should) connect. It is an initial map of the social and moral terrain in which a representative of the school meets representatives of the home as idealised courses of action.
>
> (Baker 2000: 107–8)

The teacher's diagnosis in our example above assembles the three participants in their capacities as teacher, parent and student, and offers proposals as to what sorts of things people belonging to those identity categories (should) do. This particular account proposes that teachers know their subject, teach lessons according to a structured syllabus ('all the ecology, all that early work'), set coursework, administer tests, know the nature of the demands these make on students, and monitor students' learning using such sources of information. They know each individual student; they can tell whether or not he or she is understanding the lessons; and they are alert to the dynamics of their peer groups. They expect students to work hard, try to answer teachers' questions, present their work clearly, get good test scores, follow 'what's going on', and listen to the teacher rather than talking to classmates. They experience pleasure when students meet those expectations. They have a sense of humour. Parents, in so far as they assent to these proposals (which this parent implicitly, and at times explicitly, does), are the sort of people who share the teacher's goals and aspirations for the student, and who recognize their daughter or son in the teacher's description. And so on.

This list probably seems both banal, as a description of a teacher's activities (nothing new there) and inflated, as an interpretation of the identity work initiated by the teacher's diagnosis (all that from so few words?). But ethnomethodologists, on whose work Baker draws, suggest that this kind of 'membership categorization analysis' is routinely done by people in order to assign one another to relevant identity categories (mother, wife, teacher, daughter, etc.), and to hold one another accountable for 'proper', moral conduct within those categories (see Jayyusi 1984). People do not simply 'belong' to these various categories; rather, belonging is 'made to happen' in and through the talk. And it is done anew each time people speak or write. It is not the case that you simply 'are' a teacher, a mother or a student. You have to 'bring off' each particular identity as a practical accomplishment, repeatedly, every time afresh.

As already noted, this identity work always has a *moral* dimension. Claiming a particular identity brings obligations to (be seen to) act in consensually 'appropriate' ways. Part of the accomplishment of 'being' a teacher (however minor a part) is precisely the ability to carry off a parent–teacher consultation. Suppose that, instead of using test scores or coursework to represent a student's attainments, you reported intimations gleaned during a seance, or brought along a picture you had painted? You could have trouble being accepted as a bona fide teacher. Questions might be raised about your sanity, or at least your qualifications. There are numerous other, more subtle ways in which participants can court failure 'as' parents or teachers in these consultations, and these are explored below. For the moment, note that the opening episodes are highly significant as markers of what will count as relevant information and activities for the participants. It scarcely needs pointing out that the agenda is emphatically that of the school rather than the home at this point in the proceedings.

'Asymmetries' of power and status

Parents' silence during the opening episode mirrors the 'remarkable passivity' noted by Heath (1992) in patients' responses to diagnoses in general practice consultations. Heath noted that patients did not respond to doctors' diagnoses as 'newsworthy' – that is, with 'news receipts' of the kind identified by conversation analysts, such as 'Oh' or 'Really', or follow-up assessments. He argued that minimal responses are characteristic of responses to <u>'expert' talk</u>. So the expert status of one of the participants is *jointly* established through the interactional contributions of both or all parties.[6]

Parents' passivity may seem surprising, given that the consultations concern a person whom parents might claim to know better than the teacher. Indeed, parents often did challenge teachers on the implicit grounds of 'privileged' knowledge of the student, but not usually until later in the interaction. This is perhaps because these opening sequences firmly locate the teacher's knowledge of the student in domains to which the parent does not have direct access – test scores, reading ages, exam

predictions. Parents are encouraged to defer to teachers' superior knowledge of their own child in matters of schooling, and to wait until they
are invited (at the closing of the diagnosis episode) to take a more active
part in the interaction.

These features might seem to confirm a view of parents' evenings
as events over which, 'like a server in tennis, the teacher still has the
advantage' (Macbeth 1989). Teachers claim, and are granted, the right
to speak first, and at some length, to control the topic and the release of
specialist information and to sum up what the diagnosis 'means'. Parents
and students are positioned as passive recipients of expert information
and advice (which, moreover, may be 'pre-packaged' to an extent).[7]
These are typical features of 'institutional talk'. This is not to say that
parents were powerless in these interactions. Parents could, and did,
challenge teachers' judgements or practice. However, it could be argued
that even their resistance is constrained by the terms of engagement
offered and accepted in the consultations and, more generally, by norm-
ative assumptions about the nature of institutional talk. It is important
to recognize, all the same, that the 'asymmetries' in these interactions,
as in institutional talk in general, are *collaboratively produced*. Parents
cooperate, by and large, in assuming the conversational role of 'client' or
layperson offered by teachers.

Opening up a space for dialogue: the entry of the parental 'voice'

Teachers usually brought their opening statements to an end with some
kind of summary statement which marked a conversational 'juncture' –
that is, a point at which topic shifts and even possible 'closings' were up
for negotiation. Closing junctures are places where speakers indicate to
one another that the topic in hand is 'understood to be either exhausted,
concluded or suspended' (Button 1991: 260). Speakers do this in several
ways; for instance, by providing a summary of the 'gist' of the talk or by
doing a series of mutual agreements about what has been discussed. You
can see a summary statement in the example above ('But you're a great
girl and I'm very impressed').

Parents almost always took the option of continuing the dialogue at
this point rather than allowing it to close down completely, no matter
how positive the teacher's diagnosis. Annabel's mother, for instance, in
the example above, asked a question about double science. The following
examples show similar 'junctures' where a teacher's summary statement
is first endorsed by the parent(s) and then followed by a question which
inaugurates a new topic:

Example 2

T	– and I'm quite pleased with the way that Martin is working
M	Oh that's good
T	I really can't say much more than that
M →	I was a bit worried, although I wanted him in the middle group, I was a bit worried that he might have trouble keeping up

Example 3

T	But on the whole he's working, you know, pretty well –
M	– good
T	– coping very well with all the work
M →	How do you find his spelling, 'cause that's quite a weak point with him?

Example 4

T	So you know, it's all good news
M →	Great, he doesn't find it hard going or anything?

Since conversational junctures can be heard as offers to bring the conversation to a close, the onus is on the parents to keep them 'open' past this first juncture.[8] As noted, most parents in our study took this option, however positive the report. Indeed, there seemed to be a certain resistance to unmitigated 'good news' diagnoses. Most parents want to hear nice things about their child; but good news stories can be problematic. They may insinuate that the teacher has not given her full attention to the student, especially if they lack detail. This possibility seems to be tacitly acknowledged by this teacher, who jokingly offers to 'make up' some problems [see also example (2) above]:

Example 5

T	. . . I mean, really, on the whole, erm, I think she's doing well, no problems at all
M	None at all?
T	No
M	<u>Keeping up with her work?</u>
T →	<u>I mean I could find</u> some if you want me to try, I'll make some up
M	No, no, no, no, if –
T	– honestly, she's really, you know, I'm quite happy with the <u>work she's</u> doing
M	<u>Brilliant!</u>
F	Good

Teachers may find themselves in something of a 'double bind', therefore, in trying to meet parents' expectations – obliged *both* to deliver good news *and* to display a 'proper' degree of engagement with the specific needs and abilities of this particular student. A further problem with good news stories is that they deny parents the chance to fulfil one of the main symbolic purposes of these encounters – namely, offering 'moral versions of themselves' as concerned parents (Baker and Keogh 1995: 263). They also offer little in the way of specific, practical things for parents to *do* by way of further supporting their child. In short, parents may need to *open up a space* within the consultation process, in which they are able to demonstrate their knowledge of such matters as their child's previous attainments, home-working habits, subject preferences, and so on, and thus display their active support for the school's work.[9] Issues of identity and accountability are thus intimately bound up in the fine details of the structure of these interactions.

Resisting and securing closure

There is a kind of *inertia* in these consultations, therefore – a tendency towards closure from the point where the teacher indicates that she has finished her diagnosis. From that point onwards, the possibility of closure hovers over the talk, and the onus of deferring it generally rests with the parent(s). It was clear that keeping the dialogic space open was often something of a struggle for parents, not just at the first juncture, but also at later points, when teachers again offered to bring the consultation to a close via summary statements and other 'pre-closing' turns. It was not uncommon to find a series of junctures in a consultation at which a parent deflected offers of closure by asking another question or pursuing the existing topic. Equally, it was not uncommon to find some *resistance* by teachers to these attempts to keep the dialogue open. A closer look at an example may help to explain why negotiations over closure can be tricky for teachers as well as parents (beyond the obvious reason that teachers must keep a tight rein on the length of consultations if they are to keep on schedule). Let us look, for instance, at how the dialogue that was initiated in example (2) above continued.

Example 6

[Student present, but silent throughout]

| T | (concluding his diagnosis) . . . and I'm quite pleased with the way Martin is working | **Proposed closing #1** [*closing summary*] |

M Oh that's good

T I really can't say much more than   [*overt closure*]
       that

M I was a bit worried, although I   **Reopening #1**
       wanted him in the middle group,
       I was a bit worried that he might
       have trouble keeping up

T Well, I mean [inaudible] . . . fairly
       good effort. Mrs X, who is Head
       of English, has looked at the files
       recently – [M: Yes] – and really he's,
       he is a little bit quiet in class and
       maybe he doesn't fully sometimes
       – sort of things like he's not sure
       what he's doing, but he really is
       getting in there with the work and **Proposed closing #2**
       getting it done –   [*closing summary*]

M – does he ask if he's not sure?   **Reopening #2**

T (hesitantly) Not as much as he
       ought to, I'm sort of aware that he
       doesn't, so I tend to check that he
       – [M: – yeah] – he hasn't shown
       any problems, everything has been
       done, he's coped with everything –

M – yes

T – so, I mean he's doing well   **Proposed closing #3**
                                            [*reiterated summary*]

M He takes so long, I'm not just saying **Reopening #3**
       English, but he takes a long time
       over his homework, so I didn't know
       whether he was sort of keeping up
       the pace in class, he sits there, but
       then there's five children at home –

T – oh right

M – and whether he's distracted or not

T No, he does well, he really is doing a
       good job, he's working . . . he's not a
       fast worker –

M – no

T but he's working and I mean the   [*T and M beginning
       thing is, he's working along, he's   to negotiate closing
       trying, he's getting neat working, it's via agreements and
       completed correctly, and the time   overlapping speech
       he's spending on it has proved he's   from about here on*]

	actually looking at the errors and making sure he's not making them	
M	Yes	
T	So, in fact, it's working to his benefit, instead of rushing it – [M: Yes] – which a lot, some, <u>lots of children</u> –	
M	<u>want to get it over with</u>	
T	<u>– get it</u> over and done with, he's consistently trying to make sure it looks good	
M	yeah	
T	And I'm pleased with the way he's working	**Proposed closing #4**
M	Oh that's good	
T	Yeah, no, he's doing a good job	
M	Oh that's good	
T	Don't forget, if you're not sure of something ask me [to S]. That's important [M laughs], I won't bite your head off [laughs] OK?	[*finalizing closure*]
M	It's just, it's confidence, I think with youngsters anyway, especially with special needs, there's so many different teachers aren't there?	**Reopening #4**
T	mmm [inaudible]. But no, he's doing nice – doing well	**Proposed closing #5**
M	Oh that's good	[*accepted*]
T	I'm pleased	
M	Very good then	
T	Right?	
M	Yes?	
T	Good lad! Keep it up	
M	All right, thank you for seeing us	
T	That's all right. Ni . . . b'bye	
M	b'bye	

The teacher proposes closure five times in this example, each time via a summary of his opening diagnosis, the 'gist' of which is that Martin is doing well. His mother averts the closure four times. Her re-openings represent a challenge to the teacher's version of Martin's progress, setting in motion a series of justifications by the teacher, and something of a tussle over whether Martin is or is not 'keeping up'.

Refusals of closure always carry the potential to be heard as challenges, however courteously and tentatively framed, because they indicate, at the very least, that the teacher's account up to that point is *not* complete and self-sufficient. They also signal a subtle shift in the interactional dynamics, since it is the parent who is now taking the initiative in prolonging the talk. Moreover, they usually take this initiative in order to raise some concern about their child, and there is always the risk that concern about the child will trigger concern about the *teacher* and his or her competence. The teacher, in the example above, appears to be alert to this possibility. When Martin's mother expresses her worry about whether her son has been 'keeping up', the teacher's response is justificatory. He cites the agreement of his head of department. He also partially acknowledges Martin's mother's concerns by describing some aspects of Martin's demeanour in class that *could* lead one to conclude that he was not keeping up ('a little bit quiet in class . . . not sure what he's doing') but dismisses these as not significantly changing the overall positive message. Note that this partial acknowledgement of the mother's point also allows the teacher to demonstrate further his knowledge of Martin.

Martin's mother picks up on an aspect of the teacher's justification in order to reopen a second time: 'Does he ask if he's not sure?' At this point the spectre of blame, which hovers over *any* mention of students' difficulties in these consultations, becomes more overt. For if Martin is 'not sure', or if he does not ask for help, whose 'fault' is it? The teacher locates the fault with Martin ('Not as much as he ought to') and describes the steps he takes to compensate for this, testifying once more to his alertness to Martin's needs in the classroom ('I'm sort of aware that he doesn't, so I tend to check . . .'). Martin's mother is still not ready to accept the teacher's 'good news' summary and move towards closure, and reopens on another tack, with new 'evidence' of Martin not keeping up ('He takes so long . . . over his homework'), which is grounded in her *personal* knowledge of her child in his home circumstances. This does not shift the teacher's positive summary; on the contrary, he incorporates the point about Martin's not being 'a fast worker' as further evidence for his *own* view – that unlike 'lots of children', Martin does not rush his work.

At this point in the consultation, the teacher and parent begin to converge. Martin's mother actively endorses the teacher's position by reformulating his point about children who rush it ('want to get it over with'), which he, in turn, mirrors ('get it over and done with') and both start to move towards closure. There is one further reopening, around the teacher's instruction to Martin (the first time he has been addressed directly during the consultation) to ask 'if you're not sure of something', an injunction which, though humorously phrased, decisively confirms the location of the fault with Martin. His mother attempts to develop this topic by introducing the issue of students' confidence to ask for help, when they have 'so many different teachers', especially in the case of those who, like Martin, are in special needs classes. The teacher only minimally acknowledges this contribution and restates his summary/closing proposal. On this fifth occasion, he secures the mother's acceptance of his offer and the consultation moves through mutual agreements to a speedy conclusion.

A sense of muted struggle runs through this consultation. Martin's mother has to struggle to keep the consultation open in the face of the teacher's repeated offers of closure. And although she achieves some success in this through her persistence, she is less successful in her struggle to modify the teacher's opinion of Martin's progress. Although she is able to avert the teacher's proposals for closure, she is not very successful in securing any *extended* discussion of the points she raises. The teacher is, of course, engaged in a complementary struggle to maintain his version of Martin's progress in the face of his mother's counter-ascriptions.

Identity

Most of all, perhaps, the consultation enacts a struggle over *identity*. There are at least two Martins produced in this interaction – the careful non-rusher who is coping well under the teacher's careful eye, and the silent child who is failing to thrive in his school work.[10] Intricately woven into this struggle over Martin's identity is another over the identity of the teacher: as careful monitor and astute judge of his students' needs, versus one who is not alert to the problems of a child in difficulty.

Is there a *third* 'Martin' – that is, the student who was actually 'there', sitting at the table beside his mother? It is interesting – although not in any way unusual during such consultations – that this person was not consulted about the competing versions of Martin's progress and welfare that were being negotiated. The adult participants might have asked Martin whether or not he felt able to ask for help; whether or not he was 'keeping up'; whether he was 'distracted' by his siblings, and so on. But this Martin was not consulted and was not addressed in any way until the end of the consultation when he was 'brought in' in order to be encouraged to ask for help. In this sense, there were indeed only two Martins produced in the interaction itself. The living, breathing embodied boy was, in the sense foreshadowed above, a kind of spectre at the table. This is not to conclude that those other two Martins, the ones produced in and through the consultation, had no link to, or effect upon, the third Martin. It is quite possible that descriptions such as these offer possible versions of himself for Martin's contemplation.

Blame and responsibility

Struggles over identity are intimately linked to issues of competence and are, therefore, a fertile site for accusation, blaming and justification. Negotiations over where the blame should 'settle' were sometimes more protracted than those in the above example. An extended 'blaming' sequence can be found in Appendix 3, where the blame for the student's reported difficulties in understanding his homework assignment is 'shifted' around several possible locations, as it were (i.e. parent, student, teacher, external circumstances), before finally being allowed to 'settle' with mother and student.

Negotiating expertise: the 'management' of personal talk

Martin's mother, in the example above, referred at one point to his home circumstances as a 'warrant' for her anxiety as to whether he was doing as well as his teacher stated. The teacher made very little acknowledgement of this personal information. This disregard of personal matters by teachers was widespread across the consultations. Overwhelmingly, teachers paid scant attention to personal information relating to students' home circumstances, emotional well-being, and so on, *where this was volunteered by parents*. Teachers often elicited this kind of information themselves (for example, about students' work habits, social pursuits, emotional well-being, friendship choices, etc.). But they tended to give it minimal acknowledgement when parents introduced it without being asked. This was the case even when such information appeared to be potentially relevant. For example:

Example 7

> T   [advising M to test her (year 10) daughter's German vocabulary] . . . 'cause again, I've a really strong suspicion that Mary doesn't learn because –
>
> M →   – My cousin speaks about seven languages and teaches five here in Norwich, so she's always said that she'll give her all the extra tuition that she needs
>
> T →   Mmm. This is the classic Mary [referring to mark sheet] – a test we did . . . [continues]

This tendency to pass over personal information ('girlfriend problems', family troubles, unhappiness, anxiety, withdrawal, 'acting up', etc.) is all the more surprising given the rhetoric of home–school communication that underpins parents' evenings. The teachers interviewed in this and an earlier study (see Walker 1998) stated that parents' evenings were of value precisely because of the insights they could give into personal circumstances that might be influencing students' achievement or behaviour. However, the tendency to 'downgrade' unsolicited personal information is characteristic of 'asymmetrical' talk in professional situations (cf. Ten Have 1991). Teachers, like doctors, may feel a need to 'manage' the emergence and deployment of personal information, not least because unsolicited information introduces an element of unpredictability into encounters that need to be kept to strict time limits. The management of the personal dimension of the talk also allows teachers to define what will count as *educationally relevant* personal information, and thus to maintain their 'expert' status in the face of rival claims from parents to speak as experts on matters concerning their child. There are other possible reasons. Teachers may be reluctant to enter into discussion of students' personal lives because they feel that this could compromise their relationship with students. Or they may want to avoid complicity with parents over the disciplining of students (see below).

Parents sometimes attempted to engage in 'expertise trading', by displaying the kind of specialist knowledge or registers deployed by the teachers – for example, when they showed their familiarity with the National Curriculum or their awareness of controversies over testing. Displays of 'insider' knowledge could be brief and allusive, as when a father asked a craft, design and technology teacher, 'Is this all resistant materials?', or when the mother of a dyslexic student said, 'She's had no multi-sensory teaching'. These parental claims to expertise did not, on the whole, seem to be any more successful in opening up the dialogue than their attempts to claim expert status on personal grounds.

Teachers seldom attempted to trade expertise in the 'other' direction – that is, by referring to their own experiences as parents and, therefore, their personal, as opposed to their professional, understanding of young people. Overall, the teachers in the consultations attempted to manage the interaction so as to maintain the boundaries around their expertise as the 'professionals'. This boundary maintenance is rather significant, given the universal rationale for these events as occasions for home–school 'partnership' and mutual endeavour in the interests of the student.

'Double binds'

Demonstrating competence, avoiding blame and maintaining a 'virtuous' identity are not simple matters. The complexities of managing these difficult, often contradictory goals gave rise to a number of interactional 'double binds', similar to those identified by David Silverman (1987) in his study of paediatric consultations involving diabetic teenagers. To demonstrate their competence, parents in Silverman's study were obliged *both* to demonstrate that they were acting 'responsibly', by monitoring their child's behaviour, *and* that they were helping their child to take control of their own health. Parents resorted to a variety of 'rebuttal strategies' to try to demonstrate competence on one of these counts, without incurring blame on the other.

The parents in these consultations courted similar risks. Showing an interest in students' homework and classwork could be seen as exhibiting responsible concern; but it could also be construed as being over-protective, or even interfering. And, as we have already seen, it was possible for parents to know 'too much' as well as too little about educational matters. One teacher summed up this 'no-win' situation for parents in his (only half-joking) categorization of them as 'over-protective, deferential or middle class'. This points to a general dilemma about the notion of parental 'support' for schools and teachers. As Gill Crozier (1998) notes, while parental support is universally desired, it can also present a threat. Parents who take an active interest may be seen as 'watchful'. Support can transmute into perceived counter-surveillance.

A further dilemma facing parents when demonstrating support relates to the *triangular* nature of the consultation, which, as noted above, always involves three parties, even when one is not physically present. Parental support for one party (student or teacher) could tacitly be taken as 'betrayal' (though this is too strong a word) of the other. For instance, a parent who defended the student in response to the teachers' criticism could easily be seen as biased or bothersome. Yet, on the other hand, attempting to support the *teacher*, by endorsing his or her criticisms of the student, could also be read in negative ways by teachers – as 'ganging up' on the student, or even as recruiting teachers against their will to do parents' disciplinary work. One teacher was critical of parents who allegedly came to the consultation 'to tell the child off', and who were 'out to just doubly-prove what's gone on at home'. Another teacher was uncomfortable about endorsing parents' criticisms of sixth formers, on the grounds that these were responsible young adults and that his relationship with them might be threatened if he was seen to be aligning himself with their parents. Allegiances between the three parties to the consultation triangle are not, therefore, clear-cut or predictable in advance of each particular consultation.

Teachers were also subject to double binds. For instance, they could fall prey to the double imperative of making their subject enjoyable, and thus motivating the student, yet also being expected to 'push' or challenge them. A teacher who claimed to make maths fun, for instance, might be interpreted as making it too easy. Teachers could be held responsible either for overestimating or for underestimating a student's abilities. This double bind was even more acute in the case of teachers of students with special needs, where there was an obligation to demonstrate that they were taking special care of special children *and* that they were not treating them differently, in terms of lowered expectations, from other children. A further double bind, already discussed above, concerned favourable reports of students. Teachers wishing to convey their genuine appreciation of good work might disappoint by failing to demonstrate 'engagement' with the student, or by telling parents 'what we already know'.

Questions of competence are never settled in advance of the consultation. There are no 'right answers', in the abstract, to such questions as: how rigorously one needs to monitor homework in order to be seen as a 'good' parent; what is the correct balance between fun and pain in the teaching of maths; how much consideration for special needs children is too much; where are the lines between parental concern, interference and deference; who is at fault when a student does not understand. Although parents and teachers undoubtedly come to the encounter with their own apprehensions and expectations of each other (their own 'axe to grind', as one teacher said of the parents), praise, blame and esteem are traded in real time in the course of each individual consultation. It is during the talk itself that conduct comes to be construed as virtuous or blameworthy.

Conclusion

Parent–teacher consultations offer a paradoxical mixture predictability and high uncertainty for those involved. On the one hand, they are routinized and formulaic. Participants all over the country repeat the same kinds of five-minute encounters, moving through the same series of episodes, making the same kinds of moves, out of which they fashion their oppositional identities 'as' parent or teacher. On the other hand, these are unpredictable encounters, fraught with jeopardy and risk of censure for all concerned. Issues of moral conduct, accountability, identity and responsibility are (un)settled on-the-spot. This helps to explain, perhaps, why people tend both to dismiss parents' evenings as empty routine *and* to experience them as traumatic (see Walker 1998).

You begin to glimpse, in these consultations, how Foucault's notion of power as 'mutual and indefinite blackmail' actually works in practice. The adversarial structure which sets teacher and parent against one another unfolds inexorably as the consultation proceeds. This does not mean that it is impossible to 'subvert' the usual dynamics of these interactions. There were instances of parents who did not wait passively during the opening diagnosis, for example (see note 6). But there will always be interactional consequences when these (very subtle) conventions are breached, such as heightened defensiveness and hostility, or challenges to a speaker's credibility.

The consultations also show how subjects are produced in and through discourse. The identity of mother, father or teacher is not just something that a person 'has' or 'is': it has to be worked for, and worked up, during each interaction. But this process of self-elaboration is done according to criteria that are not freely chosen by the participants. It is also clear that these are *situational* identities. What will count as relevant to your conduct – and even your credibility – as a mother, or a teacher, will be only a very small sub-set of all the possible acts and experiences associated with mothering or teaching in other situations. You could say, in fact, that parent–teacher consultations offer rather stripped-down, minimalist identities for the participants.

This is not to suggest that all parents, or all teachers, are 'the same' in other contexts. Studies of parental involvement have emphasized the considerable diversity that exists across families, in terms of gender, class, family practices, attitudes towards education and benefits from it (cf. David 1993). And teachers are no less diverse in their interests and personal lives (e.g. Sikes *et al.* 1985). But it appears that such differences are generally displaced onto a more crude, binary distinction in the context of a consultation, where parent and teacher confront one another in a rather stark opposition between 'us' and 'them'. The identities of parent and teacher in these settings are *structurally oppositional*: it is impossible to be in both (interactional) places at once. And because of this fundamentally oppositional relation, it may be especially difficult for each participant to envisage the world from the position of the 'Other'. Teachers who are themselves parents, for instance, do not seem to show greater empathy with their parental 'clients' than teachers who do not have children – *within the consultation itself*. It may well be the case that teacher-parents are more sympathetic to the experiences of parents in other circumstances (see Sikes 1997). But within the confines of the consultation, teachers are obliged, it seems, to engage with parents very much 'as' teachers, leaving their parental identity at home. This non-reversibility of identities also helps to explain why teachers who are attending parents' evenings 'as' *parents* do not seem to feel any more powerful than any other parent (e.g. Walker 1998: 170). The consultations demonstrate in a particularly crystalline form, therefore, how subjects are constituted in and through discourse.

This 'up-close' look at parent–teacher consultations problematizes the ideals of 'partnership', 'parental involvement' and 'support' that underpin public aspirations for successful home–school relations. All of these aspirations depend on some kind of breaching, or dissolution, of the boundaries that insulate schools and homes. The evidence from this study suggests that the *proximity* that would ensue is something to be both feared and desired. Teachers and policy makers may want to breach those boundaries to recruit parents to do educational 'outreach' work, or even to smuggle school culture into homes (Baker and Keogh 1995). They may, in other words, want parents to act (be) more 'like' teachers. But perhaps not *too* like them. We saw above how parents could be deemed to know too much about curriculum or assessment; or how their indications of support could be construed as surveillance or interference. We saw too how personal, home-centric information is carefully (although not necessarily deliberately) managed and contained. The evidence from parents' evenings shows that the boundaries between home and school cannot simply be dissolved by good intentions or state interventions (such as home–school agreements).

Retrospect

I hope that this chapter has demonstrated something of the way in which selves and social lives are constructed through *talk*. Conversation analysis, which I have unfaithfully drawn on here, engages with discourse on what often seems like a very 'technical' level – the fine grain of turn-taking and sequential structure.[11] But I hope to have shown how these technical features 'carry' subtle meanings and effect significant social acts. Who you 'are', how you are treated, the constraints and possibilities that are open to you as a social actor, all of these are intimately tied up with interactional issues, such as who speaks when, how topics are developed and closed off, and so on. This kind of close focus on the details of mundane interaction has the potential to provide the missing link that some discourse analysts find in Foucauldian approaches, where the focus tends to be on the production of subjectivities at the level of institutions and social formations. As Poynton and Lee (2000) point out, Foucauldian discourse analysis has lacked a 'textual analytics' that is capable of tracing the effects of power in the 'specificity of what actual people actually say and do' (p. 6). A focus such as the one offered here has the potential to elaborate *how* subjects are 'constituted' in discourse, while still exercising agency and energy in their encounters with one another.

More generally, I hope you will, once again, have been able to glimpse the ways in which a discourse orientation can open up well-worn educational topics to new questions and directions. I hope this chapter has been useful in helping to see those routine and somewhat tiresome events known as parents' evenings in new ways, and to re-mobilize some rather stale concepts (such as partnership and involvement) that easily become either empty of meaning or overstuffed with discursive and ideological investments.

4

Taking a text apart: a discourse analysis of a polemical article

Introduction

This chapter provides a 'close reading' of one particular text, an article by a former chief inspector of schools, Chris Woodhead, which appeared in the centre-left weekly paper, the *New Statesman*, in March 1998. The article has been referred to in passing in Chapter 1. Here, however, I focus on the structure of the text as a whole. The article is a polemical attack on the state of educational research in the UK. As such, it is of fairly limited interest at this distance in time. My main aim in including it is to demonstrate how one might go about unravelling the structure of the arguments that hold a text together and produce its 'authority'.

New Statesman 20 March 1998

CHRIS WOODHEAD

Academia Gone to Seed

Once upon a time, educational research helped teachers and illuminated how children learn. Today's academics produce little more than badly written dross

THE INTERNATIONAL LIBRARY OF SOCIOLOGY:
THE SOCIOLOGY OF EDUCATION
Karl Mannheim (founder), *Routledge, 28 vols.*
various prices [. . .]

Around £63 million of taxpayers' money is spent each year on educational research. A good deal of this research is broadly speaking sociological. Much of it is 'poor value for money in terms of improving the quality of education provided in schools'. The comment is not mine. This is the professor of education at the University of Cambridge, David Hargreaves, speaking. In his view, much of the educational research published today is 'frankly, second-rate'. It neither helps teachers nor makes 'a serious contribution to fundamental theory or knowledge'. It simply 'clutters up academic journals which virtually nobody reads'.

I agree. I used to try to read these journals. I have given up. Life is too short. There is too much to do in the real world with real teachers in real schools to worry about methodological quarrels or to waste time decoding unintelligible, jargon-ridden prose to reach (if one is lucky) a conclusion that is often so transparently partisan as to be worthless.

But it was not always like this. In the 1940s Karl Mannheim founded the International Library of Sociology; it became the forum for pioneering research and theory across the whole range of sociological inquiry: into religion, politics, culture, work, the family and so on. Up to 1970, 275 volumes were published; Routledge has now reissued them, including 28 volumes on education.

To browse through these is to be reminded that sociologists used to engage with serious issues in a humane and accessible way.

[. . . .]

Professor Hargreaves' own contribution to the series, *Social Relations in a Secondary School*, remains a highly relevant text. He spent a whole year in his chosen school. He is painstakingly thorough. He is tentative in his conclusions and frank with regard to the limitations of his methodology. He is both perceptive and wise. Above all, he can *write*: 'The smoke and grime give an air of dilapidation to the larger buildings of churches and schools. For much of the year this little world seems grey and dismal, but on sunny days women and old people sit at the front door, on the step or a chair, and call to one another across the street, above the noise of the countless small children who play undisturbed'.

Just for a moment I thought Ursula Brangwen might appear at the end of that street. This is a book that, 31 years after its first publication, ought to be read by every young teacher who is baffled by the behaviour of his pupils and by every politician who is tempted to believe that the latest managerial intervention will suddenly and miraculously transform the social and psychological realities that define classroom life. Take this passage: 'During the art lesson, the teacher picked up a painting done by Derek and took it to the front of the class. When he called the form to attention and said, "Boys. Look what Derek's done", Derek was overwhelmed with confusion and embarrassment. He had assumed that the teacher was using his picture as an illustration of *bad* work'.

It is ridiculous to complain that books like that are not published every year. But it is reasonable to ask why so much that is now published in the sociology of education is of such dismal quality.

As it happens, the Office for Standards in Education is about to publish a study of educational research undertaken for us by James Tooley, senior research fellow at Manchester University School of Education. Tooley concludes: 'Not only was much of the research "partisan" in nature, . . . but this was actively condoned by influential researchers. Many of the papers reviewed raised severe doubts about methodology, in particular over the issues of sample size, the reporting of how samples were selected, and the difficulties inherent in the conduct and reporting of qualitative research. Much theoretical research was of dubious value, in particular that concerned with unquestioning adulation of particular "great" thinkers. Finally, the focus of educational research raised some cause for concern, particularly the lack of attention paid to the way learning and access could be improved for young people'.

Tooley is careful to state that some educational research is of high intellectual quality and of both theoretical and practical interest. But too much is not. Do we really need research into 'how schools, as patriarchal institutions that are ideologically and culturally heterosexual, create and maintain a set of inequitable circumstances that exercise a level of control over the "private" lives of lesbian teachers'? What about papers premised on unthinking acceptance of the belief, held by Professor Stephen Ball of King's College, London, that the Conservative government's reforms were driven by the wish that schools should be 'run and managed like businesses with a primary focus on the profit and loss account'? Do they really add to our understanding of how the development of an educational market can, for better or worse, influence what happens in schools? Does anyone really believe that an attempt to find out how Pierre Bourdieu's notion of 'habitus' can be applied to the primary classroom will in any sense raise standards?

These are not extreme examples picked to caricature the truth. They are taken from Tooley's stratified sample of articles selected from the prestigious *British Journal of Sociology of Education*.

So why has the quality of what is written declined so much? I think there are two explanations.

The first is something that government, if it wanted, could do something about. It is that the expansion of higher education, coupled with the demand that every academic institution produce more and more research, has inevitably resulted in a lot of nonsense being published.

The second explanation is much more problematic and even more controversial. It is that the sociology of education is a subject without a future. Its intellectual trajectory is doomed. On one hand, as I fear recent history shows, sociological researchers can go further and further down the ethnomethodological road, probing the interaction of everyday life in ever more minute detail; on the other, they can struggle to develop ever more complex and abstruse theories that purport to offer macro-explanations of what happens in our educational institutions. Neither possibility is likely to generate much that is of intellectual interest or, indeed, practical use.

There is, perhaps, a third way. This is to recognise that the future lies, if it lies anywhere, in the rediscovery of the importance of historical perspective; in the patient application of disciplines such as economics and philosophy to the understanding of our education system; in the suspension of political and professional prejudice; and above all, in a return to what was once the classical terrain: issues, that is, concerning social class and educability and schools as social systems.

I have quoted Cambridge's professor. Let me give the final word to Richard Pring, professor of Education at Oxford, who wrote in 1995 that 'so much of the educational bookshelves is covered with the kind of dross that a decade ago would never have seen the light of day'.

The Department of Education is about to embark on its own review of educational research. All of us who care about education and who worry about the misuse of public funds must hope that it manages to eliminate at least some of this dross. Is it possible for the sociology of education to regain the intellectual high ground it occupied when Karl Mannheim began putting his library together?

The policy context

First, it is necessary to sketch in a few details of the context. Woodhead was appointed Chief Inspector of Schools and head of the Office for Standards in Education (Ofsted) by a Conservative government and retained by the incoming Labour government after the 1997 general election. Throughout his term of office, which ended in 2000, Woodhead sustained a high public profile as the perceived scourge of teachers and defender of 'standards'. Woodhead's attack on educational research was part of a wider current of critique which emerged in the mid- to late 1990s. In addition to the Ofsted review commissioned by Woodhead and referred to in his article, another review was instigated around the same time by the Department for Education and Employment (Hillage *et al.* 1998). Critical voices had also been raised by hostile witnesses internal to the profession, such as David Hargreaves, whom Woodhead quotes. Woodhead was nevertheless a prime mover in the emergent critique, with his widely publicized appointment of James Tooley in September 1997 to carry out the Ofsted review of the quality and cost-effectiveness of educational research. Tooley was a controversial appointee, an academic already known for his right-wing views and his antipathy to educational research. Woodhead's *New Statesman* article, although ostensibly a book review, was also an advance announcement of the conclusions of Tooley's report. When that report was eventually published a few months later, in July 1998, with another public endorsement from Woodhead, the newspapers tended to focus on the same issues that Woodhead flagged up in the article under consideration here – that is, waste of public money, poor scholarship, irrelevance to classroom practice and alleged 'bias'.

The article that we are going to look at here was thus part of an intertextual fabric of press and policy criticism of educational research.

The article contains further traces of those intertextual threads, in the quotes from the two eminent professors, David Hargreaves and Richard Pring. Hargreaves' remark about 'second rate' research which 'cluttered up academic journals that virtually nobody read', quoted at the beginning of Woodhead's article, had, for instance, already been quoted in September 1997 in the right-wing *Spectator* (Leo McKinstry, 'Sending out research parties', 20 September 1997), and was quoted again in the *Telegraph* on the day of publication of Tooley's report (John Clare, 'Ofsted says £70m wasted on biased schools research', 23 July 1998). Pring's allegation of *dross* on the education bookshelves had a particularly lively intertextual career. Dated back to 1995 by Woodhead in the article above, it was quoted again in the papers on the day of publication of Tooley's report. Moreover, the word 'dross' became detached from its originator, and began to appear in headlines or sub-heads without attribution to Pring (as, indeed, it does in the sub-heading of the article under consideration here). For instance, the headline of *The Times* coverage of Tooley's report ran: 'Education research is dross, says Woodhead' (Victoria Fletcher, 23 July 1998). The deployment of quotable professors has been an important part of the rhetorics of this issue, as we shall see below.[1]

The article under scrutiny here is, therefore, part of a wider intertextual weave. As with all discourses, the edges of that weave are ultimately indeterminable. Towards the 'outer' edges, the critique of educational research shades into the more general discrediting of education 'experts' – teachers, teacher educators, subject specialists etc – that has been a feature of policy and press discourse for well over a decade. The critique of educational research also connects, intertextually, with a general and long-standing critique of academic writing as irrelevant, unreal, frivolous and biased.[2] As Chapter 6 argues, this is a very old and recurring hostility, directed towards the work of scholars, philosophers and others whose business is *writing*. While firmly lodged in the circumstances and politics of its 'own' time, Woodhead's article, as we shall see, deploys some venerable tropes and rhetorical devices.

'Spot the binaries: taking the text apart

Let us turn, then, to the *New Statesman* article. I want to focus on the binary oppositions around which the article is structured. Such binary structures are a general characteristic of texts, as we have already seen. Woodhead's article, in common with many polemical texts, wears its binaries on its sleeve. This makes them easy to spot and interrogate.

Perhaps most obviously, the article as a whole is structured around the opposition between *past* and *present*, flagged up in the sub-heading, with its opposition between 'Once upon a time' and 'Today's academics'. The pretext for this past/present opposition is the reissue of the Karl Mannheim International Library of Sociology, which Woodhead is purportedly reviewing, although he devotes only two paragraphs and a final sentence to it. As with all such binaries, this one is not forged on equal terms. Woodhead is telling a golden age story, in which the sociological past of Karl Mannheim, the 'intellectual high ground', is elevated above the present state of intellectual decline. This basic opposition between past (good) and present (bad) provides the structure onto which a range of other oppositions is mapped. In the past educational research (or sociology – the distinction is somewhat blurred throughout) was (intellectually) *serious*, where now it is *frivolous*. It was *accessible*, where now it is *unintelligible*. It was *relevant*, where now it is *irrelevant*. It was *impartial*, where now it is *partisan*. There is also the opposition, already mentioned in Chapter 1, between the *real world* (of 'real teachers in real schools') and the *unreal* world of research, with its preoccupation with prose and jargon. This dichotomy is mapped onto the past/present distinction, at the point where Woodhead first mentions the Karl Mannheim Library: 'It was not always like this'. This linkage ties together two main strands of critique that run through the article; that is, that in comparison with a better past, educational research is both intellectually inferior and of little practical use (because it is not grounded in the 'real' world).

A related binary opposition involves notions of science and objectivity. Tooley's critique, as reported by Woodhead, centres on the alleged failure to meet scientific criteria of adequacy such as impartiality and reliability (the latter evidenced in the concern about 'samples'). So there is a 'scientific/unscientific' opposition running through the text. Good research is scientific, bad research (i.e. most existing practice) is unreliable and biased. Tooley is clearly lined up by Woodhead on the scientific side of the binary: his review is (inaccurately) described as being based on a 'stratified sample' of articles.

The intellectual competence of present-day researchers is also attacked less overtly, through ascriptions which insinuate an *absence of thought*: 'unquestioning adulation' of great thinkers; 'unthinking acceptance' of Stephen Ball's 'belief'. There is tacit opposition at work here, between *proper* appreciation of the thinkers recruited to one's 'own' side, and *improper* reactions to the thinkers placed on the 'other' side. Proper appreciation equates to (earned) respect; improper appreciation is 'adulation'. Readers are not, I think, encouraged to interpret Woodhead's appreciation of Hargreaves, whom he describes as wise, perceptive, frank, thorough and literary, as 'adulation' or unthinking acceptance. Again, it should be stressed that this lop-sided strategy of valorizing the people on one's own team is not a quirk or pathology on the part of Woodhead, but a pervasive device used to construct textual authority.[3]

Accusations of failure to be properly 'scientific' can carry a moralizing aspect. 'Rigour', for instance (not used in the present article), may slide from its technical meaning to its more general sense of exactitude or (proper) severity. The charge of lack of rigour may impute moral laxity or at least intellectual laziness. Something of this dynamic is going on here. Hargreaves is characterized (in tacit opposition to present-day researchers) as 'painstakingly thorough', a commendation that might be taken to apply to his character as well as his methodological preferences. A similar slight on the diligence of educational researchers is implied when Woodhead recommends the '*patient* application of disciplines such as economics and philosophy'. The notion of methodological impartiality also carries a sense of moral propriety. Woodhead's description of present-day research as 'partisan' carries an imputation of impropriety, especially when (in the quotation from Tooley) 'influential' researchers are described as having 'actively condoned' this. No-one ever condones something that was morally unimpeachable in the first place.

More than half-way through the piece, three examples of poor-quality journal articles are cited from Tooley's report. Woodhead does not explicitly state why these particular articles are to be judged negatively, but simply describes their contents and poses rhetorical questions as to whether they are 'really' needed or relevant. We may assume that, by this point in the text, educational research has been lined up on the 'wrong' side of so many binaries – intellectual, moral, practical – that there is no need to spell out or justify the demerits of particular instances. The offending articles are suspended in the net of aspersions woven in the preceding paragraphs. This allows a good deal of the argumentation to be done without calling attention to itself in propositional language. It is likely, for instance, that the long quotation from one particular journal article is to be taken as an example of 'jargon ridden prose' (as opposed to real-world relevance); and that an interest in the lives and conditions of lesbian teachers, or the ideological and cultural dimensions of schools, is also irrelevant, and possibly 'partisan'. Ball is easily read as the 'bad' professor who either practises or promotes in others (it is not entirely clear) 'unthinking acceptance' of belief (in implicit contrast to the painstaking and thorough Hargreaves, and the properly scientific Tooley).[4] Bourdieu is presumably an example of one of the 'great' thinkers who are subject to 'unthinking adulation' and whose work is irrelevant to real-world concerns about standards.

The deployment of named education professors (Hargreaves and Pring 'versus' Ball) is worth exploring a little further, as a source of the text's claim to authority. Woodhead assigns particular authority to the views of Hargreaves and Pring, not only by quoting them directly, but by placing their quoted remarks at the beginning and the end of the article, so that they 'frame' the text. Moreover, Woodhead explicitly draws attention to the institutional affiliations of his professorial 'allies': 'I have quoted Cambridge's professor. Let me give the final word to Richard Pring, professor of education at Oxford'. Woodhead is invoking the intellectual authority of the two elite universities, and perhaps also the authority of history and tradition associated with them, given the past/ present axis on which the text is hung. The views of these professors are to be believed, not just because of their rational or persuasive force, but because they emanate from noted seats of learning, tradition and prestige.

It might be helpful to list the binary oppositions that have been identified in this text, although this carries the risk of oversimplifying and schematizing textual operations that are much more mobile and complex.

Positive	Negative
past	present
serious	frivolous
high ground	decline
relevant	irrelevant
impartial/objective	partial/partisan
accessible	inaccessible
sense	nonsense (unintelligible)
real world	writing (jargon/prose)
real people (teachers, children, Woodhead)	researchers
world of practice	world of 'theory' (Bourdieu; patriarchy)
good theory	bad theory
good writing	bad writing
proper appreciation of thinkers	improper appreciation of thinkers
scientific	unscientific
moral propriety – painstaking/ thorough/frank/impartial	moral impropriety – lax/prejudiced/ inclined to adulation
practical	impractical
social class (as topic)	gender, sexuality
high intellectual quality	low intellectual quality
thinking	unthinking
good professors (Hargreaves, Pring)	bad professors (Ball)
Oxford and Cambridge	The rest
value:	waste:
– for money	– of money
– use	– useless
– quality	– dross

The accumulation of negative terms in the various binary oppositions is amalgamated in the last two paragraphs into Pring's resonant word: *dross*. And in a familiar device of polemical language, Woodhead appeals to the readers as 'us', calling on 'All of us who care' to eliminate the dross.

Some items in the list above appear on both sides of the line. Theory, for instance, is negative when contrasted with the real world of real schools. But there is also good theory, when it is opposed to the bad theory of contemporary educational research. Woodhead's critique is anti-intellectual and intellectually elitist at the same time, therefore. Educational research is condemned for failing to concern itself with the real world of practice and standards *and* for failing to be properly theoretical. In other words, Woodhead plays the *theory/practice* opposition 'both ways'.

Woodhead acknowledges the binary nature of his analysis in proposing a 'third way' – a keyword in the political lexicon of New Labour in its first term, as Fairclough (2000: 4–6) notes. Although the notion of a third way suggests some kind of transcendence of opposites through reconciliation, Woodhead's third way for the sociology of education amounts to going back to the future. It is a strategy of *rediscovery* (of historical perspective), of *return* (to the 'classical terrain' of social class), of aiming to '*regain* the intellectual high ground'.

Contradictions

Where do Woodhead's binary oppositions break down (as all such oppositions do) into contradiction? The paragraph in which he formulates his third way encapsulates several, including the use of the term 'third-way' itself. There is irony in using a pre-eminently politicized keyword to urge 'the suspension of political and professional prejudice'. And in calling for a return to a concern for social class and disadvantage in a voice which is so clearly impressed by the elite credentials of Oxbridge professors. The advocacy of 'disciplines such as economics and philosophy' seems to contradict the disapproval, expressed earlier, towards Ball's market analysis of reform, and the application of Bourdieu to primary schooling.[5] In recommending philosophy for the third way, Woodhead is also, somewhat paradoxically, recommending a return to something that has *already* returned, with the growth of research informed by postmodernism, pragmatics and deconstruction, and the use of insights from philosophers such as Derrida, Foucault, Rorty and Lacan. However, this work would presumably be exempt under the 'adulation of great thinkers' clause as the wrong sort of philosophy.

Perhaps the most entrenched contradiction concerns the notion of 'historical perspective'. For the article is rather adrift in terms of its own history. The past/present axis of the article does not stand up to much critical pressure. For instance, in advocating politically neutral research, Woodhead overlooks the fact that the golden age of the sociology of education which he invokes was emphatically one of socio-political critique. The 'new sociology of education' which he celebrates was highly critical of schooling, viewing it as a mechanism for the reproduction of social inequality. The influential ethnographies of schooling that were carried out from the late 1960s to the early 1980s were directly and explicitly engaged in the public debate about secondary education and how best to achieve the dissolution (more or less) of the two-tier system of secondary modern and grammar schools. Woodhead does not mention that Hargreaves' book was a study of a *secondary modern* school, and that it suggested that the two-tier system perpetuated the cultures and conditions of disadvantage. Hargreaves' (1967) study of Lumley School was, in fact, the first in a series of critical ethnographies of different types of secondary schools, including *Hightown Grammar* by his fellow researcher at Manchester University at the time, Colin Lacey (1970). So if one were inclined (as I clearly am) to disorganize the past/present economy of Woodhead's binary structures, one might argue that contemporary educational research is no more politically invested these days than it was in the 'once upon a time' of Hargreaves and the old new sociology of education.

There are further intricacies around the deployment of Hargreaves as the exemplary figure in a vanished sociological past. Take, for instance, the juxtaposition of Hargreaves with Stephen Ball, whose article was singled out by Tooley/Woodhead as an example of contemporary decline, in contrast to the high-ground of Hargreaves' ethnography. The relation between Hargreaves and Ball could be read otherwise. It would be quite possible, for those 'inside' the discourses of educational research, to find a historical link, rather than a sharp divide, between these two figures. For Ball was a student of Lacey, and his study of a comprehensive school, *Beachside Comprehensive*, published in 1981, was widely held to take its place alongside Hargreaves' and Lacey's books as the last in a trilogy of 'classic' ethnographies of secondary schooling.

In the time-frame of Woodhead's argument, Hargreaves does not, of course, only stand for 'the past'. He exemplifies that fragment of the past which persists into the present, and is presumably also part of the 'third way' that will lead research forward/back to the intellectual high ground. But it is possible, again, to unsettle the terms of Woodhead's argument. Hargreaves is a controversial choice as a figure of intellectual and educational continuity, whose public career has often been interpreted, in academic and educational circles, in terms of *discontinuity*.[6] The education press often refers to him, usually approvingly, as a 'maverick' (see, for example, Swain and Williams 2000).

One of the most interesting contradictions revolves around the two paragraphs extolling Hargreaves' book. It is striking that, in an article which prioritizes the 'real world', Woodhead approves 'above all' the quality of the *writing*. It is the sub-Lawrentian prose style which most impresses. The line between fiction and real world is quite blurred. Hargreaves' writing is so 'realistic' that Woodhead thinks for a moment that Ursula Brangwen might appear. His comments unintentionally point to the textual fabric of the real world, and the power of fiction to pass itself off as reality.

Conclusion

I have looked in some detail at a text that would not normally receive, or perhaps merit, close examination. My main point is not (or not just) to argue, as other commentators have done, that Woodhead is himself biased, or that he oversimplifies the complexities of past and present. Nor do I want to simply reverse the poles of Woodhead's dichotomy to argue that all education research is, on the contrary, excellent. Such blanket assertions mean very little. I would not want to argue, either, against taking a historical perspective. The loss of focus on social class as a research topic, for instance, is a matter which deserves to be taken seriously in my view. But my main aim here has been to uncover the tropes – the figures of speech and rhetorical devices – on which arguments depend (that is, literally, 'hang').

It is important to recognize, though, that taking texts apart is not necessarily a guarantee of political effectiveness. Policies or prejudices do not simply fall apart once their binaries have been disassembled – not in any immediate and direct way at least. The intertextual 'after-life' that any particular critique enjoys is always a knotty and tangled matter. It may be ignored or dismissed; or it may, on the other hand, get caught up and be more widely disseminated, if it connects with other sentiments and allegiances that are in circulation at the time.

But there are longer-term arguments for mobilizing the kind of 'discursive literacy' which is capable of doing this kind of 'disarticulating' work on the texts of education. The capacity to interrogate, or at least to 'interrupt', the flat pronouncements of common sense or polemic offers a new kind of agency to teachers, students and researchers, by providing resources for asking how particular interests and views are stitched up in texts.

The fabrication of research

The writing of Realism is far from being neutral, it is on the contrary loaded with the most spectacular signs of fabrication.

(Roland Barthes 1967: 73)

I confess that I still have difficulty uncoupling myself from the persuasive promises of ethnography. I desire to construct good stories filled with the stuff of rising and falling action, plots, themes and denouements.

(Deborah Britzman 2000: 32)

Introduction

Educational research is, unavoidably, a rhetorical affair. Like any other texts, research texts – reports, articles, instruments – are 'fabrications'. Their truths and findings are put together – that is, built or woven (depending on the sense of 'fabric' that one prefers) to achieve particular effects and structures – rather than artlessly culled from a pre-existing world Out There. As we have seen, this is never an innocent business. Texts assemble and deploy the objects and phenomena to which they seem to refer, so as to invest them with particular moral and epistemological significances. For instance, 'the teacher' is no less rhetorical a figure in the discourses of educational research than in the press and policy discourses that have been discussed in previous chapters (cf. Nespor and Barber 1991; and see below). In all of these discourses, 'the teacher' is a made, rather than a found, personage, woven into fabrics of differing personal, moral and theoretical resonances, depending on the text into which 'she' is insinuated. The notion of 'fabrication' also reminds us that texts work somewhat like lies. This is not to say that there is nothing but falsehood, or that no research can be trusted. But like lies, texts are artful, and they succeed when they *persuade* us that some state of affairs, proposition or argument is as it appears to be.[1]

Moreover, texts are often at their most persuasive when they don't seem at all rhetorical, but rather pass themselves off as fact or realistic description. Barthes (1967) called this 'degree-zero' writing – that is, writing that appears to be free of rhetoric and bias, and impervious to dissenting interpretations. Scientific writing has also long been thought of as rhetoric-free and interpretation-proof; or at least as coming closer to these conditions than other kinds of writing, such as literature, journalism and polemics. It is this supposed absence of style, animus and literary artifice that allows scientific texts to conjure an uncontestable world of objective facts and independently existing realities. But studies of scientific texts have shown that the no-style, no-guile quality of scientific writing is *itself* a stylistic accomplishment. A fabrication, in other words. 'The style of non-style is itself the style of science', writes J. Gusfield (quoted in Atkinson 1990: 43). Latour and Woolgar (1979) show how scientific papers use rhetorical and literary devices to persuade readers of the facticity of their arguments. The signal achievement of scientific rhetoric, they say, is to *erase* its own workings: 'The function of literary inscription is the successful persuasion of readers, but the readers are only fully convinced when all the sources of persuasion have disappeared' (p. 76).

What these studies of scientific texts show is that it can be hard for readers to spot the rhetoric in non-fictional and scholarly texts. Texts conspire to erase the traces of their fabrication. Just as in other disciplines, research texts in education often pose themselves as unproblematic, in terms of their relation to the 'external' situations that they describe, the knowledge claims that they make, the subjects that they depict and, indeed, the kind of *reader* that they tacitly summon to the act of reading.

This chapter, then, will begin to explore the textuality of educational research. The point is not to take the rhetoric out of research, or the research out of its rhetorical dress. There is no external, non-textual vantage point from which research knowledge can be grasped. 'No outside-text', as Derrida (1976: 159) famously, and contentiously, stated.[2] The point is to interrupt, or disrupt, the processes by which research knowledge is customarily produced, and treated by those who read it as self-evident. As the words 'interrupt' and 'disrupt' suggest, with their shared etymology of rupture, this involves finding and forcing *openings* in the smooth fabric of research texts (see Stronach and MacLure 1997). It is important to stress again that the kind of opening that is demonstrated and practised in this book is not a form of unmasking or illumination, in which the true meaning is revealed behind the surface deceptions of the text. Texts cannot be reduced to singular meanings. But they can be unsettled – shaken up, breached, disturbed, torn – so that new questions and meanings are generated. And while my focus is upon qualitative research texts, and ethnographies in particular, it is also worth reiterating that qualitative research writing is no more susceptible to this kind of shaking up than quantitative or scientific genres. *All* forms of writing can be subject to interrogation along the lines of the questions listed below.

Here are some general questions, then, that I might ask in order to 'open up' a research text:

• How do politics and poetics intertwine in this text?
• Does this text carry the 'scent' of an institution (e.g. the law, education, medicine etc.)?
• How are knowledge claims established and defended?
• How does this text make its bid for believability?
• Where does this text get its authority?
• How does this text persuade?
• Where does power reside in this text?
• What other kinds of texts is this text 'like'?
• What might be so taken for granted in this text that it is almost impossible to 'see' it? (A trick question, of course, but no less important because of that.)
• Whose 'voices' are privileged in this text? Who is silenced?
• What kinds of oppositions structure the arguments and the moral framework of this text? How might these oppositions be broken down?
• How are subjects drawn in this text? Who gets agency?
• What kind of reader is this text 'hailing'? Where am I supposed to 'stand'? – 'What am I participating in when I read it?', as Johnson (1987: 4) writes.
• What are the questions that this text cannot pose to itself?
• Where are the gaps, silences and inconsistencies in this text?

The remainder of this chapter will be given over to asking questions of some examples and fragments of research texts. Or – better perhaps – to responding to the questions posed by those texts. Because, in a sense, there is no general checklist of questions, no blueprint for opening up a text. The questions that I have listed above are some of those that, looking back, it seems I have been moved to ask. But they were not used to guide my inquiries except in the most loose and dimly felt way. It's more a matter of being attentive to the questions that each individual text raises for you, at least as a starting point. Barbara Johnson (1987), attempting to describe deconstruction without reducing it to a formula, writes of trying to preserve your capacity for *surprising yourself* (p. 15). I think this is as good a guideline as any for the acts of close reading that this book recommends. The hardest thing to see in any text is that which poses itself as natural and unquestionable. So a first step towards opening up any text would be to watch and wait for something – often a little, seemingly inconsequential thing – that somehow catches your attention, puzzles you. For instance, in the first example below, I think the question that first occurred to me was, *What are the half-moon glasses doing here?*

The discussion of the text fragments below may well seem like gross over-attention to small, mundane pieces of research writing. I will certainly be producing many more words 'about' these snatches of text than the texts themselves comprise. It might be helpful to think of the examples as 'pre-texts' rather than traditional objects of analysis – as starting points, and excuses, for fabricating further texts. In the course of this fabrication, methodological questions of realism, of intertextuality and of boundaries – between self and other, writer and reader, inside and outside – will emerge.

'The off-stage miracle': getting 'the field' into the text

Here are two short fragments from an evaluation report. The report deals with the work and careers of researchers employed on a programme of linked research projects. The first fragment describes one of the project directors in a meeting with her team of researchers. The second fragment comes from the concluding section of the report, which attempts to build a theory of how research careers operate in the economy of academic production. I am primarily interested in the first extract, but I include the second because it is partly from the *contrast* between the two passages that we can get a glimpse of what the first one might be 'up to'.

> Ros takes them methodically and carefully through the workplan. She leans forward, back straight, gaze direct over half-moon glasses, punctuating her listening with nods and a slow procession of 'yes', 'yes', 'OK', that's right'.

> A first step towards that might be to regard these intellectual goods as a 'complex totality' rather than as some kind of economic exchange (even if only metaphorically expressed) – in the manner of Mauss and Levi-Strauss . . .
> (Stronach and Macdonald 1991: 31 and 65)

The most obvious point about this example is the sharp differences of discourse that can reside within a single research text.[3] The first part is descriptive and factual, the second analytic and conceptual.[4] The first seems closer to reality, perhaps, since it describes a (reportedly) real person, in terms of visual attributes and observable behaviours. It does not use 'technical' terms and it is easy to understand. The second deals with ideas and theoretical concepts. It is more 'abstract' and it might be hard to decipher by readers who were unfamiliar with the authors and concepts invoked, even if those readers had access to the full text of the report. It has many of the features of 'technical discourse' as described by Lemke (1995) – that specialized register that appeals to a cognoscenti of readers with a shared knowledge of other texts, who are familiar with oblique grammatical constructions and who are able to decode allusions to theoretical models and respected 'ancestors' (see also Lofland 1974; Atkinson 1990).[5]

Why would you need both kinds of discourse? Or, to put it another way, what might these two different kinds of writing be intended to *do* in this text? One answer is that they seek to establish two different kinds of *authority*. Taking the second fragment first, it is fairly clear what kind of authority is claimed: this is the author-evaluator addressing an academic or professional readership.

The first fragment, which is the one I want to concentrate on, testifies that the author-evaluator was actually present in 'the field', and that the theory elaborated elsewhere in the report, concerning research careers, is therefore grounded in up-close observation of actual researchers in action. As analysts of anthropological writing have pointed out, one of the main tasks facing ethnographers has always been to establish that they were truly, fully and deeply 'There' – that is, immersed in the 'other' world about which their monograph or report theorizes. In order to trust the theory, readers must also trust the description of what the ethnographer saw in the field and the meanings that he or she attached to this. They must be persuaded that had they too been there, they would have seen pretty much what the ethnographer saw. Clifford Geertz (1988) famously called this the challenge of 'Being There', and he stressed that it is a textual accomplishment: a matter of writing in such a way that readers are persuaded that 'this off-stage miracle has occurred' (p. 5). This is a challenge that confronts every qualitative researcher whose analysis, theory or conclusions rest on 'data' gathered in that Other place called the field.

Geertz showed that there are many different ways of bringing off the trick of Being There, depending on the style and the authorial 'signature' of the writer. The example above is a simple and familiar one, in the form of a quasi-objective description. It relies heavily on the *visual*, a common source of authority and 'veracity' within the realist genre of writing (see Crapanzano 1986: 57; and see below). On my reading of this fragment, this is one of the functions of the 'half-moon glasses' which first caught my eye in this text. They provide information that *only a co-present observer* would have had access to.

The first fragment derives further authority from the fact that it is taken from observation notes made on-the-spot. Field notes have a special significance in ethnography, as we will see later in this chapter, because they bear the traces of the 'field' itself. As first-order jottings done in the midst, so to speak, of the field experience, field notes seem to be 'closer' to reality, or to experience, than the more polished texts of the final report or monograph. As James Clifford (1990) observes, field notes have often been thought of as the embodiment of 'pure inscription' – of that moment of alchemy that effects 'the passage of experiential phenomena into writing' (p. 56). But as Clifford points out, and as we shall see in more detail later, the idea of pure inscription does not hold up. Other texts and discourses have always gone before, shaping the conventions available for writing. And, as Clifford also notes, even to *notice* some activity or fact, as an observer, is to assume some frame or inscription within which that which is noticed achieves significance – that is, comes to count as notice-able. Nevertheless, the first fragment can be read as claiming the authority of first-hand witness: it carries a little piece of the field 'back' into the final text.

What else might be going on in this short, fairly unremarkable piece of writing? It is obviously a description of one of the researchers carrying out one of the research tasks. More than this though, it assembles, indirectly, an *identity* for Ros – as the kind of person who carries out tasks in this way. We are intended to 'read' Ros, I think, as careful, methodical, attentive, patient, receptive to others' contributions. What else are we invited to know about her? Well, there are the half-moon glasses, which possibly suggest something about Ros's age (reading glasses being commonly associated with middle age). Or perhaps they invoke a scholarly aspect. In any event, we might conclude that the description in these two short sentences is far from direct, spontaneous or disinterested. It is carefully wrought to assemble a portrayal of 'Ros'. Again we see that there are no 'innocent' inscriptions of people or facts.

Returning to the idea of catching the 'surprise' in the text: why did the half-moon glasses particularly catch my eye here? Well, I don't really know. But one possible reason is that they took on a kind of hyper-specificity in contrast to the rather neutral words used in the rest of the passage – leaning, listening, gazing, punctuating. They called attention to themselves, as it were – or, rather, called attention to the textual machinery that had produced this piece of 'factual' description. And thus, for this particular reader, alert to the issue of textual work, the glasses paradoxically opened up a little hole in the fabric of the text's unassuming facticity, through which the *writing* could be glimpsed.

Where shall I stand? Personal versus scientific authority

The next example is also taken from an evaluation report – in this case, of an innovative music course (referred to below as 'the MCPS Project') at a conservatoire, which required students to work closely with local communities. The 'evaluator' referred to below is also the writer of the report. I want to open up this text via two questions:

1 Where is 'the evaluator' located in this fragment?
2 How are we to read Simon's last remark?

> The evaluator was in conversation with students from the MCPS Project and they were questioning him about the way the evaluation worked. How would it report? Would there be, at the end of a long three years, a lengthy and unreadable report? The response (not at all frivolous) was that the more successful the evaluation, the shorter the report – the best final report would be a simple but all-encapsulating phrase. Some weeks later the evaluator was sitting with the Project Director in a bar around the corner from the Guildhall and a regular dropping-in place for students. Simon, a singing student on MCPS, came in for a quick drink before going off to hear a concert being given by singing students on the Jazz course. 'Simon', shouted Peter [the Project Director] across the bar, 'will you be joining the course again next year?' Simon hesitated. 'I don't think so, Peter. I might have a chance of getting on to the Opera course'. (An advanced course and a prestigious opportunity). 'Oh, Simon', Peter teased, 'I thought you were committed to this innovation – I thought you'd abandoned the star system!' Simon leaned over sideways as he reached for his pint at the bar – 'well, there you are. You see you're not just fighting the institution, you're fighting the dream'.
>
> (Kushner 1985: III)

There are interesting effects of voice and presence in this text. The evaluator is both 'inside' and 'outside' the reported scene. On the one hand, the writer refers to himself in the third person, as 'him' and 'the evaluator'. This helps to establish an objective, outsider perspective on the scene and all its participants, including the evaluator himself, who thus looks down on himself from an external vantage point. Yet the evaluator is also placed 'inside' the scene described, taking an active part in the bar-room conversation. By putting 'the evaluator' in two different places, textually speaking – both in the thick of things *and* on the outside looking in – this fragment claims two different kinds of authority, more or less simultaneously. First, it claims the authority of rich, subjective immersion in the culture of the research subjects. And, second, it claims the professional/scientific authority of the distanced academic.

The tension and the trade-off that this fragment enacts – between personal and scientific authority, subjective and objective perspective – is characteristic of empirical or qualitative research writing, across many disciplines. Clifford Geertz (1988), writing of ethnography, described it as the challenge of '[f]inding somewhere to stand in a text that is supposed to be at one and the same time an intimate view and a cool assessment' (p. 10). Mary Louise Pratt (1986) describes it as the contradictory call for 'engagement' and 'self-effacement' (p. 33). She describes the tension between personal and scientific authority thus:

> In terms of its own metaphors, the scientific position of speech is that of an observer fixed on the edge of a space, looking in and/or down upon what is other. Subjective experience, on the other hand, is spoken from a moving position already within or down in the middle of things, looking and being looked at, talking and being talked at.
>
> (Pratt 1986: 32)

Pratt's description of the two 'positions' required of ethnographers is immediately recognizable in the above fragment. Ethnographers, and qualitative researchers in general, write under the distracting obligation to speak from somewhere *very* particular (the specific scene of the fieldwork, case study, etc.) and yet also from nowhere-in-particular – from the distanciated position of the social scientist with no particular axe to grind.

The two positions do not always occur simultaneously. In ethnographic monographs, the place traditionally reserved for the personal narrative was the beginning – the opening chapter, which described the anthropologist's arrival at, and absorption into, the local culture. Having provided a long, vivid personal narrative of arrival, the bulk of the monograph was often devoted to the elaboration of facts, analytic categories, and so on. Pratt also notes that the oscillation between up-close personal narrative and 'objectified description' can be traced back to the antecedents of anthropology, in the travellers' tales of exotic lands that circulated in Europe from the early sixteenth century.

There are no 'pure' qualitative research texts

The contrary pull of subjective and objective authority influences the style and genre of ethnographic texts, ensuring that these are never 'pure' texts with their own unique conventions that would distinguish them clearly from other kinds of writing. Paul Atkinson (1990) draws attention to 'the elementary fact that ethnographic writing was – and is – a genre which has elective affinities with other modes of writing' (pp. 31–2). Clifford Geertz (1988) asserts, more pithily, that ethnographies 'tend to look at least as much like romances as they do like lab reports (though [. . .] not really like either)' (p. 8). Returning to our example above, this description seems particularly apt: the second half, taken out of context, could almost (but not quite) have occurred in a 'Mills and Boon' romantic novel.

This is not to suggest that this text is especially frivolous or deficient with respect to some 'proper' way to write educational research. Nor was Geertz implying that 'lab reports' are intrinsically superior to 'romances' as representations of events; or that ethnographers should emulate scientific writing. Rather, he was underlining the essentially blurred nature of the boundaries between supposedly distinct discourses.[6] My aim in identifying the traces of other genres in research and evaluation reports is to point, once again, to the inescapable *written-ness* of the descriptions and portrayals of educational research. Even in the most simple, innocent, uncontentiously descriptive passages, there is *writing*. By looking closely at how this writing has been done, it is possible to glimpse the processes of fabrication that produce research accounts, and the extent to which these processes are indebted to other modes of writing.

Even when – perhaps especially when – we think we are pretty much 'writing down' what we see, we are deeply bound by old, enduring conventions. I want to explore further the indebtedness of educational research texts to other modes of writing, and the extent to which our resources for apprehending reality are deeply *conventional*.

Framing culture: three examples

Let us approach this by looking at three paragraphs from three different ethnographic texts. Each one introduces its readers to the setting in which the research was carried out, and appears near the beginning of the book. The first comes from an ethnography of two neighbourhoods in Chicago in the 1920s, *The Gold Coast and the Slum*, by H.W. Zorbaugh (1929), a member of the Chicago School of urban sociology. The second is taken from David Hargreaves' 1967 classic, *Social Relations in a Secondary School*, a study which played a major role in the establishment of the sociology of education in the UK in the 1960s and 1970s.[7] The third comes from Marjorie Shostak's (1981) book *Nisa: The Life and Words of a !Kung Woman*, a study of a woman member of the !Kung people in the Kalahari. Note how similar these passages are.

> At the back door of the Gold Coast [an affluent area of Chicago], on Dearborn, Clark and La Salle streets, and on the side streets extending south to the business and industrial area, is a strange world, painfully plain in contrast, a world that lives in houses with neatly lettered cards in the window: 'Furnished rooms'. In these houses, from midnight to dawn, sleep some twenty-five thousand people. But by day houses and streets are practically deserted. For early in

the morning this population hurries from its houses and down its streets, boarding cars and buses, to work in the Loop. It is a childless area, an area of young men and young women, most of whom are single, though some are married, and others are living together unmarried. It is a world of comings and goings, of dull routine and little romance, a world of unsatisfied longings.

(Zorbaugh 1929: 9; cited in Atkinson 1990: 32)

Lumley [district] is rather like a small island, surrounded on two sides by the tentacles of industry and on the third by a main road, which is lined with shops and stores. These natural boundaries enclose the maze of stereotyped streets [. . .] The smoke and grime give an air of sorrowful dilapidation to the larger buildings of churches and schools. For much of the year this little world seems grey and dismal, but on sunny days women and old people sit at the front door, on the step or a chair, and call to one another across the street, above the noise of countless small children who play undisturbed.

(Hargreaves 1967: 1–2)

Walking into a traditional !Kung village, a visitor would be struck by how fragile it seemed beneath the expanse of sky and how unobtrusively it stood amid the tall grass and sparse tree growth of the surrounding bush. [. . .] A visitor who arrived in the middle of the cold season – June and July – would see mounds of blankets and animal skins in front of the huts, covering people still asleep beside their fires. Those who had already awakened would be stoking the coals, rebuilding the fire, and warming themselves in the chilly mountain air.

(Shostak 1981: 7–8; cited in Pratt 1986: 43)

The communities described in these three passages are worlds, and decades, apart. But the descriptions are very similar in some respects. First, they are all expository, 'guidebook'-type introductions, in which the locale is described as it might appear to a visitor or outsider.[8] All three are intensely oriented towards the visual – towards that which can be seen by the observer, such as topographical features and observable behaviours. Paul Atkinson (1990) notes, with particular reference to the Zorbaugh extract, that such introductions are typical of the 'classic realist' mode of writing: 'The reader is introduced, as if a stranger or outsider, in the fashion of a guidebook. The *setting* is portrayed in concrete terms, its features catalogued and some social types sketched in' (p. 32). As Atkinson explains, there were explicit textual (and, indeed, social) connections between the Chicago sociologists, of whom Zorbaugh was one, and the American naturalist novelists of the 1920s. However, the textual conventions of realism stretch back to the early nineteenth century and forward to the present day, where they continue to underpin popular culture in literary fiction, film and television (see, for example, Belsey 1980: 67).

In each of the passages above, there is also a kind of zoom effect that guides the eye 'inwards' from a broad, panoramic view of the local geography, towards the people who inhabit that space. In the first two passages, there is also a strong sense of aerial perspective – of the writer/observer hovering above the mean streets, before focusing in on the people who live in them. In the third, the writer, and the imagined visitor, approach at ground level. But all three passages describe a community seen, and approached, from the *outside*. One effect that this panoramic perspective achieves is to provide a *frame* around the community that will be the subject of the research. The Chicago slum is shown as bounded by the fashionable district and the industrial area. The !Kung village is surrounded by the grass and the sky. Lumley is clearly marked off from its surroundings – island-like and enclosed by the 'tentacles' of industry and the main road. This framing of the culture is also achieved, less obviously, through the suggestion of social or cultural *contrasts* – explicitly in the case of the slum, which is contrasted with the affluent Gold Coast, and also in the case of Lumley, where the preceding paragraph to the one quoted compares its working-class inhabitants to the 'professional people' who have moved outside the town boundaries. In the case of the !Kung, cultural contrasts are not specifically drawn, though we might assume a taken-for-granted contrast between a community of semi-nomadic hunter-gatherers in a distant country and the 'back home' cultures of the assumed readers.

There are also striking similarities in the content of the passages. In each, when the description 'zooms in', it captures the inhabitants coming to life, as it were. These are quite literally 'enlightenment' scenes. Emerging into the light after a night's sleep, or lured by the sunshine, people are depicted issuing from their houses or sleeping places to engage in the routines of everyday life – boarding cars and buses, sitting at their front doors, rebuilding the fire. They emerge into the landscapes of their environment, just as they emerge into the text.

The description continues to be made from a fixed vantage point somewhere outside the scene, even though the focus has tightened: people pass before the eye of the observer *en masse*, still at a remove. Although there is movement in each passage, it is the repetitive movement of unvarying routine. And although there is time, it is the cyclical time of day and night or the seasons. The inhabitants in all three passages are frozen in the date-less zone of the 'ethnographic present' (Fabian 1983). As James Clifford (1986b) notes, this has been one of the ways in which ethnography has constructed its subjects at arm's length, as 'Others'. By suspending the subjects in time, the ethnographic present 'effectively textualizes the other, and gives the sense of a reality not in temporal flux, not in the same ambiguous, moving, *historical* present that includes and situates the other, the ethnographer and the reader' (p. 111).

Framing devices

The cumulative effect of all these rhetorical devices is to establish boundaries and frames. The three passages are all concerned with demarcating insides from outsides. Each passage invokes, very economically, a clearly bounded culture, insulated from its surroundings and from the vicissitudes of time, viewed across an unbreached perimeter that divides, and distinguishes, the inside from the outside. The culture in question is also insulated from *ambiguity* – about who belongs on the inside and who does not; about whether some people feel they sort of half-belong; about multiple and dissenting views among participants of what it might mean to be a working man in a Chicago rooming house, a granny on the front step of a Lumley terraced house, or a member of a !Kung village.

The culture is framed in such a way that it is also insulated from ambiguities of *interpretation*. In each fragment, the authorial voice is assured, summary and unqualified. Zorbaugh and Hargreaves use the 'universal present' tense, a tense associated with 'factuality and certainty' and common in instructional texts such as school textbooks (cf. Kress 1985: 91). Both of these authors invoke a 'world' (a strange one and a little one, respectively) over which, it is implied, they have interpretive dominion. All three descriptions project a singular, stable and potentially *knowable* cultural domain.

The framing devices in these passages also set up clear boundaries between the subjects of the research on the one hand, and the writer and the reader on the other. The guidebook format, the panoramic perspective and the fixed vantage point work together to line the reader up with the writer on the outside of the frame, looking 'in' at a cohesive culture that is depicted as going about its business uncontaminated by the biases, motives or personal histories of either reader or writer. Mary Louise Pratt (1986) describes the work of the Shostak passage thus: 'here is a traditional society doing its traditional thing, oblivious to the alien observing presence' (p. 43). The pervasive 'visualism' of all three passages, noted above, contributes further to the location of the research subjects as 'others', located in a frame that separates them from the interpretive frailties and fantasies of the ethnographer or the reader, who are positioned merely as onlookers. As James Clifford (1986a) puts it, the effect of visualism is 'to confer upon the other a discrete identity, while also providing the knowing observer with a standpoint from which to see without being seen, to read without interruption' (p. 12).

There is, of course, more than purely visual information in each scene: each also contains material that would not be available to direct observation, and which goes beyond 'literal' description. Indeed, this is partly where each writer's claim to authority rests. Zorbaugh claims access to the lives and loves of the rooming house dwellers. Shostak 'knows', not just what a traditional village looks like, but also how it would strike a visitor. Hargreaves describes the emotional impact of the streets, as well as their greyness and smokiness. Nevertheless, in foregrounding the visual, the authors are able to smuggle in their knowledgeability without drawing too much attention to the question of their partiality.

The three passages all occur near the beginning of the book in question and are, therefore, themselves frames for the book-to-come. One of the jobs that each does is to begin to make the culture *available* as an object of study. Each begins to carve out a space within which the research will be located. More than that, though, each passage contains coded and highly conventionalized 'reading instructions' that tell readers many different things, as described above: how to think the notion of culture; where to 'stand' to get the best view of it; why to trust the author; what kind of knowledge to expect. There are also indirect instructions as to what sort of *reader* the text expects – that is, an autonomous individual who can dissociate herself from the subjects of the research and who can, therefore, be confident of accruing uninterrupted knowledge 'about' them.

The reading that I have offered of the three passages may seem over-wrought. Each short passage is made to bear a heavy freight of significance. Each is, after all, only part of the preamble to an entire book, which is left unexamined. Hargreaves, for instance, has not even got round to describing the school that lies at the heart of the book, at the point from which the passage is taken; and the study is not centrally 'about' the old women and the children in the streets, but about the boys in the fourth form (year 10). Still, he has already mapped out the space (geographical, cultural and epistemological) within which the school and then the fourth-form students will be placed. And he has already told us something about what kind of readers he wants us to be and where his authority resides. Although the introduction does not determine the content of the book by any means, it does set up some of the ground rules for how the book shall be read.[9]

Realism and intertextuality

I have written as if these rhetorical devices and reading instructions simply reside 'within' each individual passage. But they derive their force from the fact that, as already noted above, they repeat a familiar, pervasive and remarkably long-lived mode of representing the world (including the imagined worlds of literature) that goes under the name of *realism*. The term has a profusion of meanings, but many definitions would include the characteristics that have been noted above: the assumption of knowledgeable authors and readers, jointly engaged in the production and accumulation of knowledge 'about' an external reality, describable through a seemingly transparent language which appears to reflect it faithfully. This is why the three passages, about such disparate worlds, can look so similar. 'Realism is plausible', writes Catherine Belsey (1980), 'not because it reflects the world, but because it is structured out of what is (discursively) familiar' (p. 47).

Realist texts draw upon a shared, intertextual lineage that links them to countless other texts built on the same premises, and containing the same petitions to be read in particular ways. And when we, as readers, read them, we draw on that intertextual heritage too. We don't encounter each text as a unique and self-contained object whose meanings lie entirely 'within' it, although that is *exactly* what it usually feels like. Instead, we activate our own intertextual knowledge, which has already inducted us into a particular way of reading – one that covers up its own history, precisely so as to persuade us that meanings lie 'within'.

Much of the time, we are not aware of all this. As readers, we are profoundly attuned to what poses itself as natural and unquestionable in any text, precisely because our expectations and responses have been minutely calibrated over countless encounters with other texts, so that we register their habits of meaning, their truths and their facticity without noticing the machinery that brings these things before us. This is especially the case with realist modes of writing, since transparency of language is the paramount effect that realist writing aims for. Realism, says Belsey (1980), 'offers itself as transparent' (p. 51).

Drawing on Althusser, Belsey tells how realism works to 'interpellate' – that is, both summon and address – a certain kind of reader and, therefore, to produce a certain kind of social subject:

> The reader is invited to perceive and judge the 'truth' of the text, the coherent, non-contradictory interpretation of the world as it is perceived by an author whose autonomy is the source and evidence of the truth of the interpretation. This model of intersubjective communication, of shared understanding of a text which re-presents the world, is the guarantee not only of the truth of the text but of the reader's existence as an autonomous and knowing subject in a world of knowing subjects. In this way classic realism constitutes an ideological practice in addressing itself to readers as subject, interpellating them in order that they freely accept their subjectivity and their subjection.
>
> (Belsey 1980: 68–9)

Patricia Clough (2000) points out that ethnographic realism also has many features of the *cinematic* realism of Hollywood films of the first half of the twentieth century. This is evident in the 'zoom' effect in the three passages above, in which the gaze of the observer swoops in/down to penetrate the culture framed and laid out in readiness for this feat of interpretive prowess. Clough, drawing on feminist film theory, identifies this as 'the oedipal logic of realist narrativity' (p. 165). She quotes Teresa de Lauretis:

> [Oedipal logic is] predicated on the single figure of the hero who crosses the boundary and penetrates the other space. In so doing the hero, the mythical subject, is constructed as human being and as male; he is the active principle of culture, the establisher of distinction, the creator of differences.
>
> (quoted in Clough 2000: 165)

This oedipal logic is easily recognized in ethnographic realism, says Clough, where it stages 'the erotic fantasy of the ethnographer's penetration of the field and the final traumatic freeing of himself from immersion with the other in order to return home, as man and a hero, with a vision of the truth of reality' (p. 165).[10]

This is not to say that readers are simply and inevitably duped into becoming the kinds of subjected subjects summoned by realism. As we have seen, no text does the job of erasing its own textuality without leaving the odd gap, bump, inconsistency or residue that threatens to disturb the smooth surface of its own innocence and, therefore, the smooth contours of the reader's self-containment. Nevertheless, there are broad politico-ideological effects at work in the intertextual links that connect people, through their shared immersion in popular texts. James Kavanagh (1995) provides a comic example of the consequences of *not* answering the summons of popular texts, in his report of a conversation in front of the TV set in a Brooklyn apartment:[11]

Young man: This is a good movie, but it's not as good as *Demons I*.
Guest: I never saw *Demons I*.
Young man: Well, it's like *Halloween*. You've seen *Halloween*, haven't you?
Guest: No, I haven't seen *Halloween*.
Young man: Oh, well, it's like *Nightmare on Elm Street*, you've seen that haven't you?
Guest: No, I never saw that movie.
Young man: You never saw *Nightmare on Elm Street*? You don't know Freddie Kruger? Well, it's like *Friday the 13th*. You must have seen *Friday the 13th*, with Jason. If you don't know Freddy, you must know Jason!

Guest: No, I never saw *Friday the 13th* either.
Young man: What are you, a communist?

(Kavanagh 1995: 317)

The ties, therefore, that bind people into a polity are, partly at least, intertextual ones: ways of reading (and viewing) built on past encounters that deliver familiar ways of reading, and being in, the world. If you don't share an immersion in those texts, you mark yourself out as not belonging. The three passages above are similar because they draw on an extensive intertextual history of realist description, and invite readers to renew their membership of that realist worldview.

What, in summary, can we learn from the discussion of the three passages? Most obviously, perhaps, that there is an element of *banality* in all description. The passages demonstrate how pre-coded and conventional our descriptive resources are, even when they generate descriptions that also manage to be fresh, direct and striking. They remind us that there is no such thing as *innocent* description or observation: to describe is always to do something else at the same time – framing, foundation-building, credentialling, and so on. The passages also show, once again, how deeply *blurred* the boundaries are between research writing and other genres, such as literature, journalism and travel writing.[12] They show how the meaning that seems to reside within a text comes partly from its intertextual links with other, similar texts. Furthermore, the passages demonstrate how realist writing establishes particular kinds of relationship between researchers and 'subjects', in which the latter are very clearly demarcated as 'others' with respect to the knowing researcher.

Textual intercourse: relations between researchers and subjects

What happens when that (textual) relationship between researcher and subjects breaks down? There is an example in Marjorie Shostak's book, *Nisa*, from which the third passage above was taken. In fact – a fact that I have concealed in my commentary so far – Shostak's book contains *two* versions of arrival at a !Kung village (see Pratt 1986: 42, on whose analysis I rely heavily here). The first one, quoted above, is a generalized description of what an unnamed 'visitor' would see on arrival at an unspecified village. The second version reports what happened when Shostak and her colleague arrived at the scene of their planned field study. They came by night to a deserted village where they found the shell of a hut that had been occupied by two anthropologists four years earlier. As they got ready for bed, they were disturbed by Nisa and a friend, both wearing tattered European clothes, singing the praises of the previous anthropologists for the gifts that they had given.

As Mary Louise Pratt (1986) notes, this version tells anthropology's 'bad dream': the subjects already contaminated by Western culture and the guilt relation of economic exchange. Just as bad, they are also corrupted 'ethnographically' – their innocence stained by prior encounters with anthropologists, of whom they have troubling expectations. This second account dismantles the frame set up in the first, generalized arrival scene, within which a collectivity was envisaged going about its traditional business in the dawn light, unheeding of the gaze, or the culture, or the fantasies of the anthropologists. Here, it is the 'subjects' who approach the ethnographers, from the 'outside'. The observers have become the observed. The account displaces the ethnographer's vision as the central, organizing point-of-view and, as a result, dismantles the ethnographer's self-certainty. Shostak's reaction, as she reports it, was to try to pretend that the encounter was not happening, and to wait for morning so that the 'proper' arrival scene could be staged (see Pratt 1986: 44). Once the worlds of ethnographer and subject start to bleed into one another, and subjects betray their own, unofficial desires and demands, the assurance that comes from knowing one's Self in contrast to the Other begins to unravel.

Self/Other complications after colonialism

There is much more to be said of this. All modes of writing insinuate some kind of difference, or distance, between Self and Other, researcher and researched, as we saw in Chapter 1 with the parable of Mrs. Ph(i)nk$_o$. But modes such as realism and quasi-scientific writing aspire to erect particularly strong boundaries. As Homi Bhabha (1994) notes, this kind of writing has always offered power and security to writers, not just in terms of the status of the knowledge they are able to produce, but also in terms of their own identity as knowledge-producers and autonomous, rational individuals. Bhabha is concerned specifically with the production of identity in colonial and postcolonial contexts, and the ways in which the self-certainty of colonial administrators and missionaries was shored up by their sense of *difference* from their colonial subjects – by their complete 'otherness'. But as Bhabha also points out, that self-certainty was always fragile because of an inherent contradiction in the colonial relationship. The native subjects of colonialism were not *simply* required to be the dark, pre-rational Other of European civilization. They were also required to emulate the habits and virtues of civil subjects of the home country. They were expected to be 'Mimic Men' as Bhabha (1994: 88) puts it, borrowing the title of V.S. Naipaul's novel. Imperialism required colonial subjects who were 'almost the same but not quite' – that is, 'almost the same but not white' (p. 89). Thus, writes Bhabha, *mimicry* lies at the heart of the colonial project. And mimicry is a disturbing and ambivalent force. It plays havoc with difference. It is *both appropriate and inappropriate* to the workings of colonial authority. On the one hand, mimicry serves the ends of colonial discipline and power, quelling dissent (difference) by 'appropriating' the Other – obliging/permitting them to be almost (but never quite) the same as 'us'. But, on the other hand, mimicry is the sign of the *in*appropriate: of 'difference or recalcitrance' (p. 86), always dangerously liable to flip over into farce, mockery or menace. The colonial endorsement of mimicry made a mockery of the civic, moral and spiritual values that the nineteenth-century colonialists had ventured abroad to promote, by acknowledging that empty or 'partial' emulations of these supposedly enduring verities would do for the natives. Mimicry also profoundly destablized the colonizers' *identity*. Bhabha writes of 'the hidden threat of the partial gaze' (p. 89): by reflecting back a disorderly and incomplete version of the colonizer's self, 'the look of surveillance returns as the displacing gaze of the disciplined, where the observer becomes the observed and "partial" representation rearticulates the whole notion of *identity* and alienates it from essence' (p. 89; original emphasis).

See how close all this is to what Marjorie Shostak describes in the 'night' version of her arrival scene: the observer becoming the observed; the solemnity of the ethnographic encounter mocked by the traces of previous, 'partial' Western identification. The parallels with Bhabha's account are hardly coincidental. Mary Louise Pratt (1986) explicitly links the night-time darkness of Shostak's arrival scene to the dark history of colonialism, finding in it 'the symbolism of guilt' (p. 45). Pratt notes that Shostak's text is the latest in a centuries-old corpus of texts on the people of the Kalahari – a corpus that documents their relentless persecution and extermination at the hands of successive waves of colonizers. Shostak's text was also part of another, more recent intertextual series, as one of a collection of studies produced by the 'Harvard Kalahari Project' in the 1960s and 1970s. Pratt shows how the Harvard anthropologists were, on the one hand, acutely aware of the vicious history of European colonization and capitalist expansion, and concerned to distance themselves from it.[13] *And yet* the Harvard scholars were also strangely blind to this history. Their main interest in the !Kung was as survivors of the stone-age. The scientific orientation of the Harvard studies, which emphasized physical and biological characteristics, and expressed these in the tables and formulae of quantitative method, de-contextualized !Kung culture and ignored the legacy of centuries of violent settlement (Pratt 1986: 49).

The textual politics of good intentions[14]

Shostak rejects such a notion of the 'pure primitive' when she introduces Nisa in her Western garb; and her account is intentionally opposed to the scientism of the mainstream Harvard tradition. In fact, the night arrival scene marks an epiphany in Shostak's text. Nisa's clamorous refusal to be what was expected of her is presented as a pivotal event that forced the ethnographer to find a new fieldwork relationship, and a new way of writing that was opposed to the dehumanizing language of science. Nisa's voice predominates for most of the book, alongside Shostak's own personal narrative and a small amount of general anthropological commentary. So the night arrival not only symbolizes the guilt relation of postcolonialism, but also its *transcendence*. The trauma of the night scene provokes a new, 'polyphonic' mode of writing that acknowledges the validity of disparate voices and the claims of personal as well as scientific authority.

But Pratt argues that colonialism and scientism are not so easily transcended. She notes that Shostak still has an interest in uncovering the timeless qualities of an ancient society (as the first generalized description of a 'traditional' village at dawn suggests), and in drawing out the 'lessons' that such a society might hold for those in the West. Shostak's anticipation of what contemporary Western society might learn from 'traditional' ways of life has a specifically feminist inflection: she hopes that the study will be of value to 'the American women's movement' (Shostak 1983: 6; cited in Pratt 1986: 48). So although the book consists centrally of Nisa's 'own' story, Shostak intends that this story will resonate across cultures and through time, expressing something that is universal in women's condition. Ultimately, therefore, Shostak repeats the act of the Harvard sociobiologists, by eliding the specific history of colonialism and its significance in shaping the lives of women of the Kalahari. The text is intricately caught up in the 'discursive legacy' of colonialism that it repudiates, according to Pratt (1986: 47). She finds further evidence of this in the benevolent personal attributes that Shostak discerns in the !Kung; namely: '[c]heerfulness, humor, egalitarianism, nonviolence, disinterest in material goods, longevity, and stamina [. . .] all underscored with admiration and affection' (pp. 47–8). Pratt describes these, acerbically, as 'the characteristics that the powerful commonly find in those they have subjugated' (p. 46), and suggests that they are part of an enduring tendency to naturalize and decontextualize the subjects of ethnography and of colonialism.

Gillian Fuller (2000), who coined the phrase 'the textual politics of good intentions', describes the same de-historicizing gesture in 'eco-discourses' that celebrate the 'Native sciences' of aboriginal peoples as an alternative to Western hard science. Discussing one best-selling popular science book, she points to the ways in which '[n]atives are consistently represented as childlike, pure and most importantly intrinsically connected to the land' (p. 84). Like Pratt, Fuller emphasizes the direct link between this celebratory 'naturalizing' of formerly colonial subjects and the repression of their precolonial history.

Derrida (1976) points out that this naturalizing tendency to constitute the other as 'a model of original and natural goodness' (p. 114) goes back at least to the eighteenth century and the philosophy of Rousseau. Shostak's desire to find out what contemporary American feminism could learn from 'traditional' societies matches exactly Derrida's account of the eighteenth-century conceptualization of non-European societies – as 'a "zero degree", with reference to which one could outline the structure, the growth, and above all the degradation of our society and our culture' (p. 115).[15]

Writing (from) the 'inside': the poetics and problematics of 'voice' in educational research

Pratt's reading of Shostak's study was one of a series of influential works to appear in the 1980s that focused specifically on the *writing* of anthropology and its complicity in the workings of colonialism. Work in this vein showed, as we saw above, how the standard ethnographic monograph tended to re-inscribe, unintentionally, the power differentials that maintained the writer/scholar (and Western reader) in a position of privilege over the native as 'Other'.[16] But this recognition was not confined to social anthropology. It became clear in a whole range of other fields of inquiry, round about the same time, that the problems of 'Othering' are not confined to postcolonial settings; but that they have been the dominant mode of representation within the social sciences in general. This recognition has given rise to a widespread unease about the boundaries that writing throws up between researcher and researched – about the 'textual laminations', as Michelle Fine (1994) puts it, 'within which Others have been sealed by social scientists' (p. 71).

One response to the 'Othering' perpetuated by traditional social science has been the search for methodologies that would circumvent inside/outside problems by presenting the view from the *inside*. Shostak's attempt to get 'more' of Nisa into her ethnography, and also something of her own personal voice, reflects this widespread interest in curtailing the malign power of the outsider – the academic/scientific author – to give voice and authority more directly to those on the 'inside'. This has also been a central aspiration of some forms of feminist methodology. Importantly, it is an aspiration that has been pursued on the field of discourse. Feminist methodologists have looked for alternative ways of writing that prioritize vernacular, personal accounts such as narrative, anecdote, life stories and journals. They have championed intimate, convivial, egalitarian field methods such as 'conversational' interview styles, and forms of analysis and interpretation that intentionally curtail the authority of the academic researcher, such as self-reflexivity, collaborative interpretation or co-writing.

The project of freeing the 'voice' of the subject, and the politics of emancipation which this carries, has also been a preoccupation within educational research. The notion of the teacher's voice and the demand that it should be heard by, and in, the discourses of educational research and reform, has been central to teacher-focused research approaches, such as those that champion action research (Stenhouse, 1975; Elliott, 1991), life history (e.g. Goodson and Walker 1991), narrative (e.g. Clandinin and Connelly 2000) and 'teacher thinking' (e.g. Elbaz 1983). All of these approaches, despite their differences in other respects, share a commitment to providing more immediate access to those on the 'inside' (i.e. teachers) and to representing the lived experiences and the practical knowledge that teachers possess and use, but which have traditionally been overridden by the big theories, or the narrow psychologistic focus, or the unequal power of academic researchers. Freema Elbaz, for instance, in her 1983 study of one teacher's practical knowledge, tried to capture the 'insider' knowledge and the practical theories that a teacher actually put into effect as she went about the business of teaching. The Foreword to Elbaz' book, by the editors of the series in which the book appears, explicitly frames her study in terms of the opposition between inside and outside:

> Curriculum planning and development are activities undertaken to improve the quality of teaching and learning in schools. But, all too characteristically, they are activities seen as being undertaken *for* schools and teachers by people outside – by experts or authorities who are sometimes benign in their intentions, at other times less benign, who believe they know what the schools *should* be doing. [. . .] Writing about curriculum development reflects these all-too-common starting points for thinking about curriculum change and development. And, inasmuch as such writing typically comes from people who were teachers (but aren't now), or from people who know what good teaching should be, a further distancing of 'voice' or perspective occurs.
>
> (Editors' Foreword in Elbaz 1983: vii; original emphasis)

Counterposing Elbaz' study with the traditional view from 'people outside', the series editors welcome the study as 'a theoretically and methodologically exciting picture of what can and does happen behind the classroom door' (p. vii). This endorsement of the view from the 'interior' is reminiscent of the remarks by Bob Lewis on the subject of action research, which were briefly discussed in Chapter 1, and which are re-quoted here:

> Experience of 'action research' over the last ten years has indicated that teachers make excellent co-researchers, bringing to the research activity a sensitivity of classrooms and of children's development. What is more such practitioners are also able to communicate the outcomes of research to peers in ways which help the community at large feel a sense of ownership of the outcomes. Research outcomes will then not be imposed by clever, out-of-touch outsiders but negotiable with members of their own close community.
>
> (Lewis 1992: 1)

Again, the justification is made on the grounds of the superiority of the inside over the outside, with the classroom as the innermost bit of that inside.

Complications of 'inside' and 'outside'

I want to look a bit more closely at the construction of this short passage from Lewis and, in particular, at the ways in which the opposition between inside and outside is fashioned. For there is a lot going on in this excerpt, and I want to use it as another example of how to 'interrupt' the fabrication of a text – in particular, here, the distinction between insiders and outsiders. Do you glimpse the texture, the weave? So much is accomplished in so few words. Action research is counter-posed, favourably, to other (unspecified) kinds of research. Teachers are contrasted with the 'outsiders' (who are doubly 'outside': i.e. external to both classroom and community). A tacit appeal is made to *relevance*: teachers as the holders of useful knowledge of children's development (because of their presence in classrooms), as opposed to the irrelevant kinds of knowledge held by those who are clever but out-of-touch. Teachers will be able to feel 'a sense of ownership' and to enjoy the solidarity of a 'close community' (whose members show 'sensitivity') as opposed to the alienated, and alienating, cleverness of the outsiders. There is even a faint hint of violence perhaps, 'imposed' by a ruling group on that 'close community'. Note the warm buzz words: ownership, sensitivity, community. The oppositions are marshalled like Gulf war troops.[17]

Lewis' celebration of the 'close community' of teachers is, in Derrida's (1976) term, 'Rousseauistic'. It invokes a community that is 'immediately present to itself, without difference, a community of speech where all the members are within earshot' (p. 136). As Derrida points out, this desire for the self-contained community (a powerful and persistent desire) is another manifestation of the *desire for presence* – in this instance, for authentic, face-to-face contact with others, effected through the immediacy of speech. Derrida was writing of the ways in which anthropologists and philosophers have valorized speech, as the bearer and mark of community, over writing. Lewis' reference to the 'clever, out-of-touch outsiders' is immediately recognizable as the same guilt-driven anxiety about (academic) writing and writers, and their threat to the integrity of local communities, that Derrida traced in Levi-Strauss's anthropology.

But look again at the example above. Teachers are to be '*co*-researchers'. They will bring 'sensitivity' and practical knowledge – perhaps to complement, as 'practitioners', the theoretical knowledge of the 'clever outsiders'? They are to 'communicate' the outcomes to 'the community at large'. Are teachers being set up as the *junior* partners in the pairing – embodying a kind of warm feminine principle that operates in the restricted domestic sphere of the classroom, the close community and the children? Is their task to domesticate the abstract, theoretical knowledge of the outsiders and carry it back into the 'close community' that excludes those outsiders?

Notice the quasi-objective, formal terminology that runs through the text, alongside the warm keywords of ownership, sensitivity and community: 'research outcomes', 'peers', 'indicated' (rather than, say, 'shown'). Look at the grammar too: 'Experience . . . has indicated'; 'Research outcomes will not then be imposed by . . .'. These grammatical constructions are typical of 'technical discourse' as defined by systemic linguists, as already mentioned earlier in this chapter. Indeed, the first sentence is identical in its structure to what Jay Lemke (1995: 60) calls 'the ubiquitous "studies show" or "research proves" formula' that is, he argues, one of the ways in which technical discourse 'claims to be a value-neutral, objective reportage of the facts' (p. 61). Perhaps, then, the promotion of action research in this short passage is undermined by a counter-discourse of objectivity and abstraction. By a discourse that, in short, speaks for, and from, a very big and powerful Outside.

What I have offered here is a 'reading' of a fragment of text. Or perhaps two, conflicting readings. But I am not suggesting that either of these readings, in which first action research and then 'outsider' research comes out on top, is the correct one. I don't want, either, to use the second reading to *unmask* the first – to expose a 'technocratic ideology' (Lemke 1995) lurking in the text. And I certainly do not mean to suggest that the writer is 'secretly' a positivist masquerading as a fellow-traveller of action research.[18] This would be to do the kind of reading described by Attridge (1996: 38) as sifting through a text for 'treasonable sentiments'. Some kinds of discourse work, notably that which goes under the name of 'critical discourse analysis' (e.g. Fairclough 1995), imply just such a process of unmasking; of exposing the ideological distortions wrought by powerful elites upon a real or innocent world. But I want to reassert that, while power and violence are indeed effected by and in texts, it is also the case that ambiguity inhabits all texts. The binary oppositions that produce fundamental truths and certainties are liable to turn 'inside-out' in this fashion. It is not, therefore, that the writer of the extract above has been more inconsistent in his arguments than anyone else. Nor is this, I would argue, an especially manipulative, 'rhetorical' or 'ideological' piece of writing. But this does not mean that it is less crafted, less built to persuade, than more obviously polemical texts.

The pursuit of innocence

Methodologies that privilege the views and the knowledge of the 'inside' invoke, or seek, a kind of *textual innocence*. Troubled by guilty knowledge of how power insinuates itself when outsiders/researchers speak and write for others, researchers would, ideally, like to let the inside 'speak for itself'. Granted that this is not possible, researchers have looked for ways of minimizing the effects of power that distort the authentic voices of subjects, as we have seen above. But access to the 'inside' is always going to be a fraught and partial business. We have already seen how Nisa's voice, in Schostak's text, became inf(l)ected with the cadences of colonialism.

As my reading of Lewis' remarks above suggests, the very notion of a self-contained 'inside' as the centre-ground of research is unstable; and so too are the moral and epistemological claims that are invested in that inside. For instance, the 'close community' invoked by Lewis may 'stand for' positive qualities such as strength, mutual support, collective wisdom and solidarity. But it could also indicate conservatism, hostility to strangers and narrow-mindedness. And, importantly, it is not just a matter of choice. The phrase 'close community' carries the trace of these opposing meanings, in ways that are never fully under the control of writers or readers. Derrida (e.g. 1981) called this 'dissemination', the inescapable tendency for meanings to fragment and disperse; never to be in the precise place where you first thought they were.

The view from the inside is never, in any case, 'enough' in research terms: something else is always needed to complement or complete it. In the fragment above, the celebratory discourse of/on insider-hood is haunted by a counter-discourse of abstraction and technical rationality. You could say that there is an invisible frame *inside* the passage, which restores the inside outside relation between academic research and professional practice that it seems to dismantle. You could even say that the phrase 'close community' acts as a kind of 'hinge' or 'pivot' between these two discourses.

These complications are not an accident confined to the fragment above: the view from/of the inside is *never* self-sufficient. This is rather obvious, in the sense that there would otherwise be nothing at all for researchers to contribute, in addition to whatever was voiced by the subject. The researcher always acts as some kind of broker between the inside and outside, however minimally she envisages that role.[19]

And as soon as the 'outside' reasserts itself, we are back with the dilemmas of inequitable access to power and knowledge, and the impossibility of innocent ways of knowing and representing others. And, in some senses, these dilemmas are sharpened. The pursuit of methodological innocence often makes the workings of power *even harder to see*, by contrast to those objective or realist strategies that are (with hindsight at least) so manifestly saturated with effects of power wielded by 'outsiders'. So there is a problem with the search for innocence. It never delivers the unimpeded view of/from the inside that it promises. And it often ends up repeating the knowledge crimes that it sets out to avoid.

Conclusion

This chapter has begun to explore the textuality of educational research. We have seen how even the most seemingly artless descriptions or narratives are 'fabricated' – woven to persuade readers of their naturalness and authority. This rhetorical fabric can be difficult to 'see', especially where research uses the conventions of literary realism – that genre that covers its own tracks as writing. The ethnographic critique of realism showed how this has unwittingly perpetuated the inequalities of power and authority that research has sought to overturn. The colonialist gesture of mastery of the 'subjects' has been repeated in the *textual* mastery of authors (and readers) over the culture of the exoticized 'Other'. It might be thought that issues of colonialism are tangential to educational research, at least if one considers this a purely 'domestic' affair. But many of the methods of qualitative research are inherited from ethnography, and carry the traces of its colonial past and postcolonial guilt.[20]

This chapter has also explored the *intertextuality* of educational research. Like all textual practice, research is woven from the threads and traces of diverse discourses and genres, and we pursued here its debt to science, nineteenth-century exploration, colonial administration, 1960s counter-culture, travel narratives, journalism, novels, realist cinema, and so on. Despite the search for more 'innocent' forms of representation, in which the voices and concerns of subjects might be heard without distortion, issues of power and authority will always return to haunt research writing. The next chapter, and those which follow, pursue the ramifications of the inescapable textuality of research.

The threat of writing

What threatens is indeed writing.

(Jacques Derrida 1976: 99)

The 'unclouded', 'innocent' eye has become a lie.

(Walter Benjamin 1979: 89)

Clarity bordering on stupidity, a dog's life.

(André Breton 1986: 6)

Introduction

This chapter continues to explore questions relating to research as writing. It focuses on what might be called, inelegantly, the *written-ness* of research. I want to suggest that this is always, potentially at least, a problem both for the producers and the consumers of research, and to show how the written-ness of research produces a certain kind of *fear and anxiety*. Research method, I suggest, can be seen as the attempt to control the threat posed by writing.

Now, 'everybody knows' that research involves a wide range of writing practices. These might include transcribing interviews, taking field notes, keeping journals, labelling files, corresponding with participants, formulating codes of practice, annotating transcripts, inventing analytic categories, turning out drafts and final versions of reports, dissertations, conference papers, policy documents, curriculum frameworks and articles, to name only some of the more 'visible' writing practices.[1] But there is something a little odd about this pervasive written-ness: it is generally down-played, or even forgotten, in accounts of the research process. Writing is often considered, when it is considered at all, to be a merely technical business: a matter of finding the best words to convey, or to capture, the stuff that really counts – the meaning, the message, the ideas, the essence, the principles, the 'themes', the categories, the fundamentals, the thoughts, the writer's intentions, the participants' views, the truth, the reality, the inner self, the research 'itself'. In this view, there's writing on the one hand, and there's all that good stuff on the other. Writing is the subordinate partner in this dualism: it is the medium, vehicle or instrument – a fishing net, perhaps, or a recording device – that we need in order to capture those more important, extratextual phenomena.

But, as Chapter 1 showed with the parable of Mrs. Ph(i)Nk$_o$'s noodles, writing can never be totally reduced to this subsidiary role. I suggested there that writing is always double-edged. It is what allows us to represent reality and to produce meaning; and it also inexorably *distances* us from those coveted entities. Writing is both a good and a bad thing – both poison and remedy, as Derrida (1981) memorably put it, borrowing the Greek notion of the *pharmakon*. In this chapter, I draw out some of the ways in which research wants to, needs to, *forget* its own written-ness – the fact that it can never 'jump clear of its own language', to use a phrase of Malcolm Bowie's (1991). When the written-ness of research is foregrounded, deliberately or not, the result is often anxiety or revulsion. This is one reason why postmodern or textually oriented theory often offends. But the fear of writing is an old fear, and it has manifested itself in many different fields and disciplines, over many centuries.

Some central concerns of qualitative method can be understood as emanating from that old fear of writing and the need to handle those disturbing reminders of the written-ness of research, when they threaten to break through the amnesia that protects research from recognizing its own textuality. The chapter traces some of the ways in which methodology manages the threat of writing, and concludes by speculating on what kinds of difference it might make if research were to acknowledge its own written-ness.

It will probably be clear to readers who have stuck with the book this far that I use the term 'writing' with more than its usual meaning. In accordance with Derrida's recasting of the word, 'writing' here means both written and spoken texts.[2] It would also include the impulse or inclination to 'inscribe' which precedes the appearance of any actual piece of speech or writing. Written-ness is not only a property of the long list of 'inky' research practices mentioned above, but also of all the spoken, flimsy, seemingly 'spontaneous' texts of research – interviews, conversations, anecdotes, and so on. Contrary to common assumptions, we are not any closer to thought, imagination, our inner selves, other people or external reality when we speak than when we write. These extralinguistic desirables are still brought to us – made *present* to us – via linguistic signs. And these sound-borne signs rely on/produce that same, irreducible distance, or *difference*, between signifier and signified that is brought about by written signs. Barbara Johnson (1995) puts it much more economically: '[s]peakers do not beam meanings directly from one mind to another. Immediacy is an illusion' (p. 43). Written-ness is no less a problem for spoken than for written texts, therefore – although most of the discussion in this chapter will concentrate on examples of the latter.

Writing crimes: some examples of why writing offends

Let us start with some manifestations of the threat of writing. The first example is taken from the critique of educational research by the former UK chief inspector of schools that was discussed in Chapter 4:

> I used to try to read these journals [i.e. 'academic' journals]. I have given up. Life is too short. There is too much to do in the real world, with real teachers in real schools to worry about methodo-logical quarrels or to waste time decoding unintelligible, jargon-ridden prose to reach (if one is lucky) a conclusion that is often so transparently partisan as to be worthless.
>
> (Woodhead 1998: 51)[3]

This is a particularly clear case of the 'appeal to the real', in the face of the often-voiced 'crimes' of academic writing – jargon, unintelligibility, irrelevance and partiality. Writing fails because it is not the same as reality. Or it fails because it cannot, or will not, render itself *transparent*, so that reality can be seen through it. So researchers are consigned to a separate, un-real world of writing, in opposition to policy makers, prac-titioners, pupils, the press or the People, who supposedly *deal directly with the real*.

Concerns about writing are not restricted to external critics. They are quite widely shared, and periodically aired, within the educational re-search community. The following writing offences were listed in the newsletter of the British Educational Research Association, in a short piece entitled 'Some FRIPPERIES and FLAWS of research papers':

> *Opaqueness*: Writing in a way which is not readily understood by most potential readers. This may be due to a complex literary style, to unusual vocabulary, or to lack of progression in argument etc. It is writing which gets the research 'off the author's chest', but not 'into the minds' of the readers.
>
> *Wordiness*: Writing at greater length than is necessary to convey the required meaning.
>
> *Writing in patois*: Using the in-house jargon of the researchers instead of translating it into readily understood language.
>
> (Bassey 1993: 21)

It is worth considering some of the tacit assumptions about writing that are embedded in these criticisms. First, it is assumed that meanings, or indeed 'the research', exist *separately* from the writing, and that they exist *before* the writing. Writing is just the means of moving these pre-existent meanings 'into the minds' of readers. Furthermore, since mean-ings exist independently of and prior to writing, there are *proper* and *improper* kinds of writing. Proper writing is that which meets the demands of 'the required meaning'. It translates meaning into 'readily understood' language, which by implication is a kind of universal or standard language, in contrast to the 'patois' of improper writing, which translates meaning into the uncrackable codes of jargon. Improper writing is unfaithful to the demands of meaning: it exceeds, falls short or misses the mark of the particular meaning that it is its duty to convey.

Above all, perhaps, these remarks, and those of Woodhead quoted above, hint at a pervasive *regret* about writing. Writing is *regrettably* needed in order to get ideas into people's minds, or to broker a real world that one would rather deal with directly. In its dealings with writing, research often finds itself in the position described by Smith (1995: 7); that is, 'irremediably poisoned by a foreign body perversely necessary to it'. This being so, researchers have often seen writing as something that needs to be tamed of its excesses and shortcomings, a task that may require explicit regulation. For instance, a booklet entitled 'Good Practice in Educational Research Writing', produced by the British Educational Research Association, enjoins researchers to 'aim for *lucid prose* which communicates effectively to the intended audience' (BERA 1999: para. 2.3; my emphasis). Again there is a desire for transparency, for language that lets you see through to the truth or meaning.

But BERA's Code is only a late entrant in a long and venerable tradition of regretting and regulating language. Zeller and Farmer (1999) trace the urge to control language back to disputes about oratorical style in Ancient Greece, and note its recurrence through the centuries up to the present in the 'APA Manual' (i.e. the *Publication Manual of the American Psychological Association*), whose stylistic conventions are widely imposed by editors of social science and education journals in the USA. One example discussed by Zeller and Farmer is the attempt of the British Royal Society in the 1660s to establish a 'plain language' purged of 'expressiveness', which would allow scientists to describe faithfully the natural world. They quote the complaint of the Society's spokesman, Thomas Sprat, against 'eloquence':

> Who can behold, without indignation, how many mists and uncertainties, these specious Tropes and Figures have brought on our Knowledge? [. . .] of all the Studies of men, nothing may sooner be obtain'd, than this vicious abundance of Phrase, this trick of Metaphors, this volubility of Tongue, which makes so great a noise in the world.
>
> (Sprat 1667; quoted in Zeller and Farmer 1999: 3)

Note how Sprat's attack on 'eloquence' is *itself* eloquently fashioned. It is far from plain, and it uses a number of 'specious Tropes and Figures', including rhetorical questioning, parallelism (in the accumulation of phrases beginning with 'this', each with an identical syntactic structure) and metaphor (e.g. 'mists'; 'this trick of Metaphors', which is itself a metaphor). Later, I will return to this tendency of writing to ensnare those who attempt to evade it or tame it. For the moment, I want to turn to one further arena where the fear, or at least the regret, of writing has been documented, namely that of philosophy.

Philosophy and the fear of writing

Richard Rorty (1978) suggests that philosophy has often been resistant to its own written-ness. Indeed, he asserts that much philosophical writing is 'really aimed at *putting an end to writing*' (p. 143; my emphasis). He describes philosophy's regret over writing thus:

> [I]t is a characteristic of the Kantian tradition that, no matter how much writing it does, it does not think that philosophy *should* be written, any more than science should be. Writing is an unfortunate necessity [. . .] In a mature science, the words in which the invest-igator 'writes up' his results should be as few and as transparent as possible.
>
> (Rorty 1978: 145; original emphasis)

Philosophers, says Rorty, would prefer to do without writing if they could. He alludes to a prevailing notion of writing as 'conveying a message which (in more fortunate circumstances) might have been conveyed [. . .] by *injecting knowledge straight into the brain*' (p. 146; my emphasis). This formulation resonates with Michael Bassey's desire, quoted above, for writing that gets educational research 'into the minds' of readers.

Derrida, whose work Rorty is invoking here, has shown how philosophers from Plato to Rousseau and beyond have been troubled by the 'secondary' nature of writing – the way it seems lifeless and derivative compared with speech, which has traditionally been thought of as the immediate manifestation of thought or meaning. Writing, in this enduring view, is a poor substitute for speech, no more than the sign of a sign. In Medieval systems of thought, writing, as marks on the page, seemed a corrupt and mortal thing, compared with the vividness and grandeur of the truths of Nature and God. In eighteenth-century humanism, writing seemed fatally detached from the vitality and immediacy of the sensations, thoughts and beliefs that were held to reside 'inside' human beings, and to constitute their uniquely human subjectivity. Derrida (1976) quotes Rousseau's view that judging a person's 'genius' from books is like 'painting a man's portrait from his corpse' (p. 17). Derrida also discovers descriptions of writing in terms of clothing and disguise – as 'a garment of perversion and debauchery, a dress of corruption and disguise, a festival mask that must be exorcised (p. 35). Writing has often been considered, then, as a 'fabrication' in its most negative sense.

Writing is always stranded on the 'outside' of our bodies, therefore. It indicates 'exteriority', artificiality, frivolity and even a kind of death. 'Writing in the common sense', says Derrida (1976), 'is the dead letter, it is the carrier of death. It exhausts life' (p. 17). This is why speech has often been more highly rated: it seems to emanate directly from that rational, sensate and spiritual 'inside'. It seems more mobile; more 'alive'.[4]

The fear of literature and other genres

The anxiety of educational researchers over the written-ness of research is, therefore, one manifestation of a pervasive and chronic anxiety about writing that has animated scholars across the disciplines and throughout the centuries. Philosophy's particular fear, according to Jonathan Culler, has been that of collapsing, or straying, into *literature*. One of the recurring tasks of philosophers has been to purify philosophy of any literary tendencies:

> Relegating problems of fictionality, rhetoricity, and nonseriousness to a marginal and dependent realm – a realm in which language can be as free, playful and irresponsible as it likes – philosophy produces a purified language which it can hope to describe by rules that literature would disrupt if it had not been set aside. The notion of literature has thus been essential to the project of establishing serious, referential, verifiable discourse as the norm of language.
>
> (Culler 1983: 181)

Culler's description of the purification of philosophy recalls Sprat's prescription for seventeenth-century science, quoted above. In both cases, a major fear is that of *stylistic excess* – a concern with the stuff of language (i.e. literary or linguistic devices) at the expense of the 'serious', non-linguistic priorities – meanings, ideas, reasoning, argument or reference to an external reality. Again, this distaste is widespread in educational research. As in those other spheres, attention to style, technique or textual construction is likely to be seen as perverse, self-indulgent, trivializing ('fripperies') or even pathological. One recurring accusation is that of 'cleverness'. This charge is levelled, for instance, in this excerpt from a book review:

> the point [. . .] is not to debate whether [the writer] is wrong in his analysis or in his speculations, although I think he is. It is to point to the fact that we have a writer who appears more interested in his

own cleverness in being able to set 'phenomenological' alongside 'phenomenal'.

(Galton 1998: 112)

The offence of cleverness is not really about incorrectness. Nor is it about intellectual ability: critics of 'cleverness' are not arguing for stupidity. It is, again, a matter of *impropriety* – defined as explicit attention to style, appearance or technique. To take another example, Erica McWilliam (1993) identifies a malign influence on educational research by 'those French poststructuralists and their clones for whom "cute and clever" is preferable to "cogent and coherent"' (p. 211).

Recall, too, the passage discussed in the previous chapter, which extolled teachers' knowledge over that of 'clever, out of touch outsiders'. Cleverness is explicitly associated here with the quality of 'exteriority' that Derrida noted. Academics' knowledge is coded in alienated writing, as opposed, implicitly, to the spoken mode engaged by the 'close community' who live, in Derrida's phrase, 'within earshot'.

When researchers foreground the crafted nature of what they have written – when they point to the written-ness of their arguments, portrayals or analyses – they draw readers' attention to their own presence in or behind the text. They are often accused by critics of putting themselves before their subjects or before the demands of knowledge or meaning, hence the charge of self-indulgence or 'vanity ethnography' that has often been levelled at work within postmodernism when it attempts irony or textual 'play' (cf. MacLure 1994a). Clifford Geertz (1988) describes a similar antipathy among anthropologists: 'Excessive concern, which in practice usually means any concern at all, with how ethnographic texts are constructed seems like an unhealthy self-absorption – time-wasting at best, hypochondriacal at worst' (p. 1). Those who look at the text will be diverted from the truth.

Keeping one's distance: the purification of research writing

I have touched on a variety of writing crimes in this chapter, including jargon, obfuscation, rhetoricity, long-windedness, literariness, irony, play, cleverness and authorial self-indulgence. They look, on the face of it, like somewhat different kinds of crimes. But every piece of writing which incurs one of these labels shares one particular quality: it *exposes its own textuality*. Derrida (1980) brings all these offences of impropriety together under the name of *frivolity*. Frivolity consists in 'being satisfied with tokens' rather than 'the real thing' (p. 118). It is, therefore, pre-eminently a *linguistic* offence, a perverse indulgence in words at the expense of meaning, or of style over substance.

Underlying all of these offences is that same fear of writing. It is the fear that insinuates itself when we are reminded of the treacherous and fragile bond that exists between the tokens and the real things. Or, worse, when we are reminded that there may be no 'bond' between separately existing realms, but rather an immensely more perplexing relationship of unbridgeable difference *and* inextricable entanglement. Derrida writes that frivolity is nothing more, or less, than that fissure or crack that resides inside the sign itself, out of which meaning issues. It is this crack that makes meaning possible, by allowing one signifier to 'refer to' another. Frivolity, in short, *is* difference: 'The fragility, the frail structure of the frivolous, *is nothing but* [. . .] difference [. . .], the spacing that ontology, as such, simply could not be capable of. There is a crack there . . .' (Derrida 1980: 132; original emphasis).

The threat of writing seems to come from *outside* – as some malign intention, foreign body or cheap embellishment that compromises 'an essentially serious discourse' (Derrida 1980: 124). But Derrida shows how the prospect of frivolity lies at the heart of meaning. There is *always* the risk of being frivolous. We can always be found to have trifled with tokens rather than confronting real things, because we are obliged to *write* if we want to deal with the real.

This sense of external threat has often led the defenders of 'serious' discourse' to recommend keeping literary and other frivolous genres at a distance. Here, for example, is Martyn Hammersley, expressing his unease about postmodern arguments for a 'blurring of the genres' between ethnography and other textual practices such as literature and journalism:

> [W]hat justification is there for ethnographers trying to compete directly with Virginia Woolf or even with Tom Wolfe? This seems futile and amounts to neglect of the distinctive contribution that social science can make to our understanding of the world. There is not just one boat on the high seas but many, and we need to keep our distance from the others if we are to avoid collisions. Of course, there is nothing wrong with the humanities, political journalism or imaginative literature and poetry; indeed, we can learn a great deal from them. But they are different from social science.[5]
>
> (Hammersley 1999: 580)

But we have already seen that the task of 'keeping our distance' from other genres is problematic. Qualitative research never has been a 'pure' genre. It has always enjoyed improper relations with its neighbours. As we saw in the last chapter, anthropological ethnography, from which qualitative research has drawn many of its methods and practices, emerged out of an amalgam of older genres – travel books, personal memoirs, tall tales, journalism, colonial treatises and missionary records. Sociological ethnography has an equally mixed heritage, with strong links to journalism and literary writing. It is precisely because of these entanglements with other, seemingly more frivolous genres that researchers are obliged endlessly to try to maintain some kind of difference or distance (see Pratt 1986: 27).

Still, the business of attempting to keep one's discipline 'pure' is essential for maintaining the integrity of that discipline. As Jonathan Culler noted (above) with reference to philosophy, literature has actually been indispensable to philosophers, as the inappropriate 'Other' which must repeatedly be cast out. By defending its boundaries against the (apparently) external threat, philosophy carves out and defines its own boundaries.

Derrida (1981) compared this process of casting out impurities to the purification ceremony of the *pharmakos*, or scapegoat, in the governance of the city in Ancient Greece. The *pharmakos* was a citizen selected to be the representative of the misfortunes befalling the city and ritually cast out to keep it pure. In the same way, says Derrida, philosophy has traditionally purified itself, and thereby defined itself, by purging itself of its literary excesses – that is, of its traces as *writing*. Jonathan Culler reminds us that it is only possible to send the literary scapegoat 'outside' because it is always already 'inside':

> The *pharmakos* may be repeatedly cast out of the city to keep it pure, but casting out metaphor, poetry, the parasitic, the nonserious, is possible only because they already dwell in the heart of the city: and they are repeatedly discovered to dwell there, which is why they can repeatedly be cast out.
>
> (Culler 1983: 148)

'The ceremony of the *pharmakos*', Derrida (1981) writes, 'is thus played out on the boundary line between inside and outside, which it has as its function ceaselessly to trace and retrace' (p. 133). There are many boundaries to maintain: between speech and writing, philosophy (or qualitative research) and literature, seriousness and frivolity, meanings and words, and so on. But this boundary maintenance is a never-ending task: the 'outside' is always already on the 'inside'.

Policing the 'proper': the work of research method

> The method for reducing the frivolous is method itself. In order not to be the least frivolous, being methodic suffices.
>
> (Derrida 1980: 125)

The fear of writing, therefore, prompts a desire to regulate the relationship between writing and its objects – to (try to) maintain a secure boundary between them. This is where 'Method' comes in. Qualitative research method can be understood, partly at least, as a set of procedures for handling the threat of writing, so that a *proper* relationship between words and worlds can be maintained. There are at least two rather different methodological strategies for managing the threat of writing in contemporary research, and aspects of these have been discussed above and in previous chapters. Here I bring them together under the headings of 'puritan' and 'vernacular', respectively.

Puritan methodology

The *puritan* strategy is evident in the demand, discussed above, that research writing should be 'lucid', 'readily understood', keep to the correct length, renounce style, flourish, and so on. The puritan version of methodological propriety requires writing that is meet and obedient to the sovereignty of meaning or reality, and does its job of carrying these into the minds of readers without fuss or embellishment. Its preferred genre is a kind of folk-linguistic *non*-genre that does not really have one single name, but is often summoned under labels such as plain language, lucid prose, 'clarity of expression' or 'communicative effectiveness'. It is language that is supposed to be almost beyond or above language, to be without inflection, political investment, personal heat or scientific jargon. This kind of plain or standard language is not just promoted in some versions of educational research, but as we saw in Chapter 5, has also been favoured by colonial administrators from the beginning of empire, and by educational policy makers and advisers since the nineteenth century. Chris Woodhead's remarks above are entirely within this long tradition, as are the various other criticisms of cleverness, frivolity and literary pretension that have been discussed in this chapter.

Vernacular methodology

An alternative methodological version of propriety, which could be called the *vernacular* version, can be seen in work that valorizes the personal 'voice' of teachers and other research subjects, as discussed in the preceding chapter. It can also be seen more generally in the revival of interest in (auto)biography and life history as research methods in the social sciences (see Goodson and Sikes 2000), and in action research, which privileges practitioners' ways of knowing and doing over the procedures and bodies of knowledge of the academic disciplines. Vernacular methodology is also practised by some versions of feminism.

Obviously, there are many important differences among and within these approaches that I am labelling 'vernacular'. But they 'belong' together at least in the view that authenticity resides with the subjects of research, and in their opposition to powerful discourses that have silenced or marginalized the authentic voice or wisdom of those subjects. Those powerful discourses would include science, 'academic' research, policy, patriarchy and colonialism. The genres of writing judged 'proper' by the vernacular tendency within qualitative research are those associated with *colloquial* language – narrative, confession, conversation, testimony, anecdote, autobiography, personal journals. 'Proper' writing, from this perspective, is language (spoken and written) which is, or seems to be, *natural*. It is writing which is spontaneous, authentic, intimate, convivial, close to lived experience, concrete and local rather than abstract and universal. It is imbued with feeling. It often carries connotations of innocence, in opposition to the political or ideological inflections of science or policy. In Habermas' (1986) terms, it would be the language of the 'lifeworld' as opposed to the abstract, logical, remote language of the 'system'.

Another example of vernacular methodology, in this case entirely concerned with spoken language, can be seen in commentaries on interview technique which compare the interview at its best to a *conversation*. The assumption is that informal, colloquial speech is less troubled by power imbalances between interviewer and interviewee than interrogatory or formal interview talk, and that conversational interviews can get much closer to the lifeworld of the subject (Kvale 1996). Interviewees, it is suggested, will feel that they can trust the interviewer, and will be more likely to drop the masks of false fronts and impression management that prevent them from 'being themselves' or telling unbiased truths (e.g. Woods 1985; Butt *et al.* 1992). Again, there is a tacit assumption of *authenticity* based on the idea of a proper, natural relationship between writing/language (here, conversation) and its referents – the self of the interviewee, her lived experiences, or the truth of her account.

In their different ways, the puritan and vernacular tendencies in methodology attempt to regulate the relation between writing/language and reality, conceived of as two separate realms. It would be possible to multiply examples of how methodological issues 'boil down to', and boil up from, the threat of writing. Eventually, all these examples would lead to the place from which this chapter, and this whole book, started out: namely, the *difference* (or *différance*) that writing sets up between itself and whatever it 'stands for' – reality, the referent, the inner self, lived experience, first principles, final truths, the culture of 'others', and so on. According to Derrida, Western thought has always longed for direct access to one or other of these prizes, and he called this longing, as we have already seen, the desire for *presence*. Writing crimes are criminal because they offend against presence. They remind us that direct access to those prized entities is eternally blocked, and that we are always obliged to look at them 'awry', through the medium, or across the gap, of writing.

The politics of plain talk

So there is no one best, clearest or most virtuous way of writing. However, this does not mean that 'anything goes', or that there is nothing at stake in choosing to write plain or fancy, vernacular or high scientific, or any of the other ways that people can talk or write. On the contrary, there is always something at stake, as the previous chapter showed. 'Plain talk' or no-style style is no less a choice (whether intentionally made or not) than choosing to write your research as a Mills and Boon romance, a collage of fragments or a haiku. The latter choices would be more visible and contentious, but this is precisely because we have become accustomed to thinking of the supposedly plainer (puritanical) versions as closer to truth, more innocent, or at least more appropriate for research purposes. This means that researchers have to be more, not less, attentive to the political and ethical issues that permeate their own ways of writing, as the last chapter argued.

But, in addition to self-scrutiny, it is also important to be wary of the plain dealers – those who periodically issue those calls for plain talk, accessible language, 'clarity', effective communication, and so on. For here, too, there is always a political and moral dimension. James Scheurich, writing of calls for 'plain talk' by US policy makers and 'mainstream researchers', points out that there is no single idiom that is definable as plain talk. He argues that calls for plain talk are connected to the attempts of powerful 'discourse communities' to extend and maintain their prerogative over less powerful ones.

> [W]hen one discourse community criticises another for not talking plain, it is like saying 'you are not talking like me'. What the first discourse community wants is more of the Same and less of the Other, less of the talk of the discourse community that is Other to it. The community making the call for plain talk is calling for more of the Same [. . .] [I]f we consider that the 'talk' of any discourse community is inevitably paradigmatic and political, the call of one discourse community for plain talk is implicitly a call for the dominance of that community's paradigmatic and political position – another, even more serious, dominance of the Same over the Other.
>
> (Scheurich 2000: 341–2)

It is generally the powerful communities, according to Scheurich, who have the clout to require others to talk plain in the interests of inclusiveness. Indeed, he observes that it is often only the most powerful who invoke inclusive notions of THE community in the first place. The less powerful know that there is no all-embracing community, and that *their* talk could never get to be the universally validated exemplar of plain-ness. Scheurich (2000) concludes that powerful discourse communities, when they call for plain talk, 'are acting as if their discourse communities are *transcendental* (outside history, language, context etc)' (p. 344; my emphasis).

There is, therefore, a 'politics of clarity' (Giroux 1992) in which those without power are obliged to make themselves intelligible, and even to define themselves, in terms of the norms and language habits of the powerful. In other words, as Patti Lather (1996a) notes, clarity often serves the ends of the status quo, since it 'maps easily onto taken-for-granted regimes of meaning' (p. 528). As many writers have noted, the call for clarity is deeply connected to class and colonialism. Chapter 2 explored one manifestation, in the enduring antipathy in the UK towards local and regional dialects, and the long succession of attempts impose 'standard English' on all children. The pursuit of clarity and 'plain language' is never a neutral matter, therefore. In Roland Barthes' (1967) words, it is 'the ideal appendage to a certain type of discourse, that which is given over to a permanent intention to persuade' (p. 64).

This is not to argue for the obverse – that is, that complexity or 'difficulty' are superior, morally or cognitively. Or, that academic writers should be indifferent to the ways in which specialist registers exclude non-specialist readers, and thus consolidate the power and authority of elite institutions. It is reasonable that writers should generally aim to be understood rather than misunderstood, or to engage, rather than disengage, their potential readers. But authorial intention is a poor predictor of how a text will be 'grasped' – a metaphor which appeals to me, as it emphasizes the active work done by readers. I might, for instance, try to reassure readers that I have tried to make this book as accessible and engaging as possible – as, indeed, I have done. But this will not prevent its being read as frivolous or jargon-ridden by readers who grasp it that way, not least because it tangles with the textuality that the serious discourses of research and emancipation often prefer to ignore.

And even if this text does come across 'clearly' to some readers, this will not be because they are able to see straight through the language to the 'deeper' meanings or truths. As Donna Haraway (1995) says, clarity is 'a very strange goal because it assumes a kind of physical transparency, that if you could just clean up your act somehow the materiality of writing would just disappear' (p. 49). The notions of clarity and obfuscation both ignore the materiality of writing, since they posit just such an underlying, non-linguistic realm of 'pure' thought or meaning, which language either faithfully or unfaithfully re-presents.

As we have seen in this chapter, the risk of failing to be clear – or to be 'serious', or to communicate 'effectively' – haunts *all* acts of speaking or writing. In Derrida's (1982) words, meaning always has to pass through 'the detour of the sign'. There is *always* the possibility of the message going astray. Rather than aspiring to clarity, then, a more appropriate obligation for discourse-oriented, deconstructive writing would be to seek to *engage* readers – in the sense of catching them up in the movements of the text. This obligation would not relieve writers of their responsibility to consider the effects of power and exclusion that might be implicated in their texts. On the contrary, since power and politics are implicated both in clarity and complexity, there is a need for continuous reflection on the possible effects of one's writing, even if one can never predict absolutely what those effects will be.

Fabricating the self: metaphors of method in life-history interviews

fabrication

1. a. The action or process of fabricating [. . .]; construction, fashioning, manufacture; also, a particular branch of manufacture. Now rare.

2. In bad sense: The action of fabricating or 'making up'; the invention (of a statement); the forging (of a document). Also concr. An invention; a false statement; a forgery.

(*Oxford English Dictionary*)

Mastery or surrender? The analyst's dilemma

Life-history interviews are tricky, methodologically speaking. Or perhaps it would be more accurate to say that they crystallize some questions that also apply to method more generally. What kind of act is analysis? What do we do – to 'the data', to the interviewees – when we analyse interview transcripts? Does analysis stifle the voice of the subject? Steinar Kvale notes that research interviews have traditionally been treated as material to be *mined* for underlying truths or essential meanings. On this view, 'knowledge is waiting in the subjects' interior to be discovered' (Kvale 1996: 3). The miner-interviewer's job is to dig out the nuggets of knowledge or meaning that are obscured by the messy surface of the interview talk. In the life-history interview, it is the *self* that is to be mined. Peter Woods (1985), for instance, uses an explicitly mining metaphor when he recommends a 'conversational' technique which is 'designed to strike rich seams of data deep in people's memories and often subconsciousnesses' (p. 13).

But analysis has come to be seen by many researchers, including Kvale, as an aggressive act that stifles the voice of the interviewees and sustains the power and pre-eminence of the analyst. Within education, there has been a widespread move, already touched on in previous chapters, to reclaim the 'voice' of research subjects – especially teachers.[1]

Such a desire to preserve the authentic voice of the teacher conflicts with the interventive analytic procedures referred to above, in which the expert researcher/analyser *does things* to the raw data offered by the story giver – 'mines' it, interprets it, cuts it up into themes, strips away its surface layers, refines it, distils its essence. Consequently, researchers have looked for more equitable, less power-driven research relationships, and more congenial research metaphors such as collaboration, conversation or partnership. I want to suggest in this chapter that, despite such moves towards collaboration, empathy and voice, a certain ambivalence continues to run through life-history method, reflecting two contradictory desires (or fears) – to intervene, analyse, interpret, or to let the narratives 'stand' on their own terms. These irreconcilable desires – for mastery and surrender – can be seen in the *metaphors* that are used to describe the research process, as I show below.

It might be thought that approaching method via metaphor is something of a literary indulgence, a reduction of research to 'mere words'. But as Donna Haraway (1995: 75) notes, all enquiry relies on a 'metaphorical toolkit' which codes the taken-for-granted assumptions that prevail within paradigms – about the nature of the world, about what it means to be a person, about what counts as knowledge, and so on. In looking at the 'metaphors we live by' (see Lakoff and Johnson 1980), or at least the ones we research by, it is possible to glimpse the tacit assumptions that govern our actions as researchers. More than that though, a close look at the figurative language of research reminds us again that we are not simply 'users', much less masters, of language; not free to pick the best words to apply to a pre-existing meaning, or to describe a pre-existing self. We are caught in the web of language that gives us our worldview and, indeed, our very self-hood. Still, Haraway argues that we can aspire to new metaphoric toolkits and new stories of science or inquiry, even if we can never fully shake off the inheritance of the old ones. In this chapter, I attempt to unpick the metaphorical fabric of some recent writing about life-history method, and propose an alternative 'metaphorical toolkit' based on the metaphor of text as *tissue* or *fabric*. Using Derrida's play on these words, and their connections with other tissues – webs, weaves, folds, membranes – I explore the implications of the self as *fabrication*.[2]

'Bias', 'fronts' and fallibility: problems of voice

The analyst's dilemma of whether or not to intervene is most clearly seen at those points where researchers note the *problems* posed by personal stories. Richard Butt and his co-workers, for instance, champion the notion of teacher 'voice', but they also note that autobiographical narratives 'are subject to incompleteness, personal bias and selective recall in the process by which the narrative is constructed. The fallibility of memory, selective recall, repression, the shaping of stories according to disposition, internal idealization and nostalgia all represent the possibility of biased data' (Butt *et al.* 1992: 91). The risk of 'biased data' leads the authors to advocate a measure of intervention: although authentic, teachers' stories cannot stand alone.

Peter Woods (1985) is similarly concerned about inconsistency and bias, about 'distortional effects on data' (p. 14). Both Woods and Butt *et al.* hold that one way – perhaps the preferable way – to minimize distortion is by arranging the dynamics of the interview encounter and the research relationship to encourage mutual empathy and the 'dissolution of fronts' (Woods 1985: 14). This might involve adopting a conversational rather than a formal interactional style, taking time to build a warm and trusting relationship, or giving and accepting hospitality. The aim is to build a research relationship in which the teacher participants will feel free to 'be themselves' (Woods 1985: 14), or where both participants, researcher and subject, will be able to 'unmask' themselves (Butt *et al.* 1992: 91). Formulations such as these are sensitive to the issue of *authenticity*, to the desire to recognize the teacher's distinctive voice and avoid intervening in her narrative. By orchestrating the dynamics of the interview relationship, the researcher does intervene; but he or she does so to allow a more real self to emerge from behind the fronts or masks that people adopt in unfamiliar or threatening social situations.[3]

Yet these prophylactic measures are seldom enough. Even in texts that foreground authenticity, personal voice, interpretive restraint and equal partnerships with subjects, there is often a counter-discourse of control and intervention. Researchers report the need to take additional 'precautions' or 'safeguards', such as cross-checking or triangulation, to detect bias and 'self-justification' (Woods 1985: 17, 18). Miles Huberman (1993), in his study of the life-cycle of teachers, refers to a 'gamut of interviewing techniques' that were used for the 'control and correction of reliability of informants' statements' (p. 23).

Metaphors of method

One can detect this counter-discourse of intervention in the metaphors that are used to describe the research process. One such metaphor has already cropped up in this chapter, namely that of 'mining'. It is worth considering some others, taking as an example Peter Woods' (1985) article, 'Conversations with teachers: some aspects of life-history method', which was referred to above.[4] Woods uses a rich array of metaphors in his careful exposition of a life-history approach. Many of these, such as the mining image itself, are *depth* metaphors. They invoke a binary world of essences and appearances, depths and surfaces, in which it is the researcher's job to go beneath, behind or beyond. For instance (all emphases are mine):

- [the conversational style is] 'designed to *strike rich seams of data deep in people's memories and often unconsciousnesses'* (Woods 1985: 13: see above);
- [research relationships] 'may induce the *presentation of "fronts" which may be difficult to penetrate'* (p. 14);
- *'temporary initial fronts'* (p. 16);
- *'sheltering behind fronts'* (p. 16);
- 'only in this last stage have we *penetrated to the vitals* of the institution' (p. 19).

Some metaphors invoke *purification* rather than penetration, although the same binary economy is invoked – of cores and peripheries, essence and appearance. Here the analyst is a chemist and method is a kind of solvent:[5]

- 'The first stage in analysis is to *distil the essence* of the biography into more manageable form' (p. 23);
- 'This *distillation* is returned to the teacher for comment' (p. 24);
- *'distilled* or "secondary analysis" stage' (p. 25);
- 'correcting and *refining* the account' (p. 24).

Then there are a set of metaphors which invoke, broadly, a notion of the analyst as engineer or technologist, who activates the machinery of self, restores the 'balance' of truth, or corrects 'distortional effects' in the narrative:

- 'The researcher will also attempt to *triangulate* data in whatever ways are possible' (p. 16);
- *'triangulation* is one of the main aids to validity' (p. 17);
- 'certain *imbalances* may well need *correcting'* (p. 18);
- [the memory] 'must be *oiled and gently coaxed into action* before it begins to function more smoothly' (p. 21).

These metaphors, many of which are common currency in research parlance, invoke a world of nineteenth-century applied science and technology: mining, refining, surveying, distilling. Whether connected with penetrating, purifying or engineering, they all imply a binary universe in which the really important things – the real person, the true story, the relevant data or incontrovertible knowledge – are opposed to, and obscured by, contingent factors (social pressure, poor memory, 'self-interest', loss of coherence, poor interviewing technique, etc.). It is the researcher's job to *remove these impediments* by applying specialist treatments or procedures to the interview setting, or the unrefined data, or the half-hidden self of the interviewee. This view of research – as the search for fundamental things that are obscured by impedimenta – places it within Derrida's definition of 'metaphysics', or the science of *presence*, which we have already encountered. Method, on this view, is a metaphysical tool for mastering uncertainty and providing access to presence (see Spivak 1976: xix).

But, as we have already seen, making presence manifest is a tricky matter. The research methods or processes that are used to reveal presence (in the form, here, of the authentic self, the true story, etc.) may *themselves* end up obscuring presence. The masterful techniques of the researcher as chemist or engineer, 'questioning the universe', are unquestionably interventive.[6] They raise the spectre, already discussed above, of researchers obscuring the very 'voices' which it is their intention to make 'present'. The methods get in the way of presence, where this is apprehended as the pure, unmediated, spontaneous voice of the subject.

At what point does support for subjects become intervention? This concern runs through Peter Woods' exposition. Intertwined with the engineer/chemist's language of technological processes is a discourse of cooperation, sharing, empathy and trust. Indeed, this discourse is foregrounded in the text as a whole. The research process is referred to as a 'joint investment' (Woods 1985: 14) and 'joint work' (p. 15), life histories are 'mutual endeavours' (p. 14). In the following comments, the borderline between support and intervention is addressed directly:

> [Life-history conversations] carry a sense of empathy, whereby the life account is shared [. . .]. Certainly, the researcher will not impose on the teacher's recall, but act rather as catalyst. Teachers may need little prompting once the conversations are under way and they have a clearer view of what the research is about. Guidance may be a different matter, but any that is given must be delicate, and either framed in general terms that relate to the patterns of all careers, or conceived in the interests of validity.
>
> (Woods 1985: 16)

These comments probe the nature and limits of the researcher's role. Emphasizing the notion of a shared account, Woods cautions researchers not to *impose* on teachers' recall, and refers to the need for *delicate* guidance. It is not entirely clear what guidance might consist of, and how it is a 'different matter' from prompting. But it appears to mean that researchers should not make substantive contributions to the details of the individual teacher's life story, though they may comment on career 'patterns' at a general level, or give guidance for purposes of 'validity' – that is, for ensuring the soundness or truth of the interviewee's story. Interestingly, Woods uses another chemical metaphor here – the *catalyst*

– to describe the limits on the researcher's role. The function of the catalyst is to set processes in motion, or to accelerate processes that would have happened anyway, without itself being altered, or affecting the outcomes of the process. In distinction to the researcher-chemist as the powerful agent who 'distils' the essences from others' stories, the researcher's role here is reduced to that of simply setting in motion the processes through which selves reveal themselves.

The figure of the catalyst preserves the chemical metaphor that recurs in the text, but diminishes the connotations of mastery and technique associated with the metaphors of distilling and refining. It invokes an intervention which is also *not* an intervention, but 'just' something that sets things going. But does it really resolve the tensions between imposition and facilitation, between the voices of subjects and researchers, which the paragraph addresses? One might ask how comfortably the metaphor of the catalyst 'fits' the notion of the *shared* venture, if the researcher is to emerge unchanged at the end of the process and to make no substantive difference to the course of that process. Is it possible to take responsibility for validity – for guaranteeing soundness and truth – without imposing on subjects' recall or transgressing the limits of 'delicate' guidance? Can method be both a catalyst *and* a solvent?

'that dangerous supplement'[7]

In the 'delicate' manoeuvres of the above paragraph, the role of the researcher is trapped in the paradoxical logic of the *supplement*. Supplementary logic, a major insight of Derrida's deconstruction, sets in when writers or thinkers attempt to maintain the priority and 'presence' of a particular thing by assigning its opposite term the modest role of supplement. We have already seen, for instance, how writing has often been allocated a supplementary role in relation to speech (Derrida 1976). Here, Woods formulates the researcher's role as that of a mere supplement to a process which, ideally, would be done without outside intervention – that is, *the telling by the teacher of her own life story*. The function of the catalyst is pre-eminently that of the supplement: something which facilitates the achievement of 'presence' (such as the true life story) without compromising the integrity of the thing that is to be made present. But as Derrida showed, the supplement always points to some hole or flaw in the thing that it supplements. The supplement never merely *adds* some (minor or contingent) element: precisely by adding something, it also *replaces* something that is not present, and so takes away from the self-sufficiency and intactness of the original. In our case, the researcher's interventions take something from the integrity and self-sufficiency of the teacher's voice. As Derrida notes, if the supplement did not have this usurping function, if it really did leave the original untouched, then the supplement would be entirely useless. There would be no point in researchers intervening at all. The supplement always carries the paradoxical threat of being *both* useless and damaging.

Rather than clarifying the nature and limits of the researcher's role, therefore, the paragraph from Woods quoted above seems to set in motion further uncertainties. Similar ambivalences surface at other points in the text, sometimes in subtle forms. Consider this statement on the importance of trust: 'the whole relationship has to be bound by trust. To cooperate in this joint capacity, *teachers must be persuaded* of the value of the project, both to themselves personally and to education generally' (Woods 1985: 14; my emphasis). The italicized words contain what linguists call a 'systematic ambiguity' – that is, an undecidable choice between two meanings, stemming from differences in the underlying grammatical structure. The agent has been deleted in the passive clause 'teachers must be persuaded of the value of the project', so that it is hard to tell 'who' would be doing the persuading. Is persuading something that must be done by researchers to teachers? Or is the persuasion something that teachers must reflexively do to themselves; or even demand that researchers must accomplish, before they autonomously agree to take part? Mastery and surrender flicker backwards and forwards across the clause.

Poison or remedy? Method as *pharmakon*

> This *pharmakon*, this 'medicine', this philter, which acts as both remedy and poison, already introduces itself into the body of the discourse with all its ambivalence. This charm, this spellbinding virtue, this power of fascination, can be – alternately or simultaneously – beneficent or maleficent.
>
> (Derrida 1981: 70)

The metaphorical structure of Woods' text points to an inexorable dilemma of life-history method. In its attempts to reveal presence (in the form of the true self, the authentic voice, the unbiased story, etc.), method ends up concealing it. Where it tries to purify, it also contaminates. Its remedies (for bias, falsehood, fallibility) are also poisons. Its operations are both harmless (catalysing) and penetrative. Derrida has played with many different words for the logical impasses produced by the metaphysics of presence (including 'supplement'), and one in particular seems especially resonant here. It is the *pharmakon*. In classical Greek, 'pharmakon' meant 'drug', in the sense of both poison and remedy, together with a range of associated meanings including an enchanted potion, a spell, a perfume and lye (i.e. a strong bleach or acid used in laundering).[8]

Pharmakon is a word fraught with ambiguity, therefore: both good and bad; poisonous and curative; cleansing and contaminating; purgative and (merely) decorative. Derrida (1981) stalks the vicissitudes of the word as it was used in Plato's *Phaedrus,* where writing is described as a *pharmakon.* Writing, for Plato/Socrates, could act as a remedy for the limitations of memory or the transience of speech as carriers of truth; but it was also a regrettable and dangerous substitute, a lifeless and fraudulent imitation of speech, and a usurper of genuine memory, leading away from, not closer to, truth. Poison and remedy, then. By tracing the intricate web of appearances of the *pharmakon* in Plato's text, Derrida (1981) unravels Plato's attempts to master the danger and ambiguity of the *pharmakon*/writing by pinning it down into 'clear-cut oppositions: good and evil, inside and outside, true and false, essence and appearance' (p. 103). Far from subduing the disruptive potential of writing, by firmly discriminating its good from its bad aspects, what happens, says Derrida, is that the *pharmakon* unsettles all those 'clear-cut oppositions' on which Plato's metaphysics depends. Because the *pharmakon*/writing is always both on the 'outside', as an external support, *and* on the inside, as medicine or corrosive poison, it undoes the very notion of inside/ outside on which Plato's binary logic depends. The *pharmakon* is, in other words, another instance of the *supplement*:

> Plato maintains *both* the exteriority of writing *and* its power of male-ficent penetration, its ability to affect or infect what lies deepest inside. The *pharmakon* is that dangerous supplement that breaks into the very thing that would have liked to do without it yet lets itself *at once* be breached, roughed up, fulfilled, and replaced, completed by the very trace through which the present increases itself in the act of disappearing.
>
> (Derrida 1981: 110)

The 'pharmaceutical' or chemical aspirations of method – to disinfect, filter, strain, purify, penetrate, cure, dissolve – will always raise the spectre of the 'bad' opposites: the risk that method might infect, adulterate, poison, contaminate, obscure, corrode.

double bind . . .

My point in interrogating these metaphors of life-history research is not to hold one author to account for inconsistency, or to suggest that writers should tighten up their tropes. Nor is it to suggest that this particular article is a special case of ambivalence. On the contrary, I want to suggest that there is an *inevitable* ambivalence in methodological discussions that revolve around, and aspire to, presence. The search for ontological security – that is, for presence – does not produce the comforts of certainty or authenticity, but produces *oscillations* instead – between scientific and personal authority; between mastery and surrender; between nostalgia for the authentic voice of the subject and the desire for certainty that leads researchers to override it. Attempts at collaboration, in which power, knowledge and truth would be 'shared' between the researcher and the researched, cannot really arrest these oscillations either. The problem is not one of 'imbalances' of power, or of the loudness of speakers' voices, but of a *double bind*, to use another of Derrida's phrases – a logical dilemma that cannot be solved because 'one can only unbind one of its knots by pulling on the other to make it tighter' (Derrida 1998: 36).

Some alternative metaphors of method

Perhaps, then, we need new metaphors of the relation between researchers and subjects, such as entanglement, knots, weaves and tissues, that would remain within the problematic of the double bind: metaphors of *fabrication* in other words. Rather than trying to escape from the double bind of mastery and surrender, we could acknowledge the productive dilemma that it creates for the researcher, inescapably caught up in the weave of the life story. Derrida (1981) reminds us that the words 'text', 'tissue' and 'textile' have a common etymology, and the weaver's creations – webs, nets, meshes, knots, threads, membranes, gauzes, tissues – run through his work as figures of Writing.[9] Life-history researchers (like any other researchers) and their subjects (like any other subjects) produce *text*. Their accounts are always fabrications, in the sense discussed in Chapter 5 – weaving something new, yet assembled out of fragments and recollections of other fabrications such as the interview 'data' and field notes, as well the scattered traces of innumerable other cultural texts of identity, policy, institutional life, career, curriculum, and so on.

Notions of analysis as mastery or surrender reflect the desire to cut loose from that textuality; to escape the sticky threads of contingency, bias, self-interest and ambiguity that constitute text. But we have seen that texts cannot be subdued into a 'one-way reading' (Derrida 1981: 225) by the heavy machinery or the chemical solvents of analysis; or by the vanishing trick of the catalytic agent who leaves no traces on the text. Analysis has to involve 'getting a few fingers caught' in the weave if it is to set anything at all in motion, as Derrida observes:

There is always a surprise in store for the anatomy or physiology of any criticism that might think it had mastered the game, surveyed all the threads at once, deluding itself, too, in wanting to look at the text without touching it, without laying a hand on the 'object', without risking – which is the only chance of entering into the game, by getting a few fingers caught – the addition of some new thread. [. . .] One must then, in a single gesture, but doubled, read and write. And that person would have understood nothing of the game who, at this [*du coup*], would feel himself authorised merely to add on; that is, to add any old thing. He would add nothing: the seam wouldn't hold. Reciprocally, he who through 'methodological prudence', 'norms of objectivity', or 'safeguards of knowledge' would refrain from committing anything of himself, would not read at all.

(Derrida 1981: 63–4)

In place of mastery and surrender, then, there is always *entanglement*. It is equally impossible for the researcher/analyst to 'master the game' or to 'look at the text without touching it'.

It is important to note that, for Derrida, texts are not smooth, grid-like weaves with neat edges. That is why they do not give themselves up to unravelling by the master philosopher/analyst who knows the right thread to pull (Derrida 1998: 37–8). They are not well-wrought tapestries or close-knit fabrics that bind their arguments into grids of meaning or stitch together a coherent self. They are not colourful patchworks either, in which multiple meanings, or multiple selves, interlock and accumulate to make a harmonious whole. Texts are always incomplete and fragmentary because they are part of the unceasing fabrication of the world, which involves both making and unmaking. Bits are unravelling at the very instant that new connections are being knotted together. So texts do not have clear-cut edges; or at least, their borders only come into being at the moment that they are carved out by 'the cutting trace, the decision of each reading' (Derrida 1981: 63). And the selves that are fabricated in the course of this 'perpetual interweaving', to use Barthes' term, are equally diffuse and mutable: 'lost in this tissue – this texture – the subject unmakes himself, like a spider dissolving in the constructive secretions of its web' (Barthes 1990: 64). The life-history researcher and his or her 'subjects' are engaged in a much less secure and certain project than metaphors of collaboration, conversation, catalysis or distillation would suggest, in which identity is never fully 'there', but always subject to shifts and ambiguity.

Wrestling with identity

What might it look like, to write research texts that resist the temptations of the 'one-way reading' and try to be responsible to the shifts and ambiguities of identity? Carol Rambo Ronai (1998, 1999) offers one attempt, in her ethnography of a group of women who worked as erotic dancers/wrestlers.[10] Rambo Ronai became a participant in the research in ways that she had not originally intended, which included wrestling in 'Jell-O' with Kitty, the group's leader, in front of a paying audience of off-duty cops, as the price of the women's cooperation with her research. Rambo Ronai weaves a 'layered text' that traces the lives of her women 'subjects' through multiple forms of representation, while maintaining a sense of the perplexity of identity and the instability of interpretation. Refusing to settle on one particular representation of her subjects, or one interpretation of their lives, she constantly puts 'under erasure', after Derrida, interpretations of the events she describes and the women she portrays. Although Rambo Ronai anchors her research primarily in metaphors of sketching and drawing, there are vestiges, too, of weaves and folds in her account of the infinite deferral of identity:

> The meaning of being a researcher or a dancer is not inherently present in itself. These identities exist in the traces of the past and in the context of the unfolding situation as it dissolves into the future. The final meaning of what it means to be a dancer or a researcher is always deferred because there is no absolute starting point from which to triangulate these identities.
>
> (Rambo Ronai 1998: 411)

In the following fragment, Rambo Ronai sketches competing interpretations and evaluations of Kitty, impersonating the 'voices' of those who might make such evaluations.

> Kitty is cute and curvy. Sexy. I'd have drawn her in calligraphy strokes, varying the pressure, tapering my lines from thick to thin in pinks, peaches, corals, and other pastels. Wisps of yellow and gold would hint at her hair. She seems soft, sweet, flirtatious – somehow feline. Her stage name, which she has insisted on using for this manuscript, works well. She looks like someone who just wants to play, have fun, and be loved.
>
> Kitty is tall, intimidating, built like a fuckin' Valkyrie warrior maiden, ready to swoop down from Valhalla and kick ass. She'd be a great model for a Heavy Metal character or perhaps a 'Boris' painting. I wouldn't want to fight her, though later, I have to.
>
> Kitty is too fleshy for her frame and height. She looks good, but if she gains another five pounds she will be overweight. The tight clothes detract from rather than accentuate her figure. Something looser, more subtle, would make a more elegant statement on her potentially regal, 6'–1" frame. She teeters the line between voluptuous and vulgar.

Kitty is a blatant victim of false consciousness, buying into her own oppression and objectification by reproducing the very images that oppress her. Kitty is clueless.

Kitty is a hard-core feminist who fully embraces her power as a woman. By taking control of her body and her life, she uses the very means through which most women are typically oppressed to undermine patriarchy and get her plumbing fixed! [alluding to an incident in which Kitty asked her apartment manager to fix her plumbing: see below]

She is nothing but a tall, tacky, pathetic whore. Her teeth are crooked and her makeup flakes off her face into a kind of pink dandruff that lands in small chunks on her clothes. Leave the tanning booth alone honey!

Kitty is a business woman who owns a travelling strip show and strip-ogram service in a major metropolitan area in the southeast region of the country. Confident, strong willed, and independent, Kitty is an admirable figure of a 1990s woman.

(Rambo Ronai 1998: 409)

Throughout her 'layered text', which moves between vignettes, auto-biographical reminiscences and methodological musings, Rambo Ronai resists 'settling' on any one of these versions of Kitty, while also refusing to dispatch any of them. She maintains a pervasive sense of uncertainty – on her own part, and hence for the reader – as to how far the women dancers, and the men with whom they come into contact (customers, bouncers, landlords), are controlling the events she describes or submitting to them; what the women think of her, and what she thinks of them; whether people are joking or serious, well-intentioned or malign, exploited or manipulative; whether she herself is a good or an inept researcher – one of the girls or a figure of fun. She describes an incident in which Kitty, dressed in skimpy gear, asks the manager of her apartment building to fix her plumbing, prompting dead-pan *double-entendres* and paroxysms of barely suppressed guffaws from the manager and his friends (or, possibly, elaborate pantomimes of barely suppressed guffaws). Throughout that vignette, Rambo Ronai (1998: 405–6) conveys her uncertainty as to how far Kitty is aware of the reactions she is producing, and perhaps in control of them; and how much of this is being staged for *her* benefit, by the men, or by Kitty, or by both. For instance, the men later claim that Kitty was annoyed at being observed by another woman 'showing her ass'; but the researcher can never decide whether they were being serious or not. She remains perplexed and wrong-footed throughout, as she struggles to decipher how Kitty and her friends feel about her. She reflects on her own inept approach to Kitty to recruit her as a participant in the research, and alludes throughout to Kitty's scornful attitude to her. Yet she speculates that the crassness of her recruitment 'technique' may have been the reason it succeeded – by prompting Kitty to challenge her to take part in the wrestling match, as a test of Rambo Ronai's willingness to humiliate herself. Mastery and surrender wrestle and dance with one another throughout her text, without either ever permanently coming out on top.

Rambo Ronai's layered text weaves in copious amounts of 'data', in the form of recalled speech and detailed ethnographic descriptions; but this adds to, rather than reduces, the possibility of multiple readings. The reader is left undecided what to 'make' of the women, in any summary sense. But this does not mean that nothing new has emerged, or that nothing can be grasped of the lives of these particular working women. On the contrary, Rambo Ronai manages to convey (to this particular reader/writer at any rate) a poignant picture of complex lives, which resists dissolving or congealing into oppositions – virtue or vice, approval or censure, money or morality, 'insider' or 'outsider' – but rather sketches how these intermingle and are negotiated in the course of lives. The women dancer-wrestlers 'come across' as bristling with agency, wit and energy, but they are not portrayed as transcending their circumstances or, alternatively, as reduced to the mere victims of these.

Although there are no single, 'true' versions of a life or a person, this does not mean, according to Andrew Travers (1991), that there is no such thing as self-hood, or that we feel any less unique and full of self just because we cannot draw clear boundaries around that self, or ever say in so many words exactly who we are. On the contrary, he suggests, it is possibly at those weird moments when we are confronted with the inherent ambiguities of identity that we feel most gripped by the sense of our own self-hood.

In conclusion

In the 'bad sense', as the *Oxford English Dictionary* puts it, 'fabrication' also means a forgery – that is, a copy or imitation. I have suggested in this chapter that identity and, therefore, life history, is *always* a matter of copies, imitations and forgeries. Identity is always deferred and in process of becoming – never really, never yet, never absolutely 'there'. Here is Andrew Travers' description of that dilemma, in an article which adds the 'sequinned negligée' to the metaphorical fabrics of text:[11]

> No person in any interaction may be allowed to evidently escape from self-identification with somebody who is not there, that person known as *that* person. Each interactant must bring himself or herself to life in fulsome plastic flesh if he or she is not to invite accusations

of not being 'himself' or 'herself'. And the self-identification of bringing oneself off, in the felt absence of a fundamentally good self with whom identification has to be made, is a camp performance, see-through and opaque at the same time.

(Travers 1993: 137)

Life-history researchers and their subjects cannot escape from camp conduct and the 'squeamish reciprocity' that it induces (Travers 1993: 135). Although it might be useful for some purposes to think of the life-history interview as a managed occasion for those involved to 'unmask themselves' (e.g. Butt et al. 1992), what is revealed when the masks are lowered will always be another fabrication.

The repulsion of theory: women writing research

Arnolphe: Her writing has almost killed me.

(Moliere, *L'Ecole des Femmes*)

Men are read rhetorically; women, literally.

(Barbara Johnson 1998: 123)

Introduction

This chapter explores issues concerning women's writing and the discomforts that 'theory' has raised for some feminist researchers and scholars, especially theory that has poststructuralist or postmodernist leanings.[1] Since this is the kind of 'theory' which animates this book too, I pursue the question of why women researchers have often felt excluded from, and repelled by, Theory. Can women 'play' in a postmodern space that has become associated with masculine pursuits? The chapter also revisits topics that have been addressed in previous chapters, including voice, autobiography and the problematic status of 'literal' writing. The chapter provides further examples of how educational research can draw productively on insights from other disciplines to explore methodological questions. Here, examples are taken from literary theory, anthropology and philosophy.

The problem with theory

'Theory' has been a source of trouble for feminism. Judith Butler and Joan Scott (1992), in their edited collection of encounters between feminism and theory, describe it as 'a highly contested term' (p. xiii). Something of the flavour of that contestation is nicely caught in an advert for an academic job in an American literature department, reported by Nancy K. Miller, which invited applications from 'a feminist or a theorist' (cited in Lutz 1995: 259). I want to explore some of the ambivalence, not to mention the outright hostility, that many feminist writers have expressed towards theory, and in particular their identification of theory as a male domain from which feminism has been excluded. Or, to which feminism cannot afford to belong.

By 'theory' I have in mind that loose collection of continentally influenced approaches with literary and/or psychoanalytic leanings that often go under the names of poststructuralism, postmodernism, deconstruction and discourse analysis. I will not spend time here on describing and discriminating between these, not least because it is an impossible task (see Appendix 1; see also Stronach and MacLure 1997). But in any case they are often lumped together under the name of theory, especially for polemical purposes. Theory is linked to those funny 'turns' that are said to have befallen the disciplines as a result/cause of the 'crisis of representation' – the linguistic turn, the literary turn, the reflexive turn, the textual turn, the narrative turn, the postmodern turn. Green (1994: iii) suggests that, while these various 'turns' have many differences, they share the work of 'registering a new space' for research and theorizing across the disciplines.

However, for many feminist researchers, the space occupied by theory is a hostile terrain of exclusion, opposition or territorial aggression. By asserting the decentring of the humanist subject, and the radical undecidability of truth, being or meaning, theory undermines, or seems to, any feminist project that is organized around a specifically female subjectivity. It threatens to dissipate the energy – and the clarity – of a politics grounded in women's experience (see, among many other feminist critiques, Mascia-Lees *et al.* 1989). Moreover, many feminist writers have argued that theory is a pre-eminently *gendered* domain, a province subdued, ruled and policed by male academics. It has struck many women writers as more than coincidental that poststructuralist theory announced 'the death of the subject', just at the time when women were asserting their claim to subjectivity. This announcement has seemed all the more hollow in that theory is associated above all with the names of some very big fathers: Foucault, Derrida, Baudrillard, Lyotard, Lacan.

Feminist researchers have often felt especially excluded by, and from, the *textual* interests of 'theory' – for example, the privilege given to irony; the exhortation to engage (indulge?) in textual 'play'; the seemingly wilful difficulty of much theoretical writing; above all, the concern with texts at the apparent expense of people, politics or practice. It is fitting to say that feminist researchers have often felt *repelled* by theory (hence the title of this chapter), since this captures the sense both of a felt exclusion from the privileged work of theory and of an internally produced antipathy to such work. It also captures the almost visceral nature of the antagonism that textualist theory frequently produces in feminist critics. To give one example: Liz Stanley and Sue Wise (1990), commenting on their own earlier attempts to define a specifically 'feminist theory', insist that such theory is 'certainly not to be treated as sacrosanct and enshrined in "texts" to be endlessly pored over like chicken entrails' (p. 24).

I want to look more closely here at the claims that feminist writers have been making for several years now, across different disciplines, about the exclusion of women from the discourses of postmodernism and poststructuralism. I am not thinking here of the blatant and widespread forms of exclusion that keep women from positions of seniority within an academy that is still regulated by a largely male coterie of gatekeepers, some of whom now happen to be selling themselves as postmodernists. Though this is not to deny the relevance of that more obvious political and institutional exclusion to my theme. But I want particularly in this chapter to open up the question of women's exclusion from *writing*.[2] I want to suggest that women have often been denied full membership of the community of playful, postmodernist writers, and to explore the implications of that for feminism within educational research.

Here is a short and brutal summary of what I hope to unfold more persuasively below. I will argue that the feminist suspicion of theory as a site of masculinist discourse is well-founded, and that this is linked to the (continuing) erasure of women's writing. Specifically, I draw on some feminist work within anthropology, literary theory and philosophy that argues that women's writing has historically been – and still is – read dismissively as textually naive and, therefore, theoretically impoverished. That is, as literal, descriptive, narrative, confessional, parochial, or 'sincere'. This dismissal of the writings of specific, embodied women has not only performed the familiar masculinist gesture of trying to contain the threat of women's disruptive potential. It has also allowed male theorists of poststructuralism and deconstruction to occupy the space (now conveniently evacuated of actual women) of the *metaphorical feminine* as traditionally construed in philosophical and literary thought – that is, as a general principle or metaphor of the unruly, disorderly, disruptive, Nietzschean 'non-truth of truth'. Through this 'metaphorization of the feminine', as Rosi Braidotti (1991) puts it, 'woman' gets to be the productive, transgressive, irreducible figure of Derridean *différance*, or the Lacanian lack that sets desire and signification in motion – but at the expense of any voice, agency, history, meaning or political effectivity as living, embodied *women*.

Yet my conclusion is that feminism cannot afford to keep its distance from theory. On the contrary, I want to suggest that it is all the more urgent that feminists engage in deconstructive play to defend women's writing, and the specificity of women's voices, from erasure. But the status, and the possibility, of such play will always be problematic in a discursive space where play is always already defined as the pastime of male theoretical cross-dressers.

It may seem odd that I should devote so much space to considering feminist work within disciplines that seem somewhat at a remove from educational research. I hope the justification for this will shape itself up as we go along. But by way of preliminary, I would say that the main reason for this is that, in various different ways, the feminist writers of anthropology, literary theory and philosophy that I discuss below are all concerned with the strange and intimate association of *writing* with women's achievement of, and failure of, subjectivity. Educational research is, of course, much concerned with writing. But as this book has tried to show, we often don't realize how truly weird writing is.

Writing lesson 1: the double-binding of feminist anthropology[3]

I want to look first at the work of some feminist writers within anthropology, where the gendered politics of writing have been a preoccupation for well over a decade. This is partly due to anthropologists' comparatively long-standing awareness of their own complicity in the processes of 'Othering' that kept colonial subjects in their place. Women who aspired also to be anthropologists were especially alert to the ironies of their double status as both perpetrators and victims of the practices of Othering. Feminist anthropologists' experiences of exclusion are particularly instructive, moreover, because of a particular event that crystallized their exclusion from theory, and simultaneously highlighted the intimate association of this exclusion with *writing*. That event was the publication in 1986 of the anthology, *Writing Culture: The Poetics and Politics of Ethnography*, edited by James Clifford and George Marcus. *Writing Culture* quickly came to epitomize the textualist critique of the realist tradition in ethnographic writing. The contributors to the collection showed how the rhetorical devices employed by ethnographers constructed the realities they seemed innocently to describe, and granted voice and authority to the writer at the expense of those written 'about'. These insights were not new, but they were articulated in an authoritative manner (paradoxically enough), with an editorial introduction by James Clifford that was also a call to ethnographers to develop innovative, reflexive ways of writing that would self-consciously challenge their own claims to authoritative knowledge. The collection rapidly assumed canonical status as a manifesto of what came to be called 'experimental ethnography'.[4]

But what made the book an 'event' for feminist anthropologists was James Clifford's justification for including only one woman contributor.[5]

Clifford invoked an ingenious, and infuriating, double bind: basically, that the women who were writing experimentally were not feminist enough, while the women who were writing feminism were not experimental enough.[6] As a result, Ruth Behar (1995) suggests, '[t]o be a woman writing culture became a contradiction in terms' (p. 5). An ironic outcome of this absencing of women was the amount of 'writing back' that it provoked among feminist ethnographers, according to Barbara Babcock (1993). *Writing Culture* prompted what Ruth Behar (1995) called a 'sullen liberation': women writers who 'had had [their] wings clipped for not being analytical enough' (p. 5) were moved to renewed attempts at creativity and innovation, and to an intensified focus on the problematics of male perceptions of women's writing.

One form that this 'writing back' has taken is to recuperate the intellectual contributions of women anthropologists of previous generations, to show how their work had anticipated many of the themes of postmodernist and textual theory. The attempt to 'think back through our mothers', as Barbara Babcock (1993: 61) puts it, quoting Virginia Woolf, was part of a deliberate strategy to interrupt the homosocial citation habits of male academics, whose intellectual lineage is generally only traced back through the male line.[7] For example, Barbara Babcock has urged a 're-reading' of Ruth Benedict, emphasizing her use of irony and textual critique to deconstruct anthropology's delusions of mastery of other cultures, and her persistent attack on the notion of a singular, universal human nature (Babcock 1993, 1995). The writings of Elsie Clews Parsons, Ella Deloria, Ruth Landes and Zora Neale Hurston have likewise been given re-readings by, respectively, Louise Lamphere, Janet Finn, Sally Cole and Graciela Hernandez.[8]

According to their latter-day sponsors, these earlier women writers sharply delineated many (now) familiar postmodern concerns: the permeability of boundaries between inside and outside, self and other; the fracture of identity; the social and political construction of 'woman'; the violence inherent in notions of universality and scientific rationalism; the problematic articulation of race and gender in the 'epistemology of the oppressed'. Several of these women writers were also accomplished practitioners of the 'blurring of the genres' later championed by postmodern and textualist ethnography (cf. Geertz 1988). Benedict was a poet and a dedicated popularizer of anthropology as well as a theorist of culture, whose best-selling book *Patterns of Culture* was deliberately written for 'the Macy shopper' (Babcock 1993: 61). Zora Neale Hurston was a notable and successful boundary-crosser – a published anthropologist, folklorist and novelist, and a participant in the Harlem Renaissance. Her status as a boundary crosser is reflected in the fact that her work is, belatedly, taken seriously both by anthropologists and literary theorists (see below).

A recurring theme in these feminist re-readings is the way in which male anthropologists, at the time and subsequently, repeatedly read these women's writing as fundamentally simple and *non-serious*. Their boundary-crossing forays into poetry, journalism, cultural movements or political activism were taken as evidence of their lack of theoretical rigour or depth. Their writing was read as simple, direct, literal and, in various ways, 'merely': merely descriptive, merely confessional, merely factual, merely popularizing. The reception of Zora Neale Hurston's writing is particularly interesting, since the counter-readings of her work by Graciela Hernandez (1995) and Barbara Johnson (1987) portray a writer of complexity, ambiguity and sophistication, whose writing was insistently 'experimental' and indeed deconstructive. Hernandez and Johnson both suggest that Hurston self-consciously assumed different identities, and intentionally challenged her own authority in her writing. For Johnson, Hurston's writing continuously undermines any position of epistemological certainty. She argues that Hurston's writing deconstructs the boundaries between inside/outside, black/white, male/female, universal/local, truth/fiction, without ever losing sight of the ways in which these binaries continue to *matter*. Hurston's (1978a) study of southern black folk tales, *Mules and Men*, re-enacts the trickster logic of those tales (called 'lies' by the tellers), according to Johnson. Hurston's own authorial sincerity and veracity are thus rendered radically undecidable, in Johnson's reading at least. Through a constant changing of frames and structures of address, it becomes impossible to know who is being fooled – the reader, Hurston's rich, white female sponsor, her anthropological father, Franz Boas, or Hurston herself. Johnson concludes that Hurston's writing dramatizes the impossibility of identity:

> Hurston's very ability to fool us – or to fool us into *thinking* we have been fooled – is itself the only effective way of conveying the rhetoric of the 'lie'. To turn one's own life into a trickster tale of which even the teller herself might be the dupe certainly goes far in deconstructing the possibility of representing the truth of identity.
>
> (Johnson 1987: 183)

But this is emphatically *not* how Hurston's work was read by her male contemporaries in the 1930s. The black American critic Richard Wright, reviewing her novel *Their Eyes Were Watching God* (Hurston 1978b), pronounced: '[her] dialogue manages to catch the psychological movements of the Negro folk-mind in their pure simplicity, but that's as far as it goes . . . The sensory sweep of her novel carries no theme, no message, no thought' (cited in Johnson 1987: 167). Where Johnson (1987) sees an attempt 'to narrate both the appeal and the injustice of universalization, in a voice that assumes and articulates its own, ever-differing self-difference' (p. 170), Wright sees virtually nothing. Or at least nothing of literary, as opposed to psychological, significance. That act of reading Hurston into simplicity is repeated with her anthropological writing. Franz Boas' preface to *Mules and Men*, for instance, describes it as making 'an unusual contribution to our knowledge of the true inner life of the Negro' (cited in Johnson 1987: 182). But, Johnson argues, the book throws into permanent question precisely the possibility of any unmediated knowledge of an 'inner life', of self or other. Its rhetorical tricksterism mocks the very idea of writing as a transparent medium though which inner things – thoughts, minds, selves – can be seen without distortion or ambivalence.

Writing lesson 2: the poetics of sincerity

I would not want to say that Johnson's or Hernandez' readings of Hurston are the only possible readings. Or, that they are true while those other readings are false.[9] The question, rather, is this: why has there been a tendency to read women's writing into simplicity and sincerity, to *not-see* complexity and texture? This tendency to read straight through women's writing has a long history, as Barbara Johnson's work in literary criticism shows. It is worth considering another of her examples, since it sheds further light on the ways in which women's writing has been read *differently* from men's. In particular, Johnson shows how women's writing has often been treated as directly *expressive* of women's experience, subjectivity or sensibility. It has been read – and either valorized or dismissed – as *art-less*. That is, as spontaneous, unmediated, uninflected representation of feminine qualities. Johnson (1998) takes as one instance the work of Marceline Desbordes-Valmore, one of the few women poets to have received Baudelaire's (extremely double-edged) approbation. What made Desbordes-Valmore available as an exemplary female figure for the male literary establishment of nineteenth-century France, according to Johnson, was her extreme femininity and her seeming lack of rhetorical or stylistic artifice. These latter practices, being the province of male writers, were widely deplored as 'monstrous' in women. Johnson shows the lengths to which Marceline's male appreciators went to denigrate her artistry, while extolling her sincerity and femininity. Baudelaire liked her poetry because it preserved 'the delicious accent of woman; nothing borrowed, no artificial ornament, nothing but the *eternal feminine*' (quoted in Johnson 1998: 105; original emphasis). An even more double-dealing appreciator summed up her work thus: 'What is enchanting, more than the talent shown in her verse, when there is any, is the total absence of pose' (cited in Johnson 1998: 104).

What the 'canonical male poets' saw and liked in Desbordes-Valmore, then, was her sincerity and her absence of *pose* – that is, the seeming un-written-ness of her writing. In a critical gesture that has been repeated many times, says Johnson (1998), by feminist criticism as well as nineteenth-century French romantic poetry, the woman writer becomes the *sujet supposé sincère* – 'the absolute voice of the native informant from the field of the Eternal Feminine' (p. 108). I will return later to the issue of why such a voice should be resisted by feminist research. For the moment, I want to pursue Johnson's argument. For she goes on to claim that this 'canonical' reading of Desbordes-Valmore as sincere and artless is no more 'natural' or unforced than was Marceline's poetry. Johnson suggests that she consciously and art-*fully* wrote herself up (or down) as that artless expression of femininity that would appeal to male poetic patronage, while at the same time leaving enough clues, gaps and ambiguities in her writing to allow for other readings. She also colluded in the depiction of her own life story as the archetypal romantic narrative of the suffering woman writer inspired by the passion of the One Great Love. However, the details of her life, which included a stage career from age 10, many lovers, infidelities and illegitimate children, could, as Johnson points out, have told a different story.

Desbordes-Valmore wrote within the rhetorical conventions of lyric poetry, in which the lover-poet defines her or himself through desire for the image of the beloved. And, again in accordance with the conventions, her poetry purveyed a feminized, masochistic version of possession by love – that is, the hapless victim overwhelmed, enslaved and undone, in the sense of losing all reason and sense of an intact self. But, says Johnson, this kind of rhetorical masochism has also been written by the male poets of the love lyric, from Petrarch onwards. What interests Johnson (1998) is the way in which this male masochism was so clearly seen as *rhetoric,* while Marceline's was taken literally, as *confession.* As Johnson notes, it is the rhetorical, not the literal, that is taken seriously in poetics:

> When men have described love as an experience of fragmentation, wounding, or loss of psychic intactness and control, it has been read as an analysis of The Nature of Desire. When women have described something analogous, it has been read as an expression of What a Woman Wants. Rhetoric, in other words, is a way of shifting the domain of a poem's meaning to a higher, less referential, more abstract and theoretical level. And this is done by universalizing, that is, by denying the presence of the sexual difference out of which the poem springs.
>
> (Johnson 1998: 124)

'Seriousness', then, is produced through the transcendence of sexual difference, an elevation that is achieved by leaving women behind on the flatlands of referential literality. But as Johnson notes, sexual difference always threatens to return to challenge the universality of male self-confidence. Rhetoric, therefore, enforces masculine privilege by allowing the male writer to 'play femininity' (Johnson 1998: 127).

This leaves women writers in something of a dilemma, especially if they want to play too. And it is a continuing dilemma, as we can see if we return to the controversy in feminist anthropology outlined above. Clifford's double-binding of feminist anthropology was offensive precisely because it suggested that the infantilization of women's writing was still going on. Behar (1995) states angrily that *Writing Culture* 'took a stab at the heart of feminist anthropology, which was devalued as a dreary, hopelessly tautological, fact-finding mission – so, tell us, my dear, are women among the Bongo-Bongo indeed so terribly different?' (p. 5). Catherine Lutz (1995), in the same anthology, also finds a continuing predisposition for women's writing to be seen as 'description, data, case, personal, or, as in the case of feminism, "merely" setting the record straight' (p. 251).

The offence was compounded, in the view of feminist anthropologists, by the adoption of a 'feminine' voice by those very male critics who continued to dismiss women's writing as local, personal or confessional. 'The *Writing Culture* agenda, conceived in homoerotic terms by male academics for other male academics', says Ruth Behar,

> provided the official credentials, and the cachet, that women had lacked for crossing the border. Even the personal voice, undermined when used by women, was given the seal of approval in men's ethnographical accounts, reclassified in more academically favourable terms as 'reflexive' and 'experimental'.
>
> (Behar 1995: 4)

What is read in women's writing as literal, descriptive and conformative is read in men's as rhetorical, disruptive and deconstructive.

Writing lesson 3: critical cross-dressers and Cartesian orphans

Barbara Babcock (1993) similarly identifies the adoption of an 'imaginary femininity' as part of the new-man identity of experimental ethnography, as of postmodernism in general. As she notes, the postmodern resistance to the abstract, totalizing reach of grand narratives has often been associated with a move to a quasi-feminine stance of renunciation of patriarchal authority. But this appropriation of the feminine has, as Babcock and many other feminist writers have noticed, left women writers interested in postmodern possibilities in something of a dilemma. She quotes Jane Gallop: 'the female postmodern thinker finds herself in the position of trying to be like Daddy who is trying to be a woman' (cited in Babcock 1993: 61). Women's voices are likely to come across as flat and uninflected in the ironic discursive space occupied by the male 'critical cross-dressers'[10] who have assumed an imaginary and rhetorical femininity in order to play with, and thus deconstruct, notions of identity.

Rosi Braidotti (1991) notes that the (re)appropriation of the feminine has been a significant move within poststructuralist and deconstructive philosophy, a move that has been deeply problematic for feminist practitioners of deconstruction, such as Braidotti herself, Gayatri Spivak (1993) and Barbara Johnson (1987).[11] Derrida has caused particular consternation through his addition of *woman* to his repertoire of 'undecidables' – that is, those words which enact the irreducible alterity and the originary absence out of which meaning and identity are produced. 'Woman', or 'becoming-woman', takes the place of other Derridean words which perform deconstruction, such as *différance*, dissemination, trace, margins, hymen and 'writing' itself. Derrida deploys 'woman' as the emblem of radical indeterminacy, of that which always evades capture by truth, and which thus guarantees the very possibility of truth itself. His most notorious treatment of the subject can be found in *Spurs*, his re-reading of Nietzsche. You can see something of its potential to offend in this excerpt:

> There is no such thing as the essence of woman because woman averts, she is averted of herself. Out of the depths, endless and unfathomable, she engulfs and distorts all vestige of essentiality, of identity, of property. And the philosophical discourse, blinded, founders on these shoals and is hurled down these depthless depths to its ruin. There is no such thing as the truth of woman, but it is because of that abyssal divergence of the truth, because that untruth is 'truth'. Woman is but one name for the untruth of truth.
>
> (Derrida 1978a: 51)

So 'woman' is put to work as metaphor, to rescue philosophy from the exhaustion of logocentrism. But the downside of being pimped for poststructuralism in this fashion is that woman has no definition in her own right except, as Rosi Braidotti (1991) points out, in terms of a generalized 'lack, void, black hole' (p. 102). Braidotti identifies a similar logic of appropriation of the feminine in the writing of Lacan, Foucault and Deleuze.[12] Braidotti can see the benefits of this metaphorized femininity for the male 'Cartesian orphans' of philosophy: namely, 'to compensate for the void left by the loss of ontological security after the exhaustion of the classical subject' (p. 140). But she is less clear as to what this gender-neutral seizure of the feminine contributes to feminism, or to the specificity of women's struggles for agency and voice. 'When a whole culture in crisis "feminizes" itself, its intellectual style and modes of enunciation, what space does it make for women's language? What sort of "feminine" is this?' (Braidotti 1991: 133).

Like Johnson and Babcock, discussed above, Braidotti is troubled by the metaphorical or rhetorical femininity assumed by the cross-dressing, theoretical Tootsies who have taken to speaking in the place of women.[13] She urges caution in dealing with the postmodern figure of the 'gender-bender', to avoid 'a massive sell-out' of the material interests of women (Braidotti 1991: 122), and sees a 'fundamental dissonance' between the discourses of feminism on the one hand, and the discourses *on* the feminine provoked by the philosophy of crisis on the other (p. 146). She also wishes, though not with much hope, that the self-pitying male theorists might stop speaking for/from other people's margins, and start doing a more sophisticated job of deconstructing their own masculine pretexts.

Gayatri Spivak (1993) is also exercised by Derrida's use of 'woman' as the non-truth of truth, and its manifestly masculinist heritage which cannot, she argues, be excused (p. 128). But she opts nonetheless to 'give assent' to Derrida's text, even though this means 'negotiating with structures of violence'. The risk is worth it, Spivak argues, on account of the productive energies that deconstruction releases in opening up texts to new possibilities (p. 129). The deconstructive force of woman as 'catachresis' – that is, a name without a literal referent – is of value to feminism, Spivak argues. It serves as an active reminder of the fissures and 'impasses' that are covered over when academic feminism mobilizes itself in the name of a generalized 'woman'. As Spivak reminds us, it is inevitably the 'disenfranchised' who get excluded by such all-inclusive gestures:

> It is the disenfranchised who teaches us most often by saying: I do not recognize myself in the object of your benevolence. I do not recognize my share in your naming. Although the vocabulary is not that of high theory, she tells us if we *care* to hear [. . .] that she is not the literal referent for our frenzied naming of woman in the scramble for legitimacy in the house of theory. She reminds us that the name of 'woman', however political, is, like any other name, a catachresis.
>
> (Spivak 1993: 137; original emphasis)

It is important to stress that most of the feminist writers whose work I have discussed in this chapter would continue to locate themselves somewhere within the range of practices named by poststructuralism or deconstruction. They are not essentialists. None of them would argue for a foundational, ahistorical truth of female identity, or the universality of women's experience. They have no plans to abandon theory. Their objection to the theoretical appropriation of the feminine is not grounded in a belief in the unchallengeable authenticity of women's experience, or a distrust of mimicry, or a disinclination to engage in deconstructive 'play'. On the contrary, their argument, as I read it, would be that feminism *must* play: that this is the only way to undo 'the comforts of mastery', as Johnson (1987: 13) puts it, that inhere in the binary logics of opposition that have kept women in their subordinate place. But the question is, *how and where can feminism play*, in a discursive playground where women get pushed to the wall by the noisy games of the cross-dressing male theorists?

Writing lesson 4: the love letter and the stone

As a partial answer to this question, I want to take one last example from Barbara Johnson's work, which dramatizes the issue of women's exclusion from writing as the scene of 'play'; but also shows how that exclusion can never be total, and how this is of importance to women's struggles for voice. Johnson reads Moliere's *L'Ecole des Femmes* as a text about male fear of women's writing. She suggests that writing is a site of possible danger to masculine ambitions of mastery and control, because writing both grants and denies control over meaning. Johnson focuses on the way that Arnolphe, the middle-aged professor, tries to teach ignorance to his young bride-to-be, Agnes, whom he has educated in isolation from the age of four, so that she will love and respect only him. One of Arnolphe's pedagogic strategies for keeping Agnes ignorant, and saving him from cuckoldry, is to prevent her from *writing*. 'A woman who's a writer knows too much' he says, and attempts to keep Agnes innocent of rhyme and word-play. According to Johnson, what Arnolphe wants to keep Agnes ignorant of is *play* – 'the play of language for its own sake, the possibility that language could function otherwise than in strict obedience to the authority of proper meaning' (Johnson 1987: 80). Arnolphe wants to confine Agnes to literalness: to sustain her infantile illusion that words can mean only one thing – that is, what Arnolphe says they mean. He rightly, if dimly, suspects that once inducted into the mysteries of writing, Agnes might realize that the relation between words and meanings is far from proper, and escape his sovereignty over her deeds and thoughts.

Arnolphe's programme is fatally disrupted when Agnes meets an eligible young man, Horace. Despite her protector's pedagogy of ignorance, she does indeed evade his mastery of her affections and transfers these to Horace. As Johnson notes, an act of *writing* is the key event which precipitates Arnolphe's downfall. For it is in and through writing that Agnes learns both agency and duplicity. Faced with Arnolphe's constant surveillance, she writes Horace a secret love letter and ties it to the stone that she has been told to throw at him. Johnson attributes Agnes' quick learning of the art of the 'double message' to her encounter with 'the contradictory demands of *two* ardent teachers' with opposing pedagogical strategies – 'I am your master' versus 'I am your victim' (Johnson 1987: 80, 82). It is through the impossible demands of two incompatible subject positions that Agnes emerges as 'a fully intelligent subject – a writing subject' (p. 82).

Agnes' letter is itself a double message, both declaring love and questioning the very possibility of knowing true love from false declarations. Having begun to glimpse her own ignorance and her former gullibility in assuming that people always meant what they said, Agnes' letter expresses not only her new-found doubt about the truth of others' words, but a mistrust of her *own* words. Agnes' ability to act, and her emergence as 'a fully intelligent subject', is born from her discovery of ignorance, ambiguity and uncertainty as the enduring 'truths' of meaning.

It may come as no surprise to learn that Agnes' letter, which Johnson (1987) describes as performing 'acrobatics of subordination on every level' in its struggle for voice (p. 82), has been read into simplicity, as a candid outpouring of girlish love, by just about everyone. This would include its fictional recipient, Horace, through the critics of Moliere's day, to the editors of the various school textbook versions aimed at adolescent examination candidates. One editor, for instance, instructs students to 'analyse the freshness and spontaneity of the feelings expressed' (quoted in Johnson 1987: 81).

What is the moral of all this for feminism's engagement with theory? I would argue that, despite the repulsion of theory, we should resist the impulse to keep our distance, since this would be to collude with the male-theoretical inclination to position women's writing as *literal*. Most obviously, this would mean renouncing the practice and promotion of literalness as a writing strategy. In other words, it would mean abandoning the conviction, if we ever had it, that writing can ever *simply* be expressive of women's experience or subjectivity. This would not necessarily mean abandoning 'confessional', descriptive or personal writing. But it would mean recognizing that confession and description are rhetorical practices rather than windows onto minds, thoughts or situations. It would mean finding more complicating ways to register the personal in writing. There's almost nothing personal in the kind of personal writing that shepherds everybody along the same old path of self-discovery, to end up with 'the generic shape [and] the universal face' of humanism, as Donna Haraway (1992: 86) puts it. It would also mean accepting that there are no 'pure' texts, confessional or otherwise, and no innocent language that can represent without distortion women's voices and ways of knowing. Patti Lather (1996b) has written of the need for feminist educational research to interrupt the 'drive to innocent knowing' that has always failed to protect the subjects of research from epistemic violence (p. 2). It is clear that the drive to innocent knowing is intimately linked to the practice, or illusion, of innocent writing.

Still, there is no guarantee that renouncing innocent writing will interrupt the male-theoretic inclination to read women's writing into innocence. Or, just as bad, no way of being sure that feminist 'play', when recognized, will not be assimilated as just the same kind of play as that of male theoretical transgression. There seems to be little advantage for feminist writers in developing the ball skills to become 'Gregory's Girls' on the boys' team of theory.[14] The practice of non-innocent feminist writing will always be problematic and vulnerable to Clifford's double bind – of being seen as not 'really' playful, or else only imitatively playful in the mode of men's theory.

I don't think there is any answer, in the abstract, to the question of how women writers should play in a discursive space where play is always-already defined as the game of genre- and gender-bending male theorists, whose prerogative is won precisely through the forced reading of women's writing onto the literal 'outside' of theory. This chapter has explored one possible strategy, which is to try to read women's writing *back* into the space of theory from which it has been evacuated. This is a paradoxical business, however: to become more visible to and as theorists, women may need to be seen *less* clearly, and certainly less virtuously. Looked at in one way, the problem for women has been that they have been treated as *too* visible. The literalization of women's writing, as the 'natural' expression of women's experience, forces women out into the open where nobody can see them, except as exemplary figures of the feminine. One of the most striking insights of postcolonial theorists such as Spivak, Trinh (1989) and Bhabha (1994) has been that visibility and clarity of expression are not necessarily in the interests of the 'subaltern' subjects of colonialism, especially women. These writers would argue that the disruptive potential of the dispossessed lies in their ambivalent and partial visibility. Their capacity to frustrate the colonial desire for total knowledge (and therefore mastery) of the other, says Bhabha (1994), lies in the practice of 'the secret arts of invisibleness' – in mimicry, ambivalence and 'sly civility' (p. 98). Johnson describes the cultural work of feminist literary theory in almost the same terms:

> The *literary* ramifications [of feminism's redefinition of the political] involve the discovery of the rhetorical survival skills of the formerly unvoiced. Lies, secrets, silences and deflections of all sorts are routes taken by voices or messages not granted full legitimacy in order not to be altogether lost.
>
> (Johnson 1987: 31)

It is important to reiterate that the re-readings done by Babcock, Braidotti, Johnson and other feminist writers are more than simple acts of rehabilitation, of getting a few women players onto the field of theory. An important part of reading women's writing back into the space of theory must involve *disrupting* that discursive space. Barbara Johnson's work is, for me, especially productive, not to mention exhilarating, in this respect. It's not just that formerly unheard women's voices begin to speak, haltingly and obliquely, in her witty (and short) essays. It's also that the assurance and self-evidence of the 'canonical' male voices of the literary and critical status quo is fractured and punctured by her deconstructions of their taken-for-granted oppositions.

Which is not to say that Johnson denies her indebtedness to theory and its male custodians or hesitates to use their insights. You could say that her writing enacts the logic of Agnes' double message: the love letter tied to a stone. Perhaps the love letter tied to a stone could stand as a kind of working title for one kind of playful relationship to theory that feminists might consider. At the very least, it reminds us that there is no single, best distance to be kept from theory, but a variety of shifting ones – close enough to 'give assent without excuse', which is how Spivak (1993: 130) defines love; just close enough to throw; far away enough to run for your life.

What about educational research?

I would hope that the implications for feminism with/in educational research are fairly clear from the foregoing. For instance, I would suggest that the 'imaginary femininity', not to mention the feminist sympathies, of male theorists of the postmodern is as problematic within educational research as anywhere else. One of the more repellent examples of male territorial aggression masquerading as self-abnegation can be seen in the expansionist fervour of some of the North American critical theorists of education who have rifled their way through the politico-intellectual wardrobe of post-1960s theory, accumulating bits of hermeneutics, phenomenology, neo-Marxism, feminism, postmodernism and postcolonialism. Feminism has been just one more outfit for these postmodern cross-dressers, alongside the hard-hat proletarian, liberation theologist, Cuban revolutionary, gangsta rapper, mestizo, flâneur, nomad and campus radical.

There are also cautionary lessons to be learned from the recent backlash against research which prioritizes teacher 'voice' and narrative modes of knowing/researching – an orientation that has direct links with earlier feminist emancipatory struggles. Some eminent male academics who have been prominent in 'sponsoring' the teacher's voice and promoting biographical research have recently begun to express concern about the lack of bigger historical and socio-political frames within which to 'locate' these personal stories (see, for example, Hargreaves 1994; Goodson 1995). I take this as yet another sounding of the male-theoretic voice, and an indication of the need for feminist researchers (and other researchers too) to find more complex, less coherent and much less 'transparent' ways of registering the voices of teachers, students and researchers, to prevent their dismissal once again as 'merely' personal.

In short, and in conclusion, I would suggest that there is promise for feminism, and for educational research, in deconstructive writing as play, as questioning and – in positively my last mention of Johnson – as *bafflement*. But, of course, it will always be possible for the Nietzschean philosophical frog to come along and swallow that bafflement whole, as another tasty morsel of the 'non-truth of truth'.

The sudden laugh from nowhere: mimesis and illusion in art and research

> She was by nature an actress of parts that entered into her physique: she even acted her own character, and so well, that she did not know it to be precisely her own.
>
> (George Eliot, *Middlemarch*)

> I noticed how people played at being executives while actually holding executive positions. Did I do this myself? You maintain a shifting distance between yourself and your job. There's a self-conscious space, a sense of formal play that is a sort of arrested panic [...] Something out of childhood whistles through this space, a sense of games and half-made selves, but it's not that you're pretending to be someone else. You're pretending to be exactly who you are. That's the curious thing.
>
> (Don De Lillo 1998: 103)

> We need a nation closer to the Waltons than the Simpsons.
>
> (George Bush Sr)

Introduction

In one way or another, the chapters of this book have worried away at the boundaries that research conjures, and maintains, in order to produce truth, certainty and authenticity – boundaries between representation and reality, sincerity and pretence, rational and irrational, speech and writing, self and other, original and copy, and many others. The possibility of any breach in those boundaries is, as we have seen, generally treated as a threat to be contained, lest mischief and paradox should be unleashed upon an orderly world. But what if the (ever-present) risk of mischief and paradox were to be engaged rather than evaded? This chapter explores some instances of work that deliberately 'plays' with, and on, those boundaries, and pursues some implications for a 'playful' research practice. I start by considering some examples of illusionist artwork from different historical periods, including instances of *trompe l'oeil*,

[handwritten annotation: like Native American Ethnic Fraud.]

art that attempts to 'fool the eye' by passing itself off as the object that it depicts. It has come as something of a surprise to me to learn how long this kind of playfulness has been going on. The 'crisis of representation' is often assumed to be a relatively contemporary preoccupation, associated with high modernity or with postmodernity. But I am beginning dimly to glimpse how *old* that playfulness is.[1]

First century AD (or earlier), Pompeii[2]

The frescos that decorate the walls of the Roman villas preserved in the volcanic ash at Pompeii are covered with illusionistic paintings. These paintings 'open out' the walls of the tiny rooms onto simulations of the surrounding countryside and receding vistas of fantastic architecture, all depicted 'behind' fake pillars, dados, curtains and proscenium arches. Norman Bryson (1990) describes the effect as 'the dissolving of actual boundaries into a limitless space of fiction' (p. 45). He suggests that this play with different levels of reality, and with the boundaries between reality and simulation, was an expression of a Roman 'ideology of culture', in which patrician power expressed itself as the ability to regulate *representation*, achieved (and flaunted) through sophisticated and precise control of transitions between the real and the artificial, nature and culture, raw and cooked.[3]

This play with boundaries, thresholds, receding frames, masks, theatricality and simulation makes late Republic and Imperial Rome sound like a very postmodern sort of place. Bryson (1990) describes the Roman aesthetic, which appropriated and transfigured (or disfigured) Greek culture and art, as an aesthetic of *'secondariness, belatedness and excess'* (p. 53; my emphasis) – a virtual summary of the postmodern or deconstructive 'turn', in which origins and fundamentals (*presence*, in other words) are 'always already' displaced, delayed, infected with doubles and imitations. I don't want to argue, of course, that representational play 'means' the same irrespective of time and place. Indeed, the boundaries between past and present are themselves disturbed: the past is 'read' from the vantage point of a shifting present that nonetheless bears the traces of what has gone before. Still, I do want to say that, at some times and places, questions about the nature of reality and artifice, text and world, have been quite explicitly addressed.[4]

Thirteenth century, France[5]

A page from an illuminated bible shows little figures in the margin, hauling with ropes on a paragraph that has been omitted, apparently trying to put it in its 'proper' place in the main text. Again, there is a playfulness about the relation between words and world. The little figures emerge from the 'real' to manipulate bits of language into the text. This one made me laugh when I stumbled across it in an internet image bank, partly, I think, because of a sudden flash of connection with the 'past' – a realization that representational play was practised then, too. I cannot, of course, claim to know what this image 'really meant' for the monks who, I assume, made the page. But at the very least, I think I see here some kind of play with that endlessly mysterious and impossible place where the real irrupts into the text. And it will be worth hanging onto that notion of the laugh – the sudden frisson of delight or surprise – because I am going to return to it later.

Seventeenth century, Holland

A painting by Cornelis Ghisbrechts, dated between 1670 and 1672, depicts *the back of a painting*.[6] It is stunningly realistic. You really would have to touch the picture to know whether the grain and the joints in the wood were real or painted. You would find out soon enough, though, when you attempted to turn the painting round to see its 'front', which was, of course, the point and the joke. The painting seems strikingly contemporary, 'postmodern' even, in its playfulness with oppositions – back and front, reality and appearance, surface and depth, frame and picture.

Ghisbrechts' painting amply meets Caroline Levine's (1998) description of *trompe l'oeil* as 'the triumph of realism, the consummate mimetic enterprise' (p. 366). But as she also points out, this is a 'duplicitous and faithless' realism. It mocks our grasp of reality, since what we think is the object immediately reveals itself as its 'deceptive double'. Right at the very point where the *trompe l'oeil* painting seems to accomplish the impossible task – of dissolving that divide between reality and representation – it flips (us) over and slams us with the reminder that there is nothing behind the painted surface. The *trompe l'oeil*, writes Baudrillard (1998), is 'an opaque mirror held before the eye, and *there is nothing behind it*' (p. 58; original emphasis). Ghisbrechts' remarkable painting of the back of a painting 'says' precisely this.

One of the most significant properties of *trompe l'oeil* is that, precisely because it imitates the real so convincingly, it *draws attention to the artistry and the artifice* involved. Right at the point where it is most referential, then, art becomes *self-referential*. This, for Levine, makes *trompe l'oeil* a 'peculiarly critical art form' and a profoundly anti-realist one. The double-take that it induces when we see the real and realize it is fake prompts the 'defamiliarization of art', enabling (or forcing) us to reflect on the nature of representation itself. This is not always a comfortable sensation for the viewer. For those who bring realist conventions to the 'reading' of art, *trompe l'oeil* focuses attention on the *wrong place* – that is, on the medium itself, preventing the viewer from 'seeing through' this to the truths that are supposed to lie behind.

But the biggest threat of *trompe l'oeil*, as Levine notes, is that it stages, in a particularly disconcerting form, what is true of *all* representation – namely that there is an irreparable split between the text and what it seems to refer to. As viewers – and as readers, as I will shortly suggest – we are *always* divided. We can focus on the referent – truth, reality, meaning, the object; *or* we can focus on the material, the texture, that 'conveys' that deeper stuff. But we can't do both simultaneously. *Trompe l'oeil* forces us to try, and it is the impossibility of the task that creates the vertigo, or the nausea – the fascination at any rate – of oscillating back and forward between these two impossible positions. We are caught in the 'space between' painting and the real.

Frivolity in writing

Turning to the written word, and in particular to the texts of qualitative research, you will recall a similar antipathy, discussed in Chapter 6, towards *writing* that 'draws attention to itself'. For instance, there was the example of Thomas Sprat, Secretary of the Royal Society, arguing in 1667 against 'specious tropes' and pleading for a 'plain language' purged of 'expressiveness', that would allow scientists to describe faithfully the natural world (quoted in Zeller and Farmer 1999: 3). Compare that desire for 'plain language' with this appreciation of the 'signs' of 'truthful art' by John Ruskin, writing in the nineteenth century:

> [They] have no pretence, nor hypocrisy, nor legerdemain about them; – there is nothing to be found out, or sifted, or surprised in them; – they bear their message simply and clearly, and it is that message which the mind takes from them and dwells upon, *regardless of the language in which it is delivered*.
>
> (quoted in Levine 1998: 370; my emphasis)

Both Sprat and Ruskin want a 'language' that will effectively disappear, allowing the truth, or knowledge, to be seen clearly. Neither of them want to be surprised.

Previous chapters also discussed the widespread objections to the 'literary turn' in ethnography, when anthropologists began to look at their own writing practices and at the dislike of 'cleverness' in academic writing. All of these objections, as with painting, rest on the complaint that the reader's/viewer's attention is directed to *the wrong place* – that is, to the medium rather than the truths that lie behind. And to the fact that the text, and the truth that is folded into it, bears the traces of the interests, biases and vanities of the person who produced it. When researchers foreground the crafted nature of what they have written (intentionally or 'accidentally'), they remind readers/viewers that the text, and the truths therein, might have been otherwise.

As Derrida would say, they make the relationship of text to truth seem *frivolous*. Or rather, they remind readers of the essential frivolity of all reference. The charge of frivolity, as we saw in Chapter 6, is levelled when writers show themselves to be 'satisfied with tokens' rather than 'the real thing' (Derrida 1980: 118). Frivolity, then, is that perverse indulgence in signs, or in technique, at the expense of meaning, whether in written texts or in painting. Underlying all these objections to artistry and artifice is the same fear – of 'writing' or 'inscription'. It is the fear that insinuates itself when we are reminded of the treacherous and fragile bond that exists between the tokens and the real things. Or worse, when we are reminded that there may be no 'bond' between separately existing realms, but a much more perplexing relationship of unbridgeable space, which is simultaneously an indissoluble 'entanglement' (Bal 1999). It is this dilemma that *trompe l'oeil* art enacts so 'grippingly', to use one of Baudrillard's words.

The disconcerted subject

We are gripped because the *trompe l'oeil* deconstructs the viewing subject. Its peculiar conventions make it impossible for the viewer to 'master' the visual field and find/impose the kinds of meanings and structures that they are accustomed to. There is no depth, no vanishing point, no discernible source for the strange light that illuminates them; and, therefore, no prioritizing or ordering of elements in the picture – none of the conventions that allow the viewer to exercise the 'sovereign gaze that subordinates everything in the field to the human observer' (Bryson 1990: 144). Instead, *trompe l'oeil* counteracts the 'privileged position of the gaze', says Baudrillard (1998), and it is in that sense that it 'fools the eye' (p. 58). Other characteristics of *trompe l'oeil* similarly work to disconcert and even, briefly, deconstruct, the onlooker. Typically, there is no narrative, myth or historicity in the contents of the picture. No nature, no faces. The depicted objects are usually mundane, lowly, redolent of everyday use and habit, and disposed without the concern for composition and order that you would find in still lifes, for example. The 'letter rack' paintings that have been a popular *trompe l'oeil* subject from the seventeenth century onwards are typical in this respect.[7] They invoke 'a certain culturality without historicity' (Baudrillard 1998: 55).

All of these features conspire to make it impossible for the viewer to *elevate* the pictures onto a higher, deeper plane of meaning – to get past, or through, the painting to the truths that lie behind or above. This is exactly the blocking action that Robert Smith identifies in the 'frivolity' that has so troubled philosophy:

> The comedy or baseness of frivolity lies in the fact that unlike tragedy it cannot easily be generalised out into statements on the 'human condition' as it used to be called. Frivolity is light and unserious, and yet it is base, heavy, leaden or bathetic because it *resists elevation to generality;* not enough of the Hegelian spirit, the spirit of reason, lightens it (in both senses).
>
> (Smith 1995: 27; my emphasis)

With these paintings, too, the viewer is prevented from 'elevating' the material to higher planes of reason and meaning. It is impossible, therefore, for the viewer to perform the acts of mastery and bestowal of significance that confirm her status as the 'centre' from which meaning issues. Both Bryson and Baudrillard suggest that this gives the pictures an unholy or haunted appearance of existing before, and in the absence of, the human subject. As several critics have written, the pictures seem to 'look back' at the viewer. Norman Bryson says that this is the source of the vertigo or shock that the *trompe l'oeil* causes:

> For the split second when *trompe l'oeil* releases its effect, it induces a feeling of vertigo or shock: it is as if we were seeing the appearance the world might have without a subject there to perceive it, the world minus human consciousness, the look of the world before our entry into it or after our departure from it. [. . .] *Trompe l'oeil* is always the annihilation of the individual viewing subject as universal centre.
>
> (Bryson 1990: 143–4)

Which brings me to the shock, the vertigo. To the sudden laugh from nowhere.[8]

'Something peculiar about similarity': mimesis in (post)colonial encounters

Without exception (I suspect), everyone who writes about *trompe l'oeil,* whether theoretically or descriptively, writes of that sudden, strange sensation. The words vary – vertigo, nausea, shock, fascination, giddiness, the gasp, the charge, 'the mimetic shudder', the surprise. But they all seem to have something to do with a sense of being momentarily taken, or shaken, out of oneself, of sudden disorientation. Michael Taussig (1993), the anthropologist, uses, and quotes, many of these words in his study of mimesis in the 'eccentric history' of colonialism and post-colonialism. He is interested in the spiritual and healing practices of mimicry and imitation among 'Third and Other World' peoples – the practices that used to be called 'sympathetic magic', involving the conjuring of spirit power and energy through the use of copies, mimicry and fetish-objects. But Taussig is also interested in the mimetic relation *between* these (formerly) colonized peoples and the putatively more sophisticated Euro-American West, a relation that has often been expressed through the mimicry or appropriation of objects and signs of Western society. For example, the 'traditional' curing figurines used by the Cuna Indians off Panama as embodiments of spirit power are dressed in seventeenth-century European clothes. Taussig traces innumerable ways in which the signs and objects of Western society – and especially, latterly, consumer society – have tangled with the so-called traditional or primitive. Among his examples are the Cuna 'molas', the traditional embroidered patterns which Cuna women wear on their shirts as 'the visual signifiers of Cuna Being' (Taussig 1993: 236). (The men wear culturally nonspecific, Western gear.) These molas often incorporate 'Western' advertising images, such as RCA Victor's little 'talking dog', who listens attentively to 'His Master's Voice' emanating from the trumpet of an old phonograph (p. 224). The mimesis embodied in these molas does not stop, of course, at the mimicry and appropriation of 'Western' advertising logos by the 'traditional' culture. It circulates further when these molas *themselves* become commodities, traded (no doubt to the economic disadvantage of the Cuna sellers) as exotica among Western consumers.[9]

Taussig (1993) notes the pleasure that the 'talking dog' mola tends to produce in contemporary Western viewers: 'the catching of the breath, the delighted laugh, the stirring of curiosity' (p. 225). This laugh is, he writes, the 'sudden laugh from nowhere', the explosive discharge sparked by the trauma of a challenge to identity and, indeed, to the very nature of Being. This is his description of that laugh:

> Why this laugh? Surely this is what I call Aristotle's pleasure, the (not so) simple fact that observing mimesis is pleasurable. And just as surely there is an element of colonialist mastery in this laughter [. . .] But there is also the possibility that this sudden laugh from nowhere registers a tremor in cultural identity, and not only in identity but in the security of Being itself. This is like Bataille's laugh; a sensuous explosion of smooth muscle composing Being in the same instant as it extinguishes it. This is Benjamin's flash, as when he writes that there is something peculiar about similarity: 'Its perception is in every case bound to an instantaneous flash. It slips past, can possibly be regained, but really cannot be held fast, unlike other perceptions. It offers itself to the eye as fleetingly and as transitorily as a constellation of stars'.
>
> (Taussig 1993: 226)

'Something peculiar about similarity', Taussig writes, copying/conjuring Walter Benjamin. The 'tremor' that Taussig attributes to the mola is, I think, the same kind of *disconcertion* (to use another of his favourite words) as the one sparked by the encounter with the *trompe l'oeil* painting. It's the frisson of the brush with the 'other-ness' at the heart of identity, brought on by the dislocating effects of mimicry – the momentary 'annihilation of the individual viewing subject as universal centre', as Bryson, quoted above, put it. In the anthropological context, it is the mimicry of the (post)colonial Other that disturbs the gaze of the onlooker. This mimicry undermines the stable distinction between the Western self and colonial others on which the colonialist identity is founded.

As with painting, these disconcerting entanglements of what 'should' be stable opposites – self/other, reality/representation, past/present, nature/culture, primitive/sophisticated – have often been ignored or suppressed in anthropological writing. But once people start to look, they find examples all over the place. For instance, we saw in Chapter 5 how anthropologists began to find them in the 'arrival narratives' that constitute a key ethnographic moment: the point at which the putative opposites first confront one another, marvel at the strangeness of their stark differences, and establish some sort of first contact.[10] We saw how these scenes of pristine difference often turn out to be considerably less than 'pure'. As with the *trompe l'oeil* picture, the scientific observer may find it disturbing when the looked-at 'looks back'. Once the worlds of ethnographer and subject start to seep into one another, and subjects betray their own unofficial desires and demands, the assurance that comes from knowing one's Self in contrast to the Other begins to unravel.

The discomforts of mimesis in research

Isn't that also true of researcher–subject relations more generally? Don't interviewees sometimes exhibit mimesis? And don't we as interviewers experience something of the same discomfiture? For example, when interviewees seem to be telling us what they think we want to know. Or when we suspect they are trying to measure up to our expectations, rather than revealing what they 'really' think? Or when they (surprisingly rarely) challenge our competence, intentions or credentials? Don't we try to pretend that those moments never happened, editing out those points in the interview when interviewees allude to the context and circumstances of the interview – when they comment on the presence of the cassette recorder, for instance, or when they seem to be conforming to some pre-established notion of what an interviewee is 'supposed' to sound like? Above all, don't we get worried when subjects, or 'co-participants', seem to be acting inauthentically? When we suspect they are not being 'themselves'?

Qualitative methodology often seems to circle around the attempt to get research subjects to do, or say, what we think they would have said or done if we researchers had not been there. Or at any rate, as we saw in Chapter 7, to act 'naturally', to be 'themselves'. As reported in that chapter, there are rules and precautions for managing interviews so that they will replicate the conditions of a *conversation* – a mode of interaction that is supposedly more spontaneous and, above all, more 'natural' than the interview. And, therefore, less likely to be fraught with mimicry and tainted with expectation.

Above all, and behind all, there is a continuing methodological unease about the possibility that research subjects might *pretend to be someone else*. So commonplace that you almost don't notice them, are the kinds of comments discussed in Chapter 7, about helping interviewees to *be themselves*; to avoid *false fronts*; to *unmask* themselves; to allow the 'substantial self' to be seen behind the situational self created by habit and convention. I would argue that qualitative methodology continues to operate, most of the time, in avoidance, or denial, of the possibility that people might routinely play with personae and levels of reality, not unlike the patrician Romans of Pompeii – putting on masks, staging little research dramas in which they pretend, or believe, that they are 'unveiling' themselves, only to reveal (and conceal) further simulations.[11]

Chapter 7 ended by suggesting that self-hood is inescapably mimetic, a matter of masks and copies whether or not we (know we) are deliberately faking it. Taussig would argue this, as does Andrew Travers (1993) in his playful exploration of the notion of the 'camp' self, referred to in that chapter. Travers suggests that there is an inescapable element of mimicry and fakery in acts of identity. He inverts the usual hierarchy of value between authenticity and artifice, copy and original, which assumes that we have that essential or authentic self which is obscured by masks and fronts, and suggests that being true to yourself is irreducibly a matter of faking it. Occasionally we may catch ourselves, like Don De Lillo in the quotation at the start of the chapter, pretending to be exactly who we are.

For reasons not at all dissimilar to the ones I have sketched above in connection with illusionistic paintings and with postcolonial mimicry, the camp performance has the power to wrong-foot the onlooker. Just as the *trompe l'oeil* hovers, or shimmers, on that boundary between fake and real in ways that disturb the self-certainty of the viewer, so the camp performance disconcerts the audience. 'Exit to detached judgement is blocked', writes Travers (1993), 'because the audience can never know how to "pass through" the apparent sincerity of the performance' (p. 131).

Exercising the mimetic faculty

This is not to say that we are usually *deliberately* faking it, although that very notion starts to shimmer, if not to disintegrate, from a mimetic viewpoint. Generally we act, as Michael Taussig (1993) puts it, as 'accomplices of the real' (p. xviii). But now and then we experience Adorno's mimetic shudder, or De Lillo's 'arrested panic' – gripped by our loss of grip on reality, when we find ourselves caught in that place where real and copy endlessly copy one another, and even one's self becomes a *trompe l'oeil*, so that we can't tell the *difference* that we need to distinguish between real and copy. This does not mean that identity is all fake and pretence, or that there's no reality. It does not mean this in a conventional, nihilistic way at any rate. Rather, it is to argue that we continue to use replicas, images and simulation to summon up our realities and our real selves. Taussig says the 'mimetic faculty' is not just the quaint prerogative of 'traditional' societies, a primitive reality-machine that the West/North traded in long ago for the more powerful and streamlined model of Enlightenment reason. On the contrary, he suggests that the mimetic faculty has become even stronger, supercharged by modernity's 'mimetically capacious' machines – the camera, the phonograph, the tape-recorder – and the vastly increased power to proliferate images and copies via mass production, the cinema, and so on. This faculty has been further propelled, Taussig argues, into new conditions of 'excess' by the complications of postcoloniality.

So we continue to exercise that faculty to 'copy, imitate, make models, explore differences, yield into and become Other'. We practise 'the magical power of replication' through which 'the copy draw[s] on the character and power of the original, to the point whereby the representation may even assume that character and power' (Taussig 1993: viii). Ultimately, says Taussig, this sympathetic magic is the 'magic of the signifier'. *Writing,* in other words. Writing is 'a mimetic exchange with the world' (p. xi) and Taussig wants to *estrange it,* so that we will be able to see again its marvellous power to transport us to other worlds.

> In other words, can't we say that *to give an example, to instantiate, to be concrete,* are all examples of the magic of mimesis wherein the replication, the copy, acquires the power of the represented? And does not the magical power of this embodying inhere in the fact that in reading such examples we are thereby lifted out of ourselves into those images? [. . .] I want to estrange writing itself, writing of any sort, and puzzle over the capacity of the imagination to be lifted through representational media, such as marks on the page, into other worlds.
>
> (Taussig 1993: 16; original emphasis)

Writing – or inscription, which would include speech and also painting – is pre-eminently mimetic, therefore. A way of conjuring worlds through inky marks, smudges and chants.

Mimesis and research

What could it mean, similarly, to 'estrange' the representational practices of qualitative research?[12] To glimpse their mimetic nature? We might start by looking at the pervasive use of quotation and imitation, at the largely un-noticed peculiarity of the 'reality-effects' that qualitative research achieves through these citational practices. The excerpts of interview 'data' that are incorporated into case studies, for instance, surely work as little pieces of the 'real' that we import into our text so that they can release their magic charge of authenticity. Mieke Bal describes the reality-effects of quotation like this:

> [D]irect discourse, or the 'literal' quotation of the words of charac-
> ters, is a form that reinforces mimesis. As fragments of 'real speech',
> they authenticate the fiction. [. . .] [T]hese fragments of reality are
> the product of a manipulation. Rather than serving reality, they
> serve a *reality effect* (Barthes 1968) which is, in fact, the opposite –
> a fiction of realism. Thus they function as shifters, allowing the
> presence of multiple realities within a single image.[13]
>
> (Bal 1999: 10)

The incorporation of snippets and fragments from 'field notes' serve a similar purpose. These supposedly spontaneous, uncrafted remarks, written in the midst of the reality of the field, carry the traces of that direct engagement over 'into' the writing (see Chapter 5 and papers in Sanjek 1990). You could see interview quotes and field note fragments as doing exactly the sort of job that the little figures in the medieval manuscript were doing in the picture I discussed above: bringing a little piece of the real into the representation.

Transcription itself can be seen as essentially mimetic, the attempt to capture, or summon onto the page the words and, indeed, the person who spoke them. This is especially clear in the elaborate conventions (or rituals) for transcribing talk developed within conversational analysis (see Appendix 1), where the aim is to 'capture' every last detail of the spoken delivery, including in- and out-breaths, pauses timed to the tenth of a second, the fine detail of hesitations, and so on. More pervasively, as already noted, research methodology is strikingly concerned with conjuring the 'real' person out of the masks and surface features of their talk. And 'analysis' can be seen as ceremonial practices to make deeper/ higher truths, themes or issues manifest themselves.

It is not that any of these mimetic practices are wrong-headed or 'bad'. They are part of the machinery with which we produce the realities we live by. But we might release more of the uncanny energy or the 'profane illumination' of mimesis if we engaged with it rather than continuing in our usual mode of 'actively forgetting'.[14] 'Mimetic excess', Taussig (1993) concludes, 'provides access to understanding the unbearable truths of make-believe as foundation of an all-too-seriously serious reality, manipulated but also manipulatable' (p. 255). In other words, something might get shaken up.

Postscript: three examples

I am going to end with three examples of the antic spirit of mimesis at work in the world of research. In each case, the 'exit' to secure interpretation is barred, because of the way in which putative opposites mimic or masquerade as one another – sincerity and pretence, seriousness and frivolity, fiction and truth, copy and original. This mimetic quality is, I think, easily overlooked if you are not looking for it; but hard to ignore once you are attuned to looking in that way. In keeping with Taussig's (1993) plea to resist the 'defensive appropriation of the familiar by means of an "explanation"' (p. 237), I am not going to 'analyse' them, but merely set them up, and hopefully in motion. To help with this, I have inserted a few questions at the end of each fragment.

Example 1 Trompe l'oeil *interview fragment*

(Excerpt from a life-history interview)

Prof. X: . . . I was rescued at the eleventh hour from a life of complete complacency by going to Cambridge and being shown there was a class system [laughs].

Int: [laughs] Do you think that was a risk though?

Prof. X: I think there's always a risk, you know, I mean it was real trauma and awful at the time, but curiously I think looking back, I'm quite grateful that I, it probably was a rescue.

Int: Probably formative –

Prof. X: Yeah. I think I could, if I hadn't had that I might have just been a complete complacent bastard.

Int: [laughs]

Prof. X: As it was, this was postponed for several years [laughs].

Int: [laughs] You think you're growing into the role now?

Prof. X: Well yes, I think there's a danger.

Int: What, seriously?

Prof. X: I think it's very interesting being a professor and not slipping into that power role . . .

> *Questions*: Is 'Prof. X' unveiling, or veiling himself? Is this an instance of the 'ambivalent sincerity' of the camp performance? Are both participants camping it up?

Example 2   So real I thought it was D.H. Lawrence

(Discussed in Chapter 4)

Chris Woodhead (1998), while Chief Inspector of Schools, writes an article in the *New Statesman* attacking educational research for its 'jargon-ridden prose' and its irrelevance to the 'real world with real teachers in real schools' (p. 5). As his prime example of how today's research fails to meet the standard of the best research of the past, he cites David Hargreaves' (justifiably) famous 1967 ethnography of 'Lumley' Secondary Modern, *Social Relations in a Secondary School*. What Woodhead values 'above all' in Hargreaves' study is the realism of the *writing*. He finds Hargreaves' introductory description of the terraced streets of 'Lumley' (it's an 'arrival narrative' – see above) so 'realistic' that he thinks for a moment that Ursula Brangwen might appear.

> *Questions*: How does fiction come to 'stand for' truth? Why does the attempt to exclude writing from the 'real world' end up finding writing right at the heart of things? Compare this example with the quoted remarks of ex-president Bush at the start of this chapter.

Example 3   Doubles: the two Peter Woods

Three articles appear in a 1993 edition of the *British Educational Research* journal. The first is written by Peter Woods, a well-known sociologist and proponent of life-history research. The article sketches a life history of a school teacher, Peter, and his struggle 'to maintain the integrity of the self' against the social and institutional pressures to adopt different 'guises' (Woods 1993a: 452). Woods' life history is, apparently, partly based on a written life history which Peter has produced. The second article is a response to Woods' paper by David Thomas, another academic. It asks a few questions about the relationship between interpreters, subjects and readers, and between texts and lives. Indirectly, and quite tactfully, Thomas raises the spectre of 'scepticism' about Woods' portrayal of Peter. He goes as far as to wonder whether, given that researcher and subject share the same first name, there might have been something of an 'exchange of identities' between subject and interpreter (Thomas 1993: 472). The third article rebuts the insinuations that Thomas had raised about the authenticity of Woods' portrayal of Peter. It is written by Peter himself, under his full name of Peter J. Woods. Peter claims sole responsibility for the version of himself that the other Peter Woods had produced, and says that the latter can, therefore, be absolved of any manipulation or artifice. He also says, however, that he and the other Peter 'should not be seen as separate entities' (Woods 1993b: 482).

Questions: Did Thomas' intervention 'summon' the second Peter Woods into print? Does the second Peter's appearance settle, or unsettle, the question of the 'exchange of identities'? Who is vouching for whom? Are readers more, or less, persuaded of the truth of stories when subjects speak up for their biographers?

Conclusion: deconstruction and educational research

> The nature of things is that they are awry from the beginning.
>
> (Robert Smith 1995: 25)

> Something nauseating looms here.
>
> (Michael Taussig 1993: xviii)

> Systematic transgression. *Déjouer*.
>
> (Rosalind Krauss 1993: 168)

One final parable . . .

In the midsummer of her sixth year, Martha begins to have doubts about the existence of the tooth fairy. She decides to check it out with Father Christmas. She has discovered triangulation.

A few weeks later, she leaves a note with her latest tooth under her pillow. The note asks for a signed letter from the tooth fairy. She has discovered documentary evidence.

Come Christmas eve of that year, Martha places a note next to the plate with the mince pie and the drink and the carrot for the reindeer. The note does not enquire about the tooth fairy. It asks Father Christmas to draw a picture of himself to confirm *his* existence. She has discovered self-portrayal.

After a furious, unresolved row with her mother, Martha writes a note and carefully trims the margins close to the letters with her plastic scissors. There are two boxes (drawn squares) as well as some writing on the note. She leaves it on the stairs. It reads:

Der MuMMy	[*translation*:] Dear Mummy
Do you woNt	Do you want
Me her you	me here? You
act Lic you	act like you
don't woNt me	don't want me
here Do you	here. Do you

woNt me her	want me here?
Yes or no	Yes or No.
Tic wich wone	Tick which one.

She has discovered questionnaire design.

Is it frivolous to insinuate that Martha's adventures in the sign trade are comparable with the exertions of researchers? [Yes or No. Tick which one.] We would not apply our methods to proofs of the existence of tooth fairies, or presume to think we could distinguish intention from action, love from indifference, with the stroke of a pen. But I want to press the similarities between Martha's concerns and those of researchers as a way of circling round, one last time, to the questions that have run through this book.

Because you could say, in a sense, that Martha has discovered Method. She has a set of methodological tools whose purpose is to make language *tell her the difference* between truth and falsehood, reality and representation, sincerity and pretence, person and mask, love and hate. In these binary oppositions, she desires those good things that stand on the left-hand side of each pair. She needs to know them in their difference from those lesser, disposable, secondary, improper, mischievous or dangerous things that stand on the other side. She longs for direct access to fundamental things. In other words, Martha is expressing that 'desire for presence' that we have encountered so often in previous chapters. Martha's 'metaphysics of presence' is more shaky than the structures that ground philosophy, and her metaphysical tool box (see Spivak 1976: xix) so far contains only the equivalent of plastic scissors. But she wields them with just as fierce a 'rage for unity', as Spivak (1976: xvi) puts it.

Martha's exertions were about as successful, and as unsuccessful, as anyone else's. The proofs she sought, and received, did not settle the question of the existence of Father Christmas or the tooth fairy. She noticed that the fairy's signature seemed to be written with the same pen as her mother's. No sooner had she found Father Christmas's self-portrait, next to the plate with the reindeer-nibbled carrot, than it struck her: there was no guarantee, and – worse – no possibility of a guarantee, that he had actually drawn it. The fact that he looked pretty much like other pictures she had seen of him was no help. In fact, it was quite the reverse – an image vouching for another image; a sign pointing to a sign. In search of originals, Martha found simulacra.

Her questionnaire, though, worked well in a performative sense, as an act of mastery. It brought her mother to heel; forced her to a declaration of love, with a tick in the 'Yes' box and thirty additional yesses scrawled on the back of the note. The dispute was resolved. But it is less clear whether this provided any kind of lasting solution to Martha's basic problem, of distilling the thoughts and feelings that lie behind words.

When you ask for a sign of love, that's exactly what you get – a sign. Actually, Martha knows this too. Her humorous (and humouring) response to the excess of her mother's thirty extra signs was, 'There's no need to go over the top'. The necessity, and the impossibility, of diagnosing love, sincerity, thought and authenticity, behind the signs that both indicate and imitate them – that indicate *by* imitating them – will exercise her, as all of us, for the foreseeable future.

Writing . . .

Notice how central *writing* is in Martha's adventures. And how problematic. It's both the solution to her puzzles about how to make doubtful entities manifest themselves (fairies, Father Christmas, love) and the perpetuation of the problem. The writing that Martha solicits – the letter, the signature, the portrayal, the questionnaire 'return' – are supposed to quell her doubts; but they also create further doubts. The capacity of writing to *act at a distance* is intimately connected to this ambivalent significance. On the one hand, this is powerful magic – it has the potential to effect a reconciliation where face-to-face wrangling has failed, and to hold another person accountable for her actions by putting them 'on the record'. It holds the promise of conjuring absent entities (even supernatural ones). But the distance is also precisely the problem. Writing gets you 'closer' by condemning you always to be separated from that which you desire – separated by the very words that are bringing you closer. 'But already within imitation, the gap between the thing and its double, that is to say between sense and its image, assures a lodging for falsehood, falsification and vice' (Derrida 1976: 205). Problem and solution; poison and remedy. The *pharmakon*.

Martha has now lost her faith in the tooth fairy and Father Christmas. But she will not lose her faith in the power of language to settle questions of truth, identity and existence. Even when it fails to live up to her expectations. Or, perhaps, precisely *because* it fails to live up to her expectations. I want to suggest that Martha's faith and her scepticism about the capacity of language to speak the truth about truth, as Lacan puts it, come from the same place. 'Language installs the dimension of truth (inconceivable outside of discourse . . .) even as it excludes all guarantee of truth' (Lacan, quoted in Spivak 1976: lxiii).

Or, as Derrida would put it, preferring the word 'writing' to 'language', writing *opens* the question of truth.[1] Writing forces a space. Between words and the things or thoughts they signify, and between those other metaphysical oppositions – truth and falsehood, self and other, nature and culture, essence and appearance, and so on. It's the spacing, the *difference*, that makes it possible for us to think truth, self, nature, etc. in the first place. We saw at the beginning of this book, with the parable of Mrs. Ph(i)Nk$_0$, that without that gap, there would be no distance across which the desire for presence might spark. We would not be able to grasp others as distinct from ourselves or, indeed, to conjure a unique self that gets its one-off specialness from its difference from all others. Without the spacing that language interposes, it would be meaningless to apprehend an 'outer' reality of material objects, bodies and observable actions, insulated from an 'inner', subjective world of feelings, imaginings and delusions.

But, as we have already seen, the gap that opens the prospect of truth and all that other good stuff is the *same* gap that 'assures a lodging for falsehood, falsification and vice', as quoted above. Difference, distance and paradox lie 'at the heart' of meaning, being and reality. We are driven, like Martha, to desire that which we can never wholly attain and, indeed, which never existed in a pure and unmediated form. 'Difference produces what it forbids, making possible the very thing that makes it impossible' (Derrida 1976: 143). The spacing effected by Writing is always an uncanny one, a matter of making a space between things that cannot, yet must have, existed prior to the movement of opening.

Derrida's argument is that the dream of presence is not undermined by the abyss – that awe-ful gap that makes it possible for truth to confront its opposite and the self to confront itself. The abyss is not an avoidable error of relativistic thinking, or an accident of careless philosophizing, but a 'structural necessity'. Writing, in Derrida's sense of inscription, marks a *loss* of something that was never intact in the first place:

> loss of the proper, of absolute proximity, of self-presence, in truth, the loss of what has never taken place, of a self-presence which has never been given but only dreamed of and always already split, repeated, incapable of appearing to itself except in its own disappearance.
>
> (Derrida 1976: 159)

'Looking awry'[2]

We may fantasize about 'transparency', about unmediated access, about unimpeded self-knowledge. We may wish we could beam our thoughts straight into other people's heads, without recourse to the interference of writing, which always seems to distort or dissipate them.[3] (We may especially wish we could do this when the heads in question are those of policy makers.) We may wish we could read the minds of parents and lovers (and tooth fairies and interviewees). But imagine what would happen . . .

- Buffy the Vampire Slayer gets bitten by a demon and inherits its power to read minds. At first it's fun, picking up people's innermost fears and naughty thoughts. But soon Buffy is overwhelmed by the cacophony of voices registering directly into her head. Her sense of self dissolves under the onslaught of this relentless proximity and she becomes unable to think or move. She lapses into a coma and only recovers when her deadly power is removed.[4]

We need the intervention, the indirection, of writing/language, of *something* at any rate, to protect us from being paralysed by presence. Buffy's misadventure reworks a dilemma that has recurred in myth and literature . . .

- Italo Calvino (1996) contemplates the myth of Perseus and Medusa, which he proposes as '*a lesson in the method to follow when writing*' (p. 4; my emphasis). Perseus is able to cut off Medusa's snaky head without being turned to stone by her 'inexorable stare', by looking at her image reflected in his shield. And once he has cut off her head, he keeps it *hidden* in a bag, bringing it out to petrify his enemies only under extreme duress. Perseus wields the power of *indirection*: his strength, says Calvino, 'lies in a refusal to look directly, but not in a refusal of the reality in which he is fated to live; he carries the reality with him and accepts it as his particular burden' (p. 5).[5]

Direct access to presence would ensure that *nothing happened*: coma, stasis, stone, paralysis, autism. Or we would be '*annihilated by transparency*', which amounts to the same thing – Jean Baudrillard. . . .

- 'There is no point in identifying the world. Things have to be grasped in their sleep, or in any other circumstances where they are absent from themselves. [. . .] To see our own face as it is would be madness, since we would no longer have any mystery for ourselves and would, therefore, be annihilated by transparency. [. . .] Fortunately, the objects which appear to us have always-already disappeared. Fortunately, nothing appears to us in real time, any more than do the stars in the sky. If the speed of light were infinite, all the stars would be there simultaneously and the celestial vault would be an unbearable incandescence. Fortunately, nothing takes place in real time. Otherwise, we would be subjected, where information is concerned, to the light of all events, and the present would be an unbearable incandescence. Fortunately, we live on the basis of a vital illusion, on the basis of an absence, an unreality, a non-immediacy of things. Fortunately, nothing is instantaneous, simultaneous or contemporary. Fortunately, nothing is present or identical to itself. Fortunately, reality does not take place. Fortunately, the crime is never perfect' (Baudrillard 1996: 6–7).

All of these examples rework one of the oldest myths/metaphors for the necessity of looking awry – the danger of looking directly at the sun, or at the face of the Father/God. Derrida (1981) traces the dissemination of this notion in Plato, and its association with writing: 'If truth is the presence of the *eidos* [the idea or essential form], it must always, on pain of mortal blinding by the sun's fires, come to terms with relation, nonpresence, and thus nontruth' (p. 166).

Is this what deconstruction 'is'?

I have tried to use this pile-up of examples – tooth fairies, Greek myths and all – to sidle up to the question of what deconstruction 'is', or what it could 'mean'. As the scare-quotes around the words in the foregoing sentence indicate, it is necessary to look awry at deconstruction too. Not because it will blind you (though it might do that, in the sense of leaving you completely in the dark), but because it disappears. If you try to distil its message, or anatomize its arguments, or prescribe it as a remedy (or poison?) to Method, you are back with the desire for presence – for the essence, or fundamentals, or underlying purposes of deconstruction that deconstruction blocks.[6] But I want to say that deconstruction, for me, is something to do with that confounded, indirect, abyssal relation to truth and reality that the examples try to conjure. And all of this has something to do with *writing*, in its most general and elusive sense – that is, that intervening something that is almost, or also, nothing; which fortunately and unfortunately interposes.

Implications

So, what are the implications for educational research? Or, to put it another way, how does deconstruction tangle with research? (Entanglement being one meaning of 'implication', with its etymology of 'folding'.) One answer is that it interferes with many of the assumptions that found the projects of education and of research. The chapters in this book have worried away at some of these, such as clarity, certainty, mastery, relevance, innocence – snarling up (that is, deconstructing) the oppositions from which they draw their force.

If research is to tangle with deconstruction, it must be acknowledged that it is always possible for meanings and messages to go astray or awry – to miss their mark – because of the gap that writing interposes. We have seen that clarity of meaning and purpose can never be guaranteed in advance. Under deconstruction, meanings, intentions and messages cannot be fully disentangled from their representation in language, as if writing was just a matter of finding the most appropriate 'vehicle' for carrying them into the minds of their target audience. They issue from that knotty, folded space where *différance* sparks the oscillations out of which truth and fiction, intention and action, meaning and expression issue, confronting one another as opposites. Yet, as we have seen, the assumption is still widespread that writing is, or should be, merely the neutral vehicle for conveying pre-existing Goods. Deconstruction proposes that the methodological policing and purification of language, to make it behave properly with respect to its superiors (meaning, truth, reality, etc.), can never succeed. There is no transparent writing.

This is of more than 'academic' interest. Educational policy these days is obsessed with clarity, certainty and 'transparency' – with forcing everything out into the open where it can be calibrated and assessed for value for money and 'quality'. The higher education system in England was undergoing a so-called 'Transparency' exercise as this book was being written – an audit of the cost and quality of research and teaching (which are counted as separate and, in some respects, inimical activities). National UK policy initiatives such as the Research Assessment Exercise (RAE) and Teaching Quality Assessment (TQA) are also about ushering the purportedly hidden and, therefore, shady practices and products of research and teaching into the light, again in the interests of accountability and rationalization. As Marilyn Strathern (2000) notes, in an article entitled 'The tyranny of transparency', despite the appeal to social and moral virtues, *'there is nothing innocent about making the invisible visible'* (p. 309; original emphasis). Not only does transparency conceal many aspects of the processes that generate research or teaching, in favour of those caught in the net of the official 'indicators'; but everybody knows this. 'Realities', says Strathern, 'are knowingly eclipsed' (p. 315).

Teaching and learning in schools are likewise gripped by this policy rage for clarity and certainty of 'outcomes'. The policy-driven 'superclarity' that Strathern critiques at university level, which assumes that learning follows directly and immediately from teaching, is as nothing compared to the ruthless clarity that regulates pedagogy in mainstream schools in England and Wales, in the form of the National Literacy and Numeracy Strategies, the National Curriculum, the Standard Assessment Tests, the bullet-pointed gaze of the Ofsted inspections, the 'league tables' of examination results, and so on. *These programmes are fantasies of presence in a particularly blatant form.* They are all concerned with controlling and, if possible, collapsing the gaps out of which teaching and learning issue. They construe the teacher as little more than a vehicle for conveying pre-constructed packages of knowledge into students' heads; and assume that the knowledge thus conveyed is assimilated unproblematically, without gap, delay or indirection (cf. Strathern 2000: 318). They configure 'training' similarly as a colourless, passionless trail of tightly scripted wisdom, uttered by closely trained trainers following schedules timed to the minute. They assume that what students make visible under assessment is what they know. They hold that what inspectors look at is what matters; and insist that, when inspectors look, they should all see the same things.

These are policies of *collapse*. They sketch a dead-level landscape where clarity and transparency conceal the pain, the conflict, the unpredictability and the irrationality that are also unavoidably implicated in teaching and learning, and in teachers and learners. Deborah Britzman (1998) notes that the outcome of this continual suppression of conflict and ambivalence, this 'putting the good inside and the bad outside', is that they return to haunt education as 'unruly students, as irrelevant questions, and as controversial knowledge in need of containment' (p. 133). If there is a politics of deconstruction that could animate research, it would involve resisting the rage for clarity and closure emanating from policy and pedagogy. It would mean trying to open up the space of education against the dead-weight of given-ness that shuts it off. At the least, it would mean thinking twice, and more slowly, about the demands from policy makers to make research 'relevant' and 'accessible'.

New imaginaries of self and other

One of the boundaries that most troubles contemporary methodological debate, as we have seen, is the one between self and other, researcher and researched. Much ink has been spilled over how researchers should relate to and represent those 'others' who are the subjects of research. This is not just a question of how researchers might relinquish the authority that has suppressed the voices and the interests of those others, though it is certainly about that. It is also about what happens to the identity of the *researcher* when confidence in the boundaries between self and other start to break down. As Michael Taussig (1993) puts it, referring to the consternation felt by First World people at the mimicry of the 'natives', it is about the threat that this mimicry poses to the 'First World quest for a decent fix of straightforward Othering' (p. 143). Or, as Vicki Kirby (1997) writes, we can no longer deploy 'the imperializing gesture of benevolent humility to an Other who is not me' (p. 99).

A decent fix of straightforward Othering is no longer an option, therefore, ethically or textually. So, what kind of relations can researchers forge with their 'subjects'? A deconstructive approach to this question would be to critically examine research postures *vis-à-vis* the Other that aspire to closure or the collapse of difference. Previous chapters have discussed some of the guises that this desire to eliminate the difference between researcher and researched can take – surrender, mastery, self-abnegation, auto-ethnography, reciprocity, partnership. When these aspirations are put 'under erasure', we are able to think again about the kinds of relations we habitually form with research subjects, including those that we may not acknowledge. Perhaps we should stop trying to: befriend them, respect them, collaborate with them, worship them, pity them, empathize with them, patronize them, know them, save them, control them, surrender to them, explain them, like them, celebrate them ... Or, rather, recognize that we can never *simply* do any of these, even if we might feel impelled to try, in order to shore up our methodological or ethical self-assurance. All of these acts, however dissimilar in other respects, are attempts to quell the nausea, or the vertigo (Taussig 1993), induced by the realization that self and other are always already 'contaminated' by one another, caught up in cycles of mimicry and simulation.

To borrow the question posed by Marilyn Strathern, what does this arrested relation to the subject *conceal*? I would suggest that it conceals, first, the fact that subjects sometimes act up, make self-conscious jokes, contradict themselves, adopt different masks (without necessarily always knowing that they are masks; or that there are only masks), forge their own signatures, and deflect researchers' agendas. And that this is an entirely unexceptional (but not at all uninteresting) part of any person's repertoire of interactional strategies and, indeed, ways of 'Being'. It is not an error to be corrected by better interviewing techniques or a more relaxed setting, or filtered out in the analysis and reporting. Secondly, it conceals the fact that such ironic exchanges threaten our own methodological and, indeed, personal self-assurance. Faced by subjects who mock their own pretensions and mimic those of their interlocutors, we become like the audience of the camp performance, as discussed in Chapters 7 and 9 – trapped in the 'squeamish reciprocity of audience and performer', in Andrew Travers' (1993: 135) memorable phrase.

Deconstruction would suggest that we try to linger a bit longer on the 'squeamish' nature of that reciprocity, to see what we might learn about the difficult conditions under which self and other come into being for one another, and for themselves. Again, we would need to abandon the purported clarity of plain view for what it obscures: the ambivalence, irony, simulation and trickery that are an essential part of self-hood and social life. Again, there is a political point: the transparent virtues of clarity, righteousness, visibility and simplicity are not necessarily in the interests of those on the margins of power and prestige. As we have seen, these seemingly simple and self-evident values have sustained the political and linguistic subordination of marginalized groups and peoples. Deconstruction advocates, again, a politics and a methodology of *indirection*. To re-quote Barbara Johnson (1987): '[l]ies, silences and deflections of all sorts are routes taken by voices or messages not granted full legitimacy in order not to be altogether lost' (p. 31).

Déjouer: research as (mis)play

Research, no less than policy, is often driven by a desire for transparency. This favours the production of literal texts, by well-meaning, self-deprecating authors, 'about' benign, simple souls, who say what they mean, mean what they say, and only mean one thing at a time – like the characters in a foreign language sketch in a BBC TV Schools programme. However, in different ways, researchers are beginning to look for more complicated – and complicating – ways of reading and writing. For some, this involves new textual practices that disturb the usual conventions of research writing and baffle the boundaries between literature and science, self and other, data and analysis, fact and fiction, mastery and surrender.[7] Others write in fairly conventional genres (as I have done, by and large, in this book), but in other ways pick at the same seams that stitch together the fabric of research.

There is no general rubric for this kind of work – each writer pursues her own threads. But there is a common impulse to interrupt the 'business-as-usual' habits of education and research, and encourage new ways of 'reading' and 'writing' the social. Different commentators have given the impulse different names, some of which have been caught up in this book – to deconstruct, defamiliarize, denaturalize, surprise, entangle, baffle, disconcert, interfere, trouble. Mieke Bal (1999) captures it eloquently, when she writes of the imperative to 'refuse to honor the fleeting pace that generates indifference' (p. 65). It is partly a matter, as Bal implies, of interfering with the simple, linear *time* of research – of slowing down the facile machinery of interpretation so that it catches on the snags, the 'lucky finds', the marginalia and the odd details that fascinate the researcher and draw her into the weave of discourse, instead of allowing her to rise above it.[8] These are the snags and details that block the Enlightenment strategy of 'elevation' to generality, a process that Rosalind Krauss (1993) depicts as: 'the general principle swooping down on the powerless, aimless, feckless particular and gathering it up into the stark clarity of a demonstration of the inner workings of the law' (p. 103).[9] The snags and details – the feckless particulars – stand out against the blinding illumination that bleaches out difference.

The temporal dislocation of research is not just a matter of slowing things down, however, but also of becoming attuned to the instantaneous – to that confounding flash that was called mimesis in Chapter 9, when harmonious relations among opposites (subject and object, copy and original, looker and looked at) are momentarily jolted into disarray through their incongruous contact with one another. Walter Benjamin (1978) called such moments instances of *profane illumination*, drawing on the surrealist/Freudian notion of the 'encounter' with the strangely familiar – the 'lucky find', or the chance juxtaposition of dissimilar objects, that releases the energies of the unconscious. As Margaret Cohen (1993) notes, Benjamin and the surrealists sought moments of profane illumination in the defamiliarization of the discarded commodities, familiar places and mundane events of everyday life in industrial society – in the strangeness that inheres in the details and the feckless particulars, in other words. Benjamin was interested in the revolutionary potential of these strange encounters, as moments of 'shock' that might momentarily jolt people out of the slumber induced by ideology.

Our ways of 'seeing' education are so deeply ingrained with habit and discursive familiarity that we are pretty well insulated from shock. We can conjure a 'classroom' from the most minimal of signs, such as the little clip-art image that was discussed in Chapter 1, and populate it with well-worn rhetorical figures – 'the teacher', 'the child' – viewed by an invisible-but-omniscient 'researcher'. We need research practices that deliberately attempt to 'rearrange the terrain of the commonplace', as Rosalind Krauss puts it (1993: 168). Krauss proposes the term *déjouer*, which means to foil or baffle, but also to 'mis-play' – that is, to undermine the game from within, by using the rules against themselves.[10] This book has explored the potential of mis-playful methodologies and writing practices that might offer some resistance to the smoothing of social and educational worlds into simplicity.

Appendix I
Definitions of discourse: a sketchy overview

I am going to follow the practice of some commentators (e.g. McHoul and Luke 1989; Pennycook 1994; Lee and Poynton 2000) and make a distinction between two broad discourse traditions, distinguished by their intellectual lineage. One stems from European philosophical and cultural thought and is associated with poststructuralism. The other has its origins in Anglo-American linguistics. Readers should bear in mind, however, that definitions always shrink, compartmentalize and petrify; and that meanings have a fluidity that always exceeds such attempts to pin them down. This, then, is only one among many possible stories of the 'field'.[1]

Discourse within poststructuralism

Taking the European tradition first: this goes back (or thinks back) to philosophers such as Husserl, Nietzsche, Hegel and Heidegger, and takes in the structuralism of Saussure, Roman Jakobson and Levi-Strauss, to arrive somewhere near the present as poststructuralism. Poststructuralist notions of discourse came to prominence in what Poynton and Lee (2000: 2) call the 'theory disciplines' in the social sciences and humanities, such as cultural studies, media studies, women's studies and literary theory, which emerged as a challenge to the positivist, science-driven approaches of mainstream sociology and psychology.

The term 'poststructuralism' is itself part of the contestation over meaning referred to above, embracing a loosely connected body of work that is often associated (although not without dispute) with such names as Barthes, Lacan, Derrida, Kristeva and Foucault.[2] Poststructuralism is often defined 'oppositionally', in terms of what it sets itself *against*: notably, the rationalist, humanist worldview that is the (continuing) legacy of the seventeenth-century 'Enlightenment'. Poststructuralism anchors itself in a critique of Enlightenment faith in *reason*, as the faculty that regulates the social and moral order. Poststructuralist theorists reject the idea of universal truth and objective knowledge, delivered through the proper use of reason, and assert, on the contrary, that truths are always partial and knowledge is always 'situated' – that is, produced by and for particular interests, in particular circumstances, at particular times. Poststructuralist work also challenges belief in progress as the inevitable result of scientific and philosophical rationality. Most radically, poststructuralism dis-assembles the *humanist subject* – the thinking, self-aware, truth-seeking individual ('man'), who is able to master both 'his' own internal passions, and the physical world around him, through the exercise of reason. Poststructural theorists argue that subjects are constituted within discourses that establish what it is possible (and impossible) to 'be' – a woman, mother, teacher, child, etc. – as well as what will count as truth, knowledge, moral values, normal behaviour and intelligible speech for those who are 'summoned' to speak by the discourse in question. Foucault (1972), in one of his most frequently quoted formulations, described discourses as 'practices that systematically form the objects of which they speak' (p. 49). Deborah Britzman gives a concise account of how discourse works in the formation of subjects:

> Every discourse constitutes, even as it mobilizes and shuts out, imaginary communities, identity investments and discursive practices. Discourses authorize what can and cannot be said; they produce relations of power and communities of consent and dissent, and thus discursive boundaries are always being redrawn around what constitutes the desirable and the undesirable and around what it is that makes possible particular structures of intelligibility and unintelligibility.
>
> (Britzman 2000: 36)

Discourses within poststructuralism involve much more than language, therefore. They can be thought of, rather, as practices for producing meaning, forming subjects and regulating conduct within particular societies and institutions, at particular historical times. James Gee (1999) coined the term 'Discourse with a capital D' to distinguish such broader sociocultural conceptualizations from the more localized meanings of discourse (with a 'small d') within linguistic approaches, where it is often synonymous with text, communication or 'language in use'.

Still, questions of language are crucial, partly because of poststructuralism's debt to linguistic structuralism. Saussure's structuralist theory radically unsettled notions of the relationship between language and reality, or words and objects, by proposing that signs took their significance from *their relationships with one another*, within language conceived of as a system. Meanings, for Saussure, were *differential* – in other words, defined in terms of their relationship to other terms within the matrix of the language system. So 'dog' would get its meaning from its systematic *difference* from other elements in a family of terms – for example, 'cat', 'sheep', 'pig', etc. – and not from some intrinsic bond between the sound of the word and the 'real' hairy animal to which it refers (or the 'idea' of such a hairy animal). In Saussure's theory, language is potent: it shapes thought and disciplines reality: '[w]ithout language, thought is a vague, uncharted nebula. There are no pre-existing ideas, and nothing is distinct before the appearance of language' (cited in Kirby 1997: 17).

These two tenets of linguistic structuralism – the constitutive role of language in shaping realities and the relationship of 'difference' that generates meaning – are equally important within poststructuralism. However, poststructuralist theory challenges the notion of language as a closed, coherent system, and posits instead a radically indeterminate universe in which the relationship between words and their referents is laced with difference through and through.[3] For poststructuralist theorists, the boundary between language and what lies 'outside' (reality or materiality) is unstable; and difference is a chronic condition. The parable of Mrs. Ph(i)Nk$_0$ which opened Chapter 1 attempted to represent the peculiarly productive nature of this difference, or *différance*.

Foucault

Among poststructuralist thinkers, the theorist most frequently associated with the term 'discourse', and with discourse analysis, is Michel Foucault. Within a Foucauldian approach, discourses are inextricably linked to *institutions* (the law, education, the family, etc.) and to the *disciplines* that regularize and normalize the conduct of those who are brought within the ambit of those institutions – psychology, medicine, science, psychotherapy, pedagogy, and so on. As already noted, discourses not only circumscribe what it is possible to say, know and do, but also establish what kind of person one is entitled/obliged to 'be'. It is impossible, in other words, to speak without *speaking as* the kind of person who is invoked by one discourse or another. As Foucault (1979: 217) put it, the individual is thus 'fabricated' into the social order. People are woven into, and woven out of, discourse. Allan Luke's (1995) metaphor of the young child's identity papers being 'watermarked', discussed in Chapter 1, neatly captures the two-faced nature of 'subjection' in the Foucauldian sense, as simultaneously enabling and constraining. The individual achieves agency as an active subject by being subject-ed to the disciplinary machineries of discourse.

Discourses are also, then, about *power*. As Diane Macdonell (1986) writes, 'discipline trains, individualizes, regiments, makes docile and obedient subjects' (p. 102). However, power, in the Foucauldian sense, is not something that one person or powerful group 'has' and wields against weaker opponents. Rather, power is diffuse, circulating in a capillary fashion around and through institutions, reaching 'into the very grain' of those who are made subjects through their involvement in discourse – parents, children, prisoners, teachers, therapists, clients, claimants, lawyers, employers, and so on (cf. Foucault 1980: 39).

This is not to deny that power becomes concentrated in the hands of certain groups at the expense of others, according to social class, gender, ethnicity, and so on, and that this concentration of power is directly linked to discourse practices. To take one example, it is abundantly clear from decades of research into family literacy practices that children from white, middle-class homes are likely to have extensive experience of the kinds of discourses that are favoured in education long before they get to school. As Gee (1992) reports, parents from such homes '*mentor* or *apprentice* their children into certain Discourses that schools and the wider mainstream culture reward' (p. 123; original emphasis). He describes the sorts of things that such parents do to fabricate their children into the ways of thinking, acting and being that are valued in schools.

> They engage their children in conversations and keep them on a single topic even when the children can hardly talk at all. [. . .] They play alphabet

games, recite nursery rhymes, read books aloud with great affect. They ask their children 'What's that?' and 'What's that say?' of pictures in a book they've both seen a hundred times. [. . .] They encourage children to pretend they can read when they can't; they let them manipulate magnetic letters on a refrigerator; and they get them to watch 'Sesame Street' for hours on end. They send them to preschool and constantly relate what the children have seen or heard in books to the children's daily experience of the world.

Most important of all, they make clear to their children that *people like us* use language, think, value, and talk *in these ways, with these objects at these times and in these places*. They introduce their children to discourses that have, for [. . .] historical, political and social reasons come to overlap their homes and our schools. These Discourses are not 'natural' and 'normal' – lots of groups neither do them nor find them very senseful.

(Gee 1992: 123; original emphasis)

The social and economic benefits that come from access to 'mainstream' discourses are not, of course, evenly distributed. Children who do not get this kind of apprenticeship run the risk of not being 'heard', if their discourse habits do not fit the pattern that teachers are listening out for. Take the case of 'news time' or 'sharing time', events that rely on being able to sift, code and frame one's experience according to certain narrative conventions, as described in Chapter 1. As several researchers in the USA have found, sharing time can pose particular challenges for children who are familiar with different narrative practices at home. Children who tell their stories in the idiom of black, working-class culture are often heard as disorganized, rambling, exaggerating or repetitious (Michaels 1981; Brice Heath 1983; Gee 1992). And the hazards of failing to be 'heard' are multiple and cumulative, precisely because knowledge, expertise and identity are all implicated in discourse. You may be judged to be not only an inexpert story 'sharer', but also a poor learner, or even the *wrong sort of 5-year-old*. And you are likely to fall ever further behind in the accumulation of knowledge, as this is measured and validated in the discourses of schooling.

The discursive distribution of disadvantage, therefore, frequently falls out along lines of class, gender, ethnicity and other large-scale social categories. However, Foucault's argument is that such inequalities develop and coalesce as the result of complex movements and interactions that are not under the direct control of the group which emerges as the dominant one.[4] Moreover, power is not just repressive, in the sense of endowing some subjects with agency and potential at the expense of others; it is also enabling – it is a productive set of relations from which, for good and ill, subjectivity, agency, knowledge and action issue.

Just as power and knowledge are discursive, so too is *truth*. For Foucault, truth is not an abstract entity or a property of sentences, but an emphatically worldly matter, always tangled up with power/knowledge:

Truth is a thing of the world: it is produced only by virtue of multiple forms of constraint. And it induces regular effects of power. Each society has its regime of truth, its 'general politics of truth': that is, the types of discourse which it accepts and makes function as true; the mechanisms and instances which enable one to distinguish true and false statements, the means by which each is sanctioned; the techniques and procedures accorded value in the acquisition of truth; the status of those who are charged with saying what counts as true.

(Foucault 1980: 31)

Truth, then, is *produced*, according to the prevailing discursive regimes of different societies. Sara Mills (1997: 19) gives the example of the production of medical truth, through the opposition of 'conventional' and 'alternative' medicine. She notes that the pre-eminence of the medical paradigm, as the repository of scientific truth and authority, has to be maintained through repeated 'discursive work' that ensures that the 'alternative' paradigm is seen, by contrast, as amateurish and suspect. The key question, writes Mills, is not which of these is 'true' or more effective, but *how the truth and authority of one is continuously produced at the expense of the other*. A comparable instance in educational discourse would be the opposition between action research and 'mainstream' educational research. It could be argued that mainstream academic research maintains its status *as* mainstream through discursive work that construes action research as the subordinate, 'alternative' paradigm (cf. MacLure 1993). These examples point to another general principle of Foucauldian analysis, that of 'exteriority'. Threadgold paraphrases this principle thus:

We should not 'burrow' into discourse looking for meanings. We should instead look for the external conditions of its existence, its appearance and its regularity. We should explore the conditions of its possibility. Just how is it possible to know that, to think that, to say that – these are the questions we should be asking.

(Threadgold 2000: 49)

Discourses are invested with *power* and with *knowledge*, and Foucault often bound the two terms together as power/knowledge (*pouvoir/savoir*) to indicate their interdependence:

No body of knowledge can be formed without a system of communications, records, accumulation and displacement which is itself a form of power and which is linked, in its existence and functioning, to the other forms of power. Conversely, no power can be exercised without the extraction, appropriation, distribution or retention of knowledge. On this level, there is not knowledge on the one side and society on the other, or science and the state, but only the fundamental forms of knowledge/power.

(quoted in Ball 1990a: 17)

Meanings are produced, therefore, by power/knowledge configurations, as these are embedded in, and constitutive of, different social institutions. Thus people speak of *the discourse of* X or Y: the discourse of law, of socialism, of education, of medicine, and so on. As Alastair Pennycook (1994) puts it, discourses '"map out" what can be said and thought about what they define as their various domains' (p. 128). Equally importantly, discourses are exclusionary: they *rule out* other ways of thinking, talking or acting.

As writers and analysts have taken up and used Foucault's ideas, discourses have tended to proliferate and subdivide. Within education, for example, analysts have identified discourses of *school effectiveness* (Morley and Rassool 1999), of *empowerment* (Bates 1998), of *partnership* (Crozier 1998) and of *accountability* (Poulson 1996). Some educational writers have argued that educational discourse has, in recent times, been invaded or 'colonized' by alien discourses – for instance, by the discourse of the New Right (Ball 1990b) – or by management and business, resulting in the 'marketization' of educational discourse (Fairclough 1992).

Deconstruction

Foucault's work is only one element within the broad intellectual landscape of poststructuralism. Although I use Foucauldian notions tacitly throughout, and explicitly in Chapter 3, this book is much more deeply indebted to deconstruction and the work of Jacques Derrida. If definitions are problematic across the whole terrain of poststructuralism, they are notoriously so in connection with deconstruction. The problem stems from deconstruction's critique of the binary oppositions underpinning the logic and the value systems that are the continuing legacy of the Enlightenment. Definitions are tricky because they imply just such a binary distinction – between words and meanings, language and reality.

One of the most important propositions of deconstruction is that our dealings with/in the world are *unrelievedly textual*. This is in contrast to many other theories or philosophies, which dream of a binary universe of fundamental things on the one hand (reality, Being, thought, identity, the Idea, etc.), distinct from the textual or language systems that convey these on the other. For these latter theories, texts are a kind of unfortunate, pragmatic necessity. They are just the 'vehicles' that convey those fundamental things. A deconstructive view, by contrast, proposes that textuality is the *condition* of truth, being, substance, etc. – that these fundamentals issue out of the gap or spacing, to recall Mrs. Ph(i)Nk$_0$ again, that sets them up *as if* they were distinct from their junior partners, language or representation. Textuality, for Derrida, is this spacing, this *différance*. It is important (though also quite difficult) to grasp that textuality, in this deconstructive sense, is not just a linguistic phenomenon – not just a property of language, writing or other sign systems, though these certainly are textual too. Derrida sometimes uses the terms 'writing in the general sense' and 'arche-writing' to indicate this much-more-than-linguistic textual-izing of the world. But he also retains the word 'writing' for this expanded notion of textuality. Vicki Kirby (1997), struggling (as I am here) to capture something of Derrida's notion of text, calls it 'an efficacious spacing' (p. 79) that effects 'the worlding of the world'.

Deconstruction is not just a game of words. It carries an ethical and a political charge, since, as Michael Shapiro (2001) puts it, deconstruction has the power to show how 'every social order rests on a *forgetting* of the exclusion practices through which one set of meanings has been institutionalised and various other possibilities [. . .] have been marginalised' (p. 321; my emphasis). A deconstructive educational research could be thought of, then, as a project of resistance to the institutionalized forgetting that takes place when matters attain the status of common sense, in educational policy, pedagogy and research itself.

Deconstruction, as Derrida has written many times, cannot be reduced to a technique or a set of theorems, to be mastered and then 'applied' to individual cases, since this, again, assumes hierarchical distinctions that deconstruction interferes with – practice/theory, principles/applications. Rather, each person has to find his or her own idiom.

> [D]econstruction is not a method, nor is it a set of rules or tools. [. . .] So, if you want to 'do deconstruction' – 'you know, the kind of thing Derrida does' – then you have to perform something new, in your own language, in your own singular situation, with your own signature, to invent the impossible and to break with the application, in the technical, neutral sense of the word.
>
> (Derrida 1996: 217–18)

The chapters in this book should not be read, then, as recipes for deconstruction, but more as traces of the kind of engagement with (educational) texts and events that deconstruction urges. It is not possible to 'grasp' deconstruction in the sense of mastering its essentials. What is needed, what this book tries to provide, is a rather more oblique kind of grasp – perhaps of the sort that Jean Baudrillard (1996) had in mind when he wrote: 'Things have to be grasped in their sleep, or in any other circumstances where they are absent from themselves' (p. 6). Or the kind of grasp involved in understanding another culture, which, according to Clifford Geertz (1983), is: 'more like grasping a proverb, catching an illusion, seeing a joke' (p. 70).

Summary

Perhaps the nearest one could get to a common characteristic of poststructuralism would be a radical suspicion of reason, order and certainty as governing principles of knowledge and existence. A famous literary theorist once summarized the difference between poststructuralism and structuralism in terms of the Freudian notion of the *uncanny*. In contrast to 'canny' critics who were wedded to structure, logic and the application of reason as tools for mastering texts, 'uncanny' (poststructuralist) critics entertained no such hopes of mastery, and were instead attuned to those points in texts where logic and reason inevitably fail, at the point of the encounter with the 'impasse', where the absurd and the irrational can no longer be distinguished from the real and the rational (J. Hillis Miller, quoted in Culler 1983: 23). To borrow Barbara Johnson's (1987: 13) words, poststructural writers have given up 'the comforts of mastery' that canny critics long for.

Discourse is intimately bound up with the pervasive loss of certainty and mastery associated with such 'uncanny' modes of knowing. A crude and rather unruly summary list of propositions associated with poststructural notions of discourse might run as follows.

- 'Realities' are discursive; that is, there is no direct access to a reality 'outside' discourse.
- Language is not 'transparent'; that is, it is not a neutral medium or vehicle for providing access to the world, or to thought.
- People are 'made subjects' though their involvement as speaking subjects within discourses.

- The self is therefore *'decentred'*: instead of the self-actualizing individual conceived of in humanist philosophies, selves are multiple, fragmented and 'subjected' to the constraints of discourse.
- Power, knowledge, truth and subjectivity are interlinked and produced in/through discourse.
- Language is never innocent.
- Ambiguity, uncertainty, irrationality and indeterminacy lie 'at the heart' of meaning, reason and truth.

There is now a substantial body of work in education that is influenced by poststructuralism. It has proved particularly useful for interrogating gender, race and sexuality, since it offers resources for prying apart the institutionalized common sense that naturalizes binary oppositions and the inequalities that they distribute – male/female, straight/gay, white/black, and so on. This is not to say that poststructuralism has been wholeheartedly embraced by researchers and workers in these fields. Indeed, there are many who argue that the displacement of the humanist subject fatally impedes emancipatory struggles built on a politics of identity and experience. Feminist theorists, for instance, have asked how women can organize politically and press their claims if the category of 'woman' is deconstructed. Similarly, poststructuralism (or postmodernism) is anathema to many forms of traditional Marxist analysis. It problematizes the dualisms of class (proletariat/bourgeoisie) and consciousness (authentic and false) on which the class struggle is premised; and its refusal of 'mastery' stalls the plot of the grand narrative of the inevitable triumph of the proletariat in that struggle.[5]

In rejoinder, researchers of a poststructuralist persuasion argue that such founding categories – woman, race, class – are saturated with effects of power and prejudice, and that productive social change will not take place if these terms are kept beyond question. In comparison with the narratives and ambitions of humanist emancipatory projects, the textual operations of poststructuralist approaches are slow, dogged and localized – a matter of 'working the ruins of humanism' as Bettie St Pierre and Wanda Pillow (2000: 4) put it, in their edited collection of feminist poststructural research in education.[6]

Still, it is important to reassert the need for caution in making a binary distinction between postructuralism and its 'opposites' – before I proceed below to stitch up the other 'side' of my own illicit binary opposition, between poststructuralist and linguistic notions of discourse. Such distinctions always carry the seeds of their own dissolution, in the manner that Jonathan Culler identifies in Miller's depiction of 'canny' and 'uncanny' critics. Miller's account is a little 'parable of pride', writes Culler (1983), in which the uncanny critics get to triumph over their canny opponents: '[t]heorists swollen with scientific ambition are out-stripped by patient explicators, who are alert to the perverse, aporetical [i.e. irreparably contractory] moments of the texts they are studying' (p. 24). Culler notes that, in Miller's portrayal, the uncanny critics end up out-cannying their opponents: they 'penetrate' deeper into texts (a pre-eminently 'canny' sort of operation) than the structuralists, who misguidedly strive for depth through science and logic. The tendency that Culler identifies is an instance of a more general phenomenon. There is *always* the possibility that a poststructural politics of renunciation – that embrace of uncertainty – will invert itself into a 'parable of pride'. Humble poststructural practices such as sifting through 'ruins', 'working the hyphens' of boundaries, courting 'disappointment' and 'resisting closure' can easily become alternative strategies of inverted mastery, with their own, peculiar comforts.[7]

Linguistic discourse analysis

Let us turn now to linguistic discourse analysis. One way of distinguishing these two broad orientations would be in terms of a distinction between a 'macro' and a 'micro' level focus (see Luke 1995). Poststructuralism, as noted above, has generally concerned itself with discourse 'with a capital D', operating at the level of social formations and institutions, and has tended to pay less attention to the specifics of actual texts. Indeed, one criticism that has been levelled at Foucauldian discourse analysis has been its lack of a text-analytic dimension, which would explain how meanings, subjectivity and power relations are manifested in the details of 'what actual people *actually say and do*' (Poynton and Lee 2000: 6; my emphasis). Linguistically oriented discourse analysis takes a more micro-analytic focus, concentrating on the structure and meaning of texts, written and spoken. It is very much concerned with 'what people actually say and do'.

Linguistic discourse analysis was originally driven by the goal of describing the organization of language 'beyond the level of the sentence' (see Cameron 2000: 10). Where orthodox linguistics had traditionally focused (and often still does) on the grammatical and phonological rules for constructing sentences, discourse analysis investigates the rules for building extended stretches of talk or writing. Another definition of discourse analysis, more suited to contemporary pursuits, is the study of 'language in use', which Deborah Cameron (2001) glosses as: 'language used to do something and mean something, language produced and interpreted in a real-world context' (p. 13). There is an assumption here that language exists as an abstract system, which is then mobilized in specific contexts, according to certain rules and conventions, to achieve a range of communicative or practical purposes. Such definitions suggest that linguistic discourse analysis still operates largely within a structuralist mode of knowing and acting, where the boundary between language and the 'real world' is secure, and where discourse is conceptualized as rule-governed, systematic and logical. Conceptual 'mastery' of discourse is, therefore, possible in principle, both for linguists and lay speakers. As Alistair Pennycook (1994: 119) notes, the notion of the coherent, humanist self also persists more-or-less intact in many linguistic models of discourse.

One famous early example of discourse analysis was the analysis of classroom talk developed by Sinclair and Coulthard (1975). This identified several levels of discourse structure in lessons, including the basic interactional unit of the 'exchange', the 'transaction', consisting of a sequence of topically related exchanges, and the lesson as a whole. One of the most significant aspects of the analysis offered by Sinclair and Coulthard was their identification of a three-part structure in the typical classroom exchange, consisting of an 'Initiating' move by the teacher, a 'Response' by the pupil(s) and a 'Feedback' move by the teacher (the 'IRF' structure). This three-part structure, in which pupils generally speak only when invited by the teacher, who then provides some form of evaluative or summative follow-up, has proved remarkably widespread in classrooms across many different cultures and contexts.

Discourse analysts have studied a wide range of settings, formal and informal, public and private. These include doctor–patient talk, parent–child talk, shop and service encounters, debates, lectures, union meetings, social work case conferences, courtroom interrogations, sermons, press articles, informal chat and 'water-cooler' talk. Interviews of various kinds have been extensively studied – in chat shows, psychiatric consultations, counselling sessions, job interviews, as well as qualitative research.[8] The focus in linguistically oriented work has been predominantly upon spoken language, although studies of written language have increased in recent years.

Linguistic discourse analysis, like everything else in this muddied field, is not a 'pure' science. From its earliest conceptions, analysts have incorporated insights from other disciplines. From the philosophy of language, for instance, discourse analysts have borrowed the notion of the 'speech act', as developed by Austin and Searle; that is, the idea that speaking is a form of action or performance. When we speak we 'do things with words', to quote most of the title of Austin's (1962) famous book – promising, betting, requesting, apologizing, commanding, denying, and so on. Searle's attempt to formulate the 'conditions' for successfully performing and recognizing various speech acts was attractive to discourse analysts, as it offered to capture the *systematic* grounds on which speakers interpret and act upon one another's utterances and, therefore, achieve coordinated discourse.[9] Another philosophical influence was Grice's (1975) 'cooperative principle', expressed as a set of general 'maxims' for achieving coordinated talk, such as being relevant, avoiding obscurity and providing the appropriate amount of information. Discourse analysts have also borrowed from the 'ethnography of communication', notably from the work of Dell Hymes (e.g. 1972) on the rules for participating in different kinds of 'speech event' – from a church service or an initiation ritual to casual conversation or 'gossip'. Hymes' notion of 'communicative competence' – that is, the rules that those within a 'speech community' need to know to participate 'appropriately' – has been especially influential. Indeed, the influence of notions such as communicative competence, 'appropriateness' and 'purpose' extends well beyond academic discourse analysis. It can still be detected, for instance, in the UK National Curriculum for English, which, in its targets for 'Speaking and Listening' in the secondary school stages, prescribes that pupils should be able to: 'speak fluently and appropriately in different contexts, adapting their talk for a range of purposes and audiences, including the more formal' (National Curriculum website at http://www.nc.uk.net/home.html). There have been other interminglings between linguistics and other disciplines, some of which are touched on below with specific reference to classroom discourse.

The influence of discourse analysis on classroom research

Classrooms were a fertile ground for discourse analysts in the 1970s and early 1980s – not, originally, because of an interest in educational questions, but because teacher–pupil talk seemed to be a relatively orderly kind of discourse, whose rules would be more accessible to analysis than those of casual conversation (see Sinclair and Coulthard 1975). Still, the regularities that the linguists discovered in classroom talk proved illuminating for analysts with broader educational, sociopolitical, cultural or developmental interests, whose insights were in turn incorporated 'back' into models of classroom discourse. In particular, the strong *control* which teachers were shown to exercise over the talk through the 'IRF' mechanism resonated with a number of concerns. For sociologists of education, classroom discourse appeared to provide a form of socialization (unwittingly on the part of teachers) into the relations of subordination and authority required for the operation of capitalist modes of production.[10] For ethnographers of communication, and interaction sociologists with an interest in race, class and underachievement, the question arose as to whether children from some social and ethnic groups (i.e. white, middle class) came to school better prepared for the vicissitudes of classroom discourse than others. This led to comparative studies of home and school language, as noted above, and a fierce controversy as to whether children from some family backgrounds (e.g. working class, African American) came to school with a language 'deficit', or merely a language 'difference' with respect to the language habits of the school (see Edwards and Furlong 1978; Wells 1981; Brice Heath 1983).

The work of the discourse analysts also raised questions about relationships between classroom discourse and *learning*. Educationists noted that traditional teacher-led talk tended to position students as passive recipients of knowledge, and began to argue for collaborative, informal, non-hierarchical discursive arrangements, such as small-group talk, which would grant students greater autonomy and initiative in negotiating their own learning (e.g. Barnes 1976). Researchers also began to make links between the discourse patterns of classroom talk and children's cognitive development. The interactional models of development proposed by psychologists such as Bruner and Vygotsky seemed to endorse more flexible and supportive modes of teacher–pupil interaction which would accord children a more active role as speakers and learners (cf. Edwards and Mercer 1987). Arguments for 'democratizing' classroom discourse were also linked to the rise of 'oracy' in the curriculum in the UK: that is, the teaching of speaking and listening. Here, the argument was that traditional classrooms allowed children to exercise only a tiny range of the discourse skills that they would need in later life. Students should, it was claimed, be given opportunities to build up a varied 'repertoire' of spoken language skills – leading meetings, taking part in interviews, telling stories, and so on (see MacLure 1994c).

In this proliferation of classroom studies, a diverse range of approaches and insights mingled with one another, to a point where, again, it would be difficult to identify a 'pure' linguistic discourse method, as opposed to a 'pure' sociological, psychological, anthropological or educational one, even though analysts tended to position themselves predominantly within one particular paradigm. The body of work that emerged exemplified, rather, differing responses to the realization that classroom talk was (a) a patterned activity that was governed by rules or conventions, and (b) that these discourse structures were linked in important ways to issues of class, culture and learning.

It is worth noting that this blossoming of interest in classroom discourse coincided with other trends in UK education policy and reform of the mid-1970s to the late 1980s. For instance, it connected with a wider move towards process-driven, student-centred models of learning centred on problem solving, active engagement, team work, the acquisition of 'skills', and the attempt to make school experience more relevant to the world outside the school gates. Some of these goals had been part of an older 'progressive' education agenda, but they took on a different inflection with the introduction of the 'new vocationalism', which aimed to equip students with the 'flexible' skills required for the 'enterprise' society (see Ball 1990b). The 'opening out' of classroom discourse also meshed with the reforms of the national examination system that were instituted in the 1980s. The new General Certificate of Secondary Education (GCSE) examinations for 16-year olds moved away from end-point, written examinations which favoured the passive accumulation of knowledge, towards course work, project work, self-assessment, 'profiling' and more 'authentic' forms of assessment, including practical oral activities.[11]

Discourse analysis proved useful, therefore, to a range of disciplines and constituencies with a stake in education, and was linked to wider currents of education reform in the UK in the 1970s and 1980s. I have taken up some space in elaborating this account because it allows me to point up some of the *differences* between linguistic and poststructural discourse analysis. The linguistically informed classroom investigations described above were primarily concerned with producing 'internal' analyses of the structure and meanings inhering in classroom discourse, even if these were also related to wider questions of class, ethnicity, learning, cognitive development, workplace 'skills', and so on. This work was mainly interested, then, in 'burrowing inside' the discourse, to borrow Threadgold's phrase, quoted above. A poststructural analysis, by contrast, would be interested not just in the internal workings of classroom discourse, but in *the conditions which had given rise to its emergence as an educational concern*. It might pursue (as the discourse analysts themselves seldom did) the *coincidence* of the interest in classroom discourse with those other trends such as student-centred, process-oriented and vocationalist curricula. It might explore the extent to which 'larger' discourses – Discourses-with-a-capital-D – were implicated in this coincidence. For instance, a poststructural analysis might ask whether 'big-D' discourses of 'progressivism', 'managerialism' and 'vocationalism' were mingled in this wider current that also swept up classroom discourse analysts. It might examine the similar vocabularies of student empowerment, expertise and active participation that ran through all of these discourses, and ask whether these expressed the same, or conflicting, educational values and student identities (see MacLure and Stronach 1993; MacLure 1994b). A Foucauldian analysis might interrogate the emancipatory rhetoric shared by the classroom discourse studies and the wider innovations. It might 'read' these not as redistributions of power and agency from teacher to student, as their advocates intended, but as devices of 'governmentality' – that is, shifts in the regulation of populations from externally imposed discipline (here, via teachers) to internal *self*-regulation (see, for example, Stronach 1988; Walkerdine 1990).

From a poststructuralist vantage point, linguistic discourse analysis has often been criticized for failing to take account of such aspects of the 'bigger picture' – that is, the political, ideological, cultural and economic dimensions of communication (e.g. Pennycook 1994; Luke 1995: 11). Some critics go so far as to accuse linguistic discourse analysts of naivety in terms of their theorizing of social concepts. Cate Poynton (2000: 27), for instance, charges linguists with opportunistically borrowing social terms from various disciplines, in the service of a crude linguistic empiricism that lacks a 'sustained engagement with social theory'. On the other hand (this being, yet again, a world of binary antagonisms), linguistic discourse analysts accuse poststructural analysts, as already noted, of lacking the linguistic resources for analysing texts and, therefore, of failing to anchor (and therefore validate) their descriptions of large-scale discourses with reference to the actualities of talk and writing in specific settings (e.g. Luke 1995: 11). In other words, each 'side' in this particular binary opposition – between poststructural and linguistic discourse analysis – finds something lacking in the other. Indeed, one could say that – in precisely the same way as for 'scientific' *vs* 'alternative' medicine, or action research *vs* mainstream research – each of these orientations draws its strength from its subordination of the 'Other'.[12]

Critical discourse analysis

There now exists a body of work emanating from the linguistic 'side' of the divide, which explicitly attempts to marry the 'bigger picture' offered by social theory with the technical sophistication of linguistic analysis, to produce an integrated approach to discourse. 'Critical discourse analysis' (CDA) is the name applied to the work of a group of linguists who emphasize the social and institutional dimensions of discourse, and attempt to relate these to the textual fabric of everyday life. Practitioners of CDA do not all share the same linguistic paradigm, or draw on the same body of social and critical theory; and there is, as ever, a degree of fuzziness as to whose work belongs within the canon. Key figures who have explicitly identified their work with critical discourse analysis include Gunther Kress (e.g. 1990), Norman Fairclough (e.g. 1992, 1995), Allan Luke (1995) and Teun Van Dijk (2001).[13]

As Kress (1990: 84) states in a review article, CDA brings an 'overtly political agenda' to the study of texts. Practitioners of CDA, he writes, abjure the scientific neutrality and the non-judgemental, descriptive stance of traditional linguistic analysis. Their aim is to identify the workings of power and domination that inhere in discursive practices, and thereby to facilitate emancipatory social change.

> By denaturalizing the discursive practices and the texts of a society, treated as a set of discursively linked communities, and by making visible and apparent that which may previously have been invisible and seemingly natural, [CDA practitioners] intend to show the imbrication of linguistic-discursive practices with the wider socio-political structures of power and domination. In as far as these structures act to the detriment of particular groups in a society, critical discourse analysts hope to bring about change not only to the discursive practices, but also to the socio-political practices and structures supporting the discursive practices.
>
> (Kress 1990: 85)

Allan Luke (1995: 13), like Kress, refers to the ways in which discourses 'naturalize' power relations and the social inequalities that these distribute, and describes CDA as 'a political act in itself, an intervention in the apparently natural flow of talk and text in institutional life that attempts to "interrupt" everyday common sense'. Critical discourse analysts share a particular interest, then, in issues of power and dominance, and a political commitment to redressing social inequities, by 'denaturalizing' and exposing the effects of power at work in discourse.

Critical discourse analysts have achieved considerable success in showing how the discursive 'fabrication' of identities and realities works through the textual fabric itself – that is, the 'stuff' of everyday talk, reading and writing. Education has been a major focus, as one of the key sites for the 'disciplining' of subjects and the inequitable distribution of symbolic and material assets. Literacy practices have been extensively studied, in textbooks, classroom interactions and family discourses. As already discussed above, literacy is seen as especially significant in the formation of official knowledge and the constitution and marginalization of subjects (cf. Lankshear 1987; Luke and Gilbert 1993; Luke 1995; Gee 1999). More generally, CDA practitioners have studied the ways in which, in the everyday business of lessons, assemblies, textbooks, essay-writing, etc., certain children are marked out as 'different' with respect to mainstream educational identities and values – in terms of gender, ethnicity, physical competence, and so on (e.g. DeCastell *et al.* 1989; Davies 1993). A comprehensive overview of the field of CDA studies to date can be found in Toolan (2002).

Despite the depth and subtlety of the textual analyses achieved in some studies, CDA has been subject to criticism from commentators who find it lacking in sophistication or coherence, in terms of its theorizing of the social. Martyn Hammersley (1997) and Deborah Lupton (1995) both argue that CDA tends to rely on over-simplified notions of dominance and power, and static conceptions of the relationship between language and society, even where analysts claim to incorporate more complicating notions from Foucault or Habermas. Hammersley (1997: 245), in his scathing critique, finds CDA analysts driven by overambition and 'Enlightenment optimism' to serious methodological error. Alistair Pennycook (1994) also questions the theorizing of power, reality and subjectivity in CDA. He suggests that it rests on a covert appeal to the notion of a 'real world' that is masked by the veil of ideology, which it is the job of the critical discourse analyst to remove, to help people to see the 'truth'. This assumption of the 'unmasking' role of the analyst sits uneasily, as Pennycook points out, alongside commitments to the Foucauldian position that there is no 'outside' of discourse from which to formulate universal truths.[14]

Pennycook (1994) suggests that the basic problem with CDA is that, in attempting to reconcile the Anglo-American and the European discourse traditions, it is trying to bolt together two incompatible intellectual enterprises. The scientific-empiricist orientation of linguistics simply does not fit with the philosophical and socio-historical leanings of Continental theory. Cate Poynton (2000) reaches a broadly similar conclusion. She questions whether linguists can sufficiently overcome the rigidities of linguistic theorizing and the constraints of a 'monolithic technical apparatus' (p. 36) to pursue more fluid, poststructural forms of analysis. Even when critical discourse analysts try to be faithful to Foucauldian or other European theoretical traditions, their analytic practices, says Poynton, remain 'stubbornly "linguocentric"' (p. 34).

Conversation analysis

I want to close this hasty tour of perspectives with a short discussion of conversation analysis (CA), an approach that has generated impressive insights into the structure and organization of spoken interaction. Conversation analysis does not have its origins in linguistics or poststructuralism, but in ethnomethodology – a dissenting tendency within sociology, initiated by Harold Garfinkel (1967), which originally drew its theoretical energies from the phenomenology of Husserl and Schutz. For ethnomethodologists, the patterns and structures that are discernible in societies (e.g. regularities of social class, institutions, 'deviance', 'the family') are not a matter of external social constraints, roles or functions imposed on hapless individuals, but are *produced* through cultural and interpretive practices ('methods') that people collaboratively use to make sense of the world and render it mutually comprehensible. Social order is not an abstract set of constraints, therefore, but an ongoing 'accomplishment' of members acting in concert. The job of the sociologist, said Garfinkel (1967: 67–8), was not to treat ordinary members of society as 'cultural dopes' who acted in blind ignorance of the social forces determining their actions, but to tap into the methods that members themselves used to display to one another their common-sense understanding of the social categories and identities to which they (for the moment) belonged.

Language was a prime focus from the start, as one of the most important cultural resources (though not the only one) through which social order is produced, and as a main target of ethnomethodology's critique of sociological method. Sociologists were attacked for treating language as a transparent medium for expressing sociological categories (class, ethnicity, power, authority, deviance, etc.) and overlooking its role in creating social realities, including the reality of sociologists' *own* categories (cf. Watson 1992: 260). Garfinkel and his followers asserted that an absolute distinction between language and an external world of objects is untenable, since language is unavoidably *indexical*; that is, inescapably tied to 'context'. Utterances have no meaning independent of the specific contexts in which they are used. Yet the 'context' is reciprocally constructed through the talk that invokes/refers to it. Language and its objects are, therefore, bound together in a *reflexive* relationship of mutual constitution, and it is not possible to erase or read 'through' the language to the sociological facts or truths that supposedly exist elsewhere.

Conversational analysis as a specific branch of inquiry developed from the work of Harvey Sacks (e.g. 1992), a colleague of Garfinkel. Sacks focused on the fine details of casual conversation – an arena where people routinely apply their common-sense methods for making sense of the world for one another. Sacks developed a form of analysis that was capable of identifying the intricate machineries that speakers mobilize to dovetail their individual utterances into a stretch of coherent conversation, and bring off the seemingly mundane business of 'being ordinary' (Sacks 1984). One line of inquiry that Sacks opened up was the identification of the 'membership categorization devices' that speakers use during their talk to assign one another to social categories such as 'adult', child, 'teacher', 'mother', and so on, and to hold one another 'accountable' to the rights and obligations associated with those categories (Sacks 1974; Jayyusi 1984). Sacks also began to identify the complexity and orderliness of the interactional turn-taking mechanisms that are the basic glue that holds talk together (Sacks *et al.* 1974).

In the spirit of ethnomethodological method, Sacks and his followers insisted that analysis should attempt to capture the details of everything that speakers actually say and do, rather than imposing pre-formed linguistic categories upon the data. This refusal to rule out any interactional phenomena as irrelevant, from the smallest 'ums' and 'ers' and the most minute pauses and hesitations, to the significance of 'in-breaths', has enabled conversation analysis to capture subtleties of conversational organization that would escape most linguistic discourse models.

Educational discourse has received considerable attention from conversation analysts (though the word 'discourse' is not used in conversation analysis). Analysts have been interested in the sequential structure and organization of classroom talk, as a form of interaction whose turn-taking systems differ in some ways from those of casual conversation. For instance, the conventions for selecting the person who gets to speak next ensure that teachers get more turns at talk, and take overall responsibility for managing the complexities of interactions involving large numbers of people. This, in turn, generates differences in the categorizations, and therefore the identities, of 'teacher and pupil' (cf. McHoul 1978).[15] Many other educational researchers have similarly found Sacks' notion of membership categorization powerful as a way of understanding how educational identities and categories are transacted in the day-to-day business of school life. Carolyn Baker (1984), for instance, has looked at the negotiation of an 'adult' identity in talk between adolescents and adults, and at the attribution and maintenance of the identities of parent, teacher and student in parent–teacher interviews (Baker 2000; see Chapter 3). Baker and Freebody (1987) have looked at categorizations of 'the child' in written textbooks. As Rod Watson (1992) notes, a CA perspective on educational identities is premised on the assumption that '"children" and "adults" are cultural events that members make happen' (p. 262).[16]

In terms of the binary distinction that I set up at the beginning of this section, between Anglo-American and European discourse traditions, conversation analysis might seem to belong to the latter. To the extent that it continues the ethnomethodological programme, with its phenomenological heritage, it is clearly inflected by European philosophical thought. Notions such as the unavoidable 'indexicality' of language, and the 'reflexive' relationship between analyst and data, seem close to poststructural, or even deconstructive, notions of the textual nature of subjectivity and reality. In common with Derrida, ethnomethodologists and CA practitioners are sceptical of an objective reality and a humanist self that exists apart from the discursive resources that produce these. And there is a decidedly Foucauldian flavour to Heritage's (1984) depiction of conversation analysis as the study of the ways in which participants 'talk an institution into being' (p. 290).

Yet conversation analysis is an interestingly hybrid approach, with affinities also to the structuralist and empiricist leanings of linguistics. Sacks' theorizing of turn-taking in terms of *systems*, his attention to structure, recurrence and 'reduplicability', and his insistence on studying 'naturalistic' practices rather than abstractions, invoke a scientist orientation that has continued to run through conversation analysis.[17] The emphasis in both ethnomethodology and conversation analysis on 'members' competence' as constructors of their own social worlds carries notions of mastery of the social that would trouble poststructural notions of discourse. Exponents of conversation analysis also often adopt an explicitly anti-'theory' stance, in favour of an empiricist attention to a seemingly self-evident 'real world'; and have developed a set of highly elaborate transcription and analytic procedures to 'capture' the minute details of those real-world practices. As Cate Poynton (2000) notes, conversation analysis shares the propensity of linguistic discourse analysis to be 'highly technical and [to] proliferate analytical tools' (p. 26).

Like critical discourse analysis, conversation analysis has come in for criticism from commentators on both 'sides' of the discourse debate. Theorists less wedded to 'rigour' have dismissed it as suffering from the linguistic disease of 'hardening of the categories' (Poytnon 2000: 26). And it has long been the target of acerbic critique from sociologists and cultural theorists on the grounds that its intransigent focus on interaction as the sole locus of social order renders it impotent to address issues of power and dominance. However, linguists have also been critical of conversation analysis, accusing analysts of inventing terms and apparatuses that are not 'motivated' by a proper linguistic understanding of the systematic nature of language. As with critical discourse analysis, therefore, conversation analysis has been both embraced and repudiated by critics who themselves hold widely differing theoretical allegiances.

In conclusion

It seems that there is something of an impasse between the Anglo-American/linguistic and the European discourse traditions, which is more-or-less where this discussion started out. Despite the desire of some analysts, particularly within critical discourse analysis, to achieve a synthesis, it seems that these may be 'incommensurable discourses' (Pennycook 1994), whose adherents belong to different discourse communities. You could say that linguists and poststructural theorists are different people – differently subject-ed by the disciplines into which they have become fabricated, and to which they owe their allegiances, their academic identities and their career prospects. They hold different beliefs: about the value of science and the merits of technical 'rigour'; about the status of truth; about the power and the limitations of their respective methods to explain the world, and to change it. Most irreconcilable of all, perhaps, are the different conceptualizations of the nature of language and of the analyst's relation to language Where linguists generally assume that it is possible to 'jump clear' of language, to see it clearly and 'capture' its regularities, many poststructuralists would see themselves as obliged to work from 'inside' the textual fabric that holds them in 'an enfolded, entrapped relationship with the real world' (Bal 1999: 24).[18]

An integrated discourse theory that would seamlessly accommodate linguistics and poststructuralism would therefore appear impossible. This is not to argue, though, that analysis is inexorably trapped on one side or other of the binary, with no possibility of traffic or translation between the two traditions. Indeed, such 'traffic' takes place anyway, with ideas and assumptions from one paradigm cropping up in another, often enough 'behind the backs' of those who would defend the boundaries between them. There are neither 'pure' discourse traditions, therefore, nor the prospect of an overarching, unified discourse theory that would regulate the 'traffic' so as to accommodate the concerns of all those with an interest in discourse. But there *are* connections between the fine grain of language and action ('what people actually say and do') and the broader sweep of Discourses with a 'big-D', and this book tries to trace some of these. But the connections are not, I suggest, the stable links between intact and clearly demarcated domains that are envisaged in theories that propose different 'levels' of discourse (e.g. micro and macro; or interactional, institutional, societal). They are not the sort of connections, either, that are envisaged in Russian-doll-type models in which 'text' is nested within 'discourse', which is, in turn, nested within something called 'society'. Instead, the connections that this book traces are of the kind invoked by deconstructive or poststructural metaphors – folds, knots, insinuations and 'the trace' itself.

Appendix 2
Standard English: chronology of policy events

November 1988	Publication of first report of the Working Party for English (5–11), chaired by Brian Cox, commissioned by Education Secretary Kenneth Baker
June 1989	Publication of draft proposals of the second Cox Report (English 5–16)
July 1989	John McGregor succeeds Kenneth Baker as Secretary of State for Education
November 1989	Final version of second Cox Report published (following consultation phase). This report formed the basis of the first Statutory Order, *English in the National Curriculum*
November 1990	Kenneth Clarke replaces John McGregor as Education Secretary
April 1992	General Election: Conservatives win under John Major
April 1992	John Patten becomes Secretary of State for Education
September 1992	Patten orders National Curriculum Council (NCC) review of the English curriculum, at the behest of NCC chair, David Pascall
April 1993	NCC/Pascall proposals, *English for Ages 5–16 (1993)*, published by the Department for Education
April 1993	Sir Ron Dearing appointed chair-designate of SCAA (replacing NCC and SEAC under the Education Act 1993) with brief to review National Curriculum and assessment arrangements
May 1994	SCAA publishes Dearing's draft proposals, including *English in the National Curriculum*
July 1994	Gillian Shephard replaces John Patten as Education Secretary
January 1995	Department for Education publishes new Statutory Order *English in the National Curriculum* for implementation from September 1995

Appendix 3
Anatomy of a blaming sequence

[T = teacher; M = mother; <u>underlining</u> = overlapping speech]

T	. . . I'm, personally I think Josh is doing well and seems quite happy. Have you any problem, any questions you want to ask? . . . You look like you have a question, yeah g –	*[concluding his 'diagnosis']*
M	[Hesitantly mutters] He's . . . he has not understood on a couple of occasions the actual homework that he has been set to do. He hasn't understood.	**problem statement/ accusation**
T	Right, so he's been, what? In English, in particular?	
M	Yeah, in particular about the Diary of the erm, the Witches' Diary thing. He, he was kind of quite upset that he didn't really understand what it was he was being asked to do –	
T	– oh r –, he misinterpreted, <u>oh that's a sh</u> –	**blameshift → student**
M	– <u>no, he just</u> didn't really <u>understand</u> –	**blameshift → teacher**
T	– <u>follow it</u>.	
M	– what he was being asked to do, yeah, and he got a little bit upset about it, getting quite stressed in actual fact, that he wasn't, he couldn't understand, well not he didn't understand, he just didn't understand what he was being asked to do, you know?	*[personal information]*
T	Right, er, it's a shame in a way if he hadn't, [stutters] you could have easily phoned up, or asked him to ask me. I mean what they were doing was we'd read the play, the book sorry, 'cause it was The Witches, wasn't it? [M: Yes] And we'd actually read the book, The Witches, and what I'd said for them to do, I said, 'Right, imagine you are the main character	**blameshift → student/ parent**
		blameshift → justification
		[pedagogical explanation]

- [M: mm] – the lad that's in the story and
choose the bits you enjoy, and imagine you
just write a little diary of some of the *main*
events in the story to show' –

M   – yeah, <u>well he</u> –

T   [*loudly*] <u>and that's</u> what they were, and it was
<u>like a, a</u>

M   well he kind of

T   <u>very easy way of</u>

                                  [*talking simultaneously*]

M   <u>he kind</u> of interpreted that to mean, erm, that   **reassertion of**
he was expected to write a diary of every   **problem/accusation**
single event that happened in the book.

T   I did quite, and it was actually written on   **denial**
the book, quite clearly, it wasn't – one of the
things I actually <u>said</u> [M: <u>Yeah</u>] was at the
time, 'you are *not* expected to write the <u>book'</u>.

M   <u>Yeah I know.</u>

T   'cause if that was the case

M   <u>yeah,</u> no, <u>that's what</u> –

T   <u>– I'd have got, you'd have written the book</u> –

M   that's what, he, he seemed to, he seemed <u>to</u>   **reassertion of problem/**
<u>think that's what he was meant</u>   **accusation**

T   <u>oh, it was a misunderstanding</u>   **blameshift →**
                                            nominalization
                                            ('no fault' version)

M   – to be doing

T   But no, that was, that's unfortunate.

M   Yeah.

T   In the case of that, if he misinterprets   **blameshift → student/**
something, or he's unsure, by all means,   **parent**
contact me or tell him to come up and ask,
you know.

M   Yeah.

T   'Cause quite often, I tell the whole class,   **blameshift → 'neutral**
there's thirty of them, you know,   **object'**

M   well, I –

T   you assume that <u>they've actually</u> –

M   [*tries to interrupt*] <u>yes, so</u> –

T   – it's on the board and written, it doesn't
always <u>follow</u> –

M   – <u>yes</u> I know the problem [laughs].   **agreement**

T   So, I mean if that's the case, then by all means
make sure that <u>you</u> –

M   – <u>Yeah.</u>

T   The next day he comes up, or if either one
of you contact me and say he's not sure,
I'm quite happy to re-explain it to him.

M   Okay.   **acceptance of T's version**

Notes

Chapter I

1 Fanon (1986) writes of the way desire opens up space and distance: 'As soon as I *desire* I am asking to be considered. I am not merely here-and-now, sealed into thingness. I am for somewhere else and something else' (p. 218; original emphasis).

2 Or perhaps it is a 'textual turn', a 'postmodern turn', a 'reflexive turn', a 'poststructuralist turn', a 'narrative turn' or a 'literary turn'. All of these terms are in circulation and, as Green (1994: iii) notes, while they may have many differences, they share the work of 'registering a new space' for research and theorizing across the disciplines, in the wake of the crisis of representation.

3 The phrase 'always ready' has itself spread like a virus in writing that may broadly be called 'deconstructive'.

4 These words were relatively new at the time of writing. Of course, by the time this book is published, they may have lost their 'newness'. They may even have acquired a hint of nostalgia that locates them in a particular era, as 'yuppie' or 'filofax', for example, are now associated with the 1980s. 'Road rage' exemplifies the generative force that some coinages often possess, having spawned offspring such as 'web rage' (irritation experienced by internet surfers) and 'lane rage' (hostility towards people who obstruct fast swimmers in public pools, according to a radio item in the summer of 1998).

5 'Entanglement' is the term used by the art historian Mieke Bal (1999) to invoke the paradoxical relationship, in Baroque and contemporary art, between domains traditionally thought of as discrete – past/present, subject/object, reality/representation, surface/depth, etc. Bal's use of the word is specifically indebted to deconstruction.

6 The changes in the name of the government department responsible for education over the past decade would merit discourse analysis in their own right. At the time of finishing this book, it was called the Department for Education and Skills (DfES). In 1999, when the first issue of *Teachers* was

published, it was called the Department for Education and Employment. For many years before that it was called the Department of Education and Science.

7 Another instance is the *Captain Euro* cartoon website established, apparently, to sell the single European currency and offer 'a European identity' to young people. The square-jawed super-hero fights for a united Europe against master criminal Dr D. Vider. Again, it is doubtful whether the target audience will find themselves swayed by such an obvious strategy. Moreover, such a pastiche can carry unintended messages; for example, that the aspirational European identity is a square-jawed, adversarial, morally inflexible male 'proponent of fortress Europe' (*Captain Euro* website: http:// www.captaineuro.com).

8 The freedom fighter/terrorist example is used by, for example, Lemke (1995: 37).

9 The position was sometimes filled by a triumvirate of parents, employers and academics. For example, the following excerpt is from a leader article on teachers' alleged opposition to the teaching of 'standard English': 'Not only parents have been concerned about the linguistic competence of their offspring in their native or adopted tongue. University teachers and employers have complained too' (*The Times*, 25 June 1989).

10 For example, a report on the launch of the government's Social Exclusion Unit stated: 'its first task will be . . . to persuade children and their parents how important it is not to play truant. "For many", said Mr Blair, "being out of school is the beginning of a slippery slope to crime, drugs and exploitation by others"' (*Times Educational Supplement*, 12 December 1997).

11 The quote above from the academic who distinguished her approach from that of the educational psychologists and sociologists can also be seen as appealing to relevance (i.e. to what is happening in schools).

12 I am being disingenuous. As this chapter is at pains to point out, there is no possibility of merely stating, or innocently describing, without also 'engaging'. Harvey Sacks (1992) spells it out (referring to a seemingly innocuous remark in a group therapy session): '. . . you can't be engaged in merely [. . .] saying "This is, after all, a group therapy session". To do that [. . .] is to do other things as well, e.g., put somebody down for something they just said, propose special relevances, propose that some topic ought to be discussed or not be discussed, invoke a status hierarchy, etc.' (p. 516).

13 I am struck by the colonialist nuances of the way I have used 'the interior'. Is this fair? See Chapter 4.

14 'The Beginning of the Armadillos' (Kipling 1994).

15 Threadgold (2000) provides a helpful outline of the main elements of discourse analysis from a poststructuralist orientation. Her comment on the 'hybrid' nature of discourse is *itself* framed from within that particular orientation. My own account privileges poststructuralist notions too (see pp. 174–82).

16 Saussure also provides an example of 'delayed transmission', since his ideas spread posthumously and took many decades to arrive in literary and cultural theory.

Chapter 2

1 Some examples from headlines over the period: 'Victory to Baker' (*Daily Mail*, 23 June 1989); 'Baker accepted defeat on teaching of grammar' (*The Guardian*, 23 June 1989); 'Teachers set to win English war of words' (*Daily Mail*, 17 November 1989); 'Gillian Shephard has declared war' (*Independent*, 14 October 1994). See MacLure and Pettigrew (1996).

2 The chapter draws on a broader study, 'The Press, Public Knowledge and Education', funded by the Economic and Social Research Council, ref. R000235314 (see MacLure and Pettigrew 1996).

3 The four education secretaries who succeeded Baker were John McGregor, Kenneth Clarke, John Patten and Gillian Shephard. The various versions of the National Curriculum for English include the original, Cox-based framework (DES 1989), through David Pascall's proposed versions (DfE 1993) to the new English order (DfE 1995), based on Sir Ron Dearing's review of the whole curriculum (SCAA 1994).

4 A similar justification in terms of entitlement was made by the Labour government in the late 1990s for the imposition of the National Literacy Strategy. As the Conclusion to this chapter discusses, the policy 'heat' had, by the end of the millennium, gone out of standard English, having been replaced with high anxiety about standards of literacy. However, as I argue later, it is entirely likely that the cycle of policy interest in the English curriculum will swing round again to standard English at some point. A similar kind of analysis to the one developed in this chapter, which moves between the curriculum, policy, press and historical 'angles', could be applied to the National Literacy Strategy.

5 There is a timeless quality to some of these opinions. Compare Melanie Phillips' championing of the Prince of Wales with these comments from the educationist George Sampson, whose book, *English for the English*, published in 1925, was a key text in the policy debates around English between the wars: 'If anyone wants a definite example of standard English we can tell him that it is the kind of English spoken by a simple unaffected young Englishman like the Prince of Wales' (quoted in Crowley 1996: 165).

6 There was one notable exception to the dismissal of linguistic expertise in the figure of Sir Randolph Quirk, an eminent linguist and former president of the British Academy, whose views were taken up by the press, especially *The Times*. Quirk took a strongly pro-standard English line and an equally strong critical view of teacher dissent. A *Times* leader on a Quirk speech at the time of the second Cox Report, for example, concluded with an embedded quote that was also picked up by the other papers: ' "the stale leftovers of the 1960s" in Sir Randolph's words, continue to pollute the classroom' (*The Times*, 5 January 1989).

7 Daley's terminology also points to the symbolic link between 'grammar' and social *discipline*. She writes of 'rigid' language teaching, 'forceful assimilation', schooling 'dominated by its strictures' on grammar. Bill Green (1998) explores, from a Foucauldian perspective, the historical associations between grammar and discipline (see pp. 38–9).

8 Fairclough was referring to the discourse strategies of the 'New Labour' government in its first term of office (1997–2001). The rationale for teaching standard English as a remedy for 'cultural deficiency' is, therefore, as compatible with the Labour rhetoric of social inclusion as it was under the former Conservative government. However, standard English did not figure prominently in the public discourses of education during Labour's first term. I return later in the chapter to this issue.

9 The pamphlet, whose full title was *The Language Trap: Race, Class and the 'Standard Language' Issue in British Schools*, was published by the right-wing National Council for Educational Standards (NCES 1983).

10 Ball *et al.* (1990) account for the rise of English as a school subject as a response to the rise of the urban working class: 'English as a *school subject* originated out of the fears and panics surrounding the development of the city and the emergence of a working class population. The phenomenal growth of urban society in the nineteenth century profoundly disturbed the moral fabric of the existing social order. In the experiences and imagination of the landed ruling class and the newly emerging industrial middle class, the city was a focus and a source of political unrest, social disorder, crime and disease. In "darkest" London (or Manchester, Birmingham, Liverpool) the rule of law and the influence of the Christian religion were tenuous' (pp. 49–50; original emphasis).

11 I am not suggesting, however, that different wordings reflect the 'same' meaning, which is how the term seems to be used in systemic linguistics.

12 The term 'sentimental sociologist' is borrowed from Carolyn Steedman's (1986) reference to the left-leaning celebrants of working-class culture.

13 Note that Jenkins explicitly attempts to dissociate his revulsion towards Glaswegians from the taint of racial prejudice. Still, his fear for 'the safety of the Indian conductor' carries the traces, for me at least, of the paternalistic concern of the colonialist.

14 A related trope is to associate non-standard speech with *childishness*. Alan Coren, recalling his own dialect-speaking origins, refers to a boy overheard at the Toy Museum, and contemplates the 'appeal of a tot's gamey demotic'. But this is the appeal of nostalgia for childish whimsy, not to be considered suitable for grown-ups. Note that 'gamey' carries a whiff of the 'animalizing' of non-standard dialect.

15 Crowley (1989) points out that the term 'barbarian' itself derives from the ancient Greek word for people who did not speak Hellenic.

16 Several commentators have argued that the media colluded with the politicians to override educationally informed opinion on key aspects of the curriculum proposals, through selective focus and deliberate misreading of the various reports (e.g. Cameron and Bourne 1989; Stubbs 1989; Ball *et al.* 1990). Although I would not disagree with the assertion of allegiances between the media and policy makers or, indeed, with the proposition that these materially affected the nature of the English curriculum, my argument in this chapter is that the entanglements of these voices with those of other constituencies (e.g. linguists, teachers, curriculum committee members, etc.) are much more complex than the simple two-sided metaphor of war allows.

17 For an account of the emergence and operation of the discourses of the 'New Right', see Ball (1990b). For a detailed account of the development of English as a school subject, and its intimate association with politics, nationhood and power, see Ball *et al.* (1990).

18 Foucault (1980) described the methods used by the nineteenth-century bourgeoisie to contain the threat of the new proletariat: 'Among the methods employed some were of enormous consequence (as, for example, the morality taught in primary schools, that is, the gradual imposition of a whole system of values disguised as the teaching of literacy, reading and writing covering up the imposition of values)' (p. 20).

19 The clearest, and most famous, formulation of linguistic 'indifference' to the details of performance is Chomsky's (1965) definition of the proper object of theory as 'the ideal speaker-listener, in a completely homogeneous speech community' (p. 3). Poynton (2000) argues, however, that even those linguistic and sociolinguistic theories that explicitly avow an interest in 'performance' data, in the form of 'actually occurring' spoken language, operate with an idealized, de-materialized version of speech.

20 Gurevitch's mention of 'monkeys' here refers specifically to the foregrounding of performance described by Henry Louis Gates (1988) in his book on black American speech, *Signifying Monkey*.

21 Each individual analyst's fingers are always already 'caught' in the intertextual net, in one way or another. If I were writing this chapter in a more autobiographical or confessional mode, I might have chosen to elaborate on my own implication in some of the historical moments that I have referred to. For example, I was directly involved in the debates about English education that preceded and surrounded the National Curriculum reforms, as a researcher for the Assessment of Performance Unit, which informed the first version of the National Curriculum and Assessment framework, and an adviser on the development of the GCSE English examinations. I was involved in the controversies over class-based language differences in the 1970s. As a Scot of working-class origins, who retains something of her accent after many years in England, I am not inclined to be even-handed on the issue of standard English. Other analysts of the texts discussed in this chapter would bring their own personal involvements. Many of these investments are not even available to conscious introspection. There are, in other words, no innocent bystanders to the events about which writers write.

22 The National Literacy Strategy is certainly worthy of attention from a discourse perspective in its own right, especially in view of its apparent power to enchant critics and silence their counter-arguments. It is also noteworthy that, in primary schools, the word 'English' has virtually been replaced by 'literacy', which includes, albeit of a reduced importance, speaking and listening.

23 For instance, the 'Glossary of Terms' for use in the National Literacy Strategy states that standard English 'is not limited to a particular region and can be spoken with any accent' (DfEE 2000), while the National Curriculum objectives for listening and speaking at Key Stage 2 (7–11 years) state that pupils must be taught to 'speak audibly and clearly, using spoken standard English in formal contexts'.

Chapter 3

1 The research was supported by the Economic and Social Research Council, ref. R000222287. See the End of Award Report (MacLure and Walker 1999) for an account of the methodology and research design.

2 It depends, of course, how you construe 'control'. It is doubtful whether main grade teachers (perhaps even headteachers) feel that they have a great deal of say in how parents' evenings are organized (see Walker 1998). And although we did find many of the features of interactional dominance characteristic of professional talk, I suggest in this chapter that teachers are no more free than parents to step 'outside' the institutional identities and responsibilities that are elaborated within the consultations.

3 Classroom talk between teachers and pupils has also been shown to be 'asymmetrical' in terms of the unequal distribution (in favour of the teacher) of speaking turns, topic control and evaluative comments (see, among many others, Sinclair and Coulthard 1975; Edwards and Furlong 1978; Torrance and Pryor 1998).

4 Similar 'three-cornered' interactions do occur in other settings, however. Silverman (1987) has analysed interactions between doctors, parents and adolescent children in paediatric medical consultations concerning the management of diabetes. I am indebted to Silverman for unravelling the complexity of these interactions, in particular to his identification of the 'double binds' that they create for the participants.

5 Of 184 consultations, 126 exhibited this episodic structure. Most of the remainder took the form that we called 'socratic dialogue', where the teacher took the student through a series of 'leading questions designed to establish key points concerning behaviour or progress. Despite their dialogic structure, these consultations were strongly teacher-controlled (see MacLure and Walker 1999).

6 There were a few interesting departures from this pattern of minimal responses in opening episodes. One occurred in a consultation where it emerged later that the student's mother had a very clear agenda, which brought her into conflict with the teacher's assessment of her son. She responded immediately to the teacher's opening statement with a 'news receipt' rather than a minimal response:

   T   . . . well, Jake's, he's doing very well.
   M → Is he?
   T   He got 63% in a recent test, which compares, you know, it's on the same standard as his test marks for last year, erm . . . and . . . I think he should aim to go for a grade A because he's capable of getting it.
   M   What that's a B is it?

It is possible that this marked response is an early indication of 'trouble to come' in the consultation and, therefore, a potential challenge to the teacher's expert status. Note that it prompts a justification from the teacher.

7 The teachers in our study appeared to have an agenda of issues that provided the basic structure for their diagnoses, which they 'ran through' with each

parent. So, for example, a year 7 special needs teacher tended to include in her diagnoses: a report on the child's reading age as measured on reading tests; a description of the group in which the child had been placed (lower/ middle/upper; a 'nice' group); a description of the student's behaviour in the group or in class; and a general statement (usually positive) about how well the child was 'coping'. Other teachers had their own agendas, partly linked to the year group in question. Thus teachers of year 10 students generally included a prediction of the GCSE examination grade that the student might attain.

8 Teachers sometimes handed 'the floor' over to parents explicitly, with invitations such as 'Do you have any questions?', 'Was there anything you wanted to talk about', etc.

9 Parents who took part in the follow-up interviews confirmed their resistance to 'good news' stories. One father, for example, approved the fact that 'a couple of alarm bells' had been rung at the recent parents' evening: 'To be honest, up to the last one I've tended to find them a waste of time. 'Cause they'd all say he was doing very well. "Just keep it up. Lovely boy"'. This accords with other work on parent–teacher consultations, which has reported that parents find little value in 'progress satisfactory' messages (Clark and Power 1998: 45).

10 My commentary here is directly influenced by Carolyn Baker's (2000) description of the 'two Donnas' in her analysis of a parent–teacher consultation.

11 Conversation analysts would consider this to be a very unfaithful appropriation indeed, since it rides roughshod over some fundamental tenets, such as the proscription on using social and sociological categories (such as 'power' or 'identity'), unless there is evidence in the data that the *participants* are orienting to such abstractions. See Hutchby and Wooffitt (1998) for an introduction to conversation analysis and Appendix 1 of this book.

Chapter 4

1 It should be noted that the papers usually quoted counter-arguments from other professional 'experts', notably Professors Margaret Brown and Michael Bassey. However, their remarks did not attain the same intertextual afterlife as those of Pring and Hargreaves, the hostile witnesses from the elite universities (Pring was Professor of Education at Oxford, and Hargreaves at Cambridge, at the time in question).

2 Consider the following example, one of many that could be cited: 'Academic jargon: how to publish it: Peter Jones aims a custard pie at practitioners of cultural studies and their pretentious gibberish', *The Times*, 25 May 1996.

3 See, for example, Nespor and Barber (1991) on the textual operations used in an influential article by Lee Schulman.

4 Tooley was not a professor at the time the *New Statesman* article was published. He was appointed to a chair shortly afterwards.

5 This contradiction is contained, to a certain extent, within the recommendation of '*patient* application' of these disciplines in third-way research. Ball and Bourdieu would presumably be subject to critique, not because they exemplify

economic or philosophical disciplines, but because they do not exemplify 'patient' or otherwise proper applications of these.

6 Pigiaki (1995), for example, identifies an 'ideological gap' between Hargreaves' earlier and later career.

Chapter 5

1 The rhetorical nature of texts is recognized in the concern with meeting the needs of different research 'audiences' (see, for example, BERA 1999), although this is usually framed in terms of unstated assumptions that there is an intact 'core' of meaning or findings, and that it is just a matter of finding the right language to express these 'clearly'. Chapter 6 presents a critique of such assumptions.

2 The meaning of this statement by Derrida has been much debated. Indeed, it has become one of those 'hot spots' where criticism, and defence, of deconstruction and postmodernism concentrates. See Vicki Kirby (1997) for a discussion.

3 The 'obviousness' of this point is, of course, heightened by my juxtaposition of two fragments that were originally separated by more than thirty pages of text.

4 A linguistic analysis of the two passages would shed light on how these effects of concrete and abstract, factual and theoretical, descriptive and analytic are produced. Without embarking on a thorough analysis, we can note some key points. The vocabulary of the first fragment consists of relatively familiar, non-technical words. Grammatically, the verb processes take the form of 'direct actions' involving specified 'Participants', including a human Agent (see Lemke 1995: 60). The second fragment, by contrast, does not refer to concrete particulars or observable actions. It contains recognizably 'academic' words (intellectual goods, complex totality) and assumes familiarity with the concepts and arguments of other scholars. Grammatically, there are no direct actions or human actors. Instead, there are 'abstract relations', carried by a quite complex clause structure. This second fragment has many of the features that Lemke describes as typical of 'technical' discourse. One feature of such discourse, according to Lemke, is that it can be difficult to understand by the 'uninitiated', because of its 'thematic condensation'. This, roughly, means the packaging of complex in-formation into abbreviated grammatical structures, requiring large amounts of prior 'intertextual' knowledge on the part of the reader to fill in the thematic gaps (such as, here, knowledge of anthropology and exchange theory).

5 The sentence that this footnote is appended to is itself firmly within the conventions of 'technical' discourse, which should alert readers to one of the sources of authority to which this book repeatedly aspires.

6 Bruno Latour (e.g. 1986) has made comparable claims for the mixing of genres in the supposedly 'pure' genre of scientific writing.

7 This is the book that was extolled by Chris Woodhead in his attack on more recent educational research, as discussed in Chapter 4.

8 Shostak explicitly invokes the 'visitor', as does Hargreaves in the paragraph which precedes the one quoted here: '[. . .] to the visitor a sense of dirt, dreariness and sometimes squalor prevails' (Hargreaves 1967: 1).

9 In the case of the third passage, the expectations set up in Marjorie Shostak's description of the !Kung village are specifically *not* satisfied, as explained later. However, they are in play at the point at which the passage occurs in her book.

10 It hardly needs saying that the 'oedipal logic of realist narrativity' is not only enacted by male writers.

11 I don't know whether Kavanagh (1995) is reporting on a conversation that actually took place or, indeed, whether he wants readers to *believe* that he is reporting on an actual conversation. He introduces it as 'a conversation which took place recently in a Brooklyn apartment, while a Puerto Rican family, their guest, and several mice were watching a video of *Demons II*' (p. 317). The problem is the watching mice. Do they testify to ethnographic veracity (of a rather whimsical type)? Or to Disney-type fantasy?

12 Such links with other genres have also been intentionally developed. Researchers and evaluators at the Centre for Applied Research in Education in the UK in the 1970s and 1980s looked to journalism and documentary film making, as well as populist urban sociologists such as Studs Terkel, for styles of representing research in ways that would be engaging and accessible to sponsors and non-academic audiences.

13 As Pratt notes, the Harvard scholars were so intent on dissociating themselves from colonial discourses, that they rejected the widely used European word, 'bushmen', in favour of !Kung.

14 This phrase is taken from the title of an article by Gillian Fuller (2000).

15 In *Of Grammatology*, from which this quotation comes, Derrida (1976) explores the links between anthropology and writing. These 'zero-degree' societies do not have writing systems and Derrida pursues, via an extended reading of Levi-Strauss, the intimate associations between writing, violence, penetration and anthropological guilt. Chapter 6 explores the ways in which writing has traditionally been seen as a threat to all things 'natural', 'pure' or original.

16 Pratt's study forms one chapter in an edited book that came to be seen as something of a watershed – *Writing Culture: The Poetics and Politics of Ethnography*, edited by James Clifford and George Marcus (1986). This book, and the gendered politics of anthropological writing which it sparked, are discussed again in Chapter 8.

17 Compare this with the example of news coverage of the Gulf War in Chapter 1, as an instance of the construction of binary oppositions.

18 If one were to go further in reading this extract, it might be possible to explain its ambiguities in terms of the 'liminality' of action research; that is, its location on the boundaries of the discourses of theory and practice, and its somewhat ambivalent status with respect both to academia and schools. See Stronach and MacLure (1997: ch. 7).

19 This would be the case even where the researcher and subject *coincide* – for example, in autobiographical research or in instances of 'reflective practice', as later chapters will make clear.

20 Delamont *et al.* (2000) trace the ethnographic origins of educational research and its differential trajectories in the USA and Europe.

Chapter 6

1 Other writing practices relating to research might include: taking notes of project meetings; constructing websites; sending emails; doing keyword searches of library catalogues; taking part in discussion groups; designing seminars and student assignments arising from one's research; marking those assignments; writing examiners' reports on dissertations, and so on.

2 Derrida's deconstruction of writing, and its significance in the development of Western thought, can be found in three books, all originally published in 1967: *Writing and Difference* (Derrida 1978b), *Of Grammatology* (1976) and *Speech and Phenomena* (1973). See Gayatri Spivak's preface to *Of Grammatology* for an extended discussion of the major threads in Derrida's treatment, and Alan Bass' introduction to *Writing and Difference* for an explication of key terms in Derrida's work on writing. Writing is also the subject of 'Plato's Pharmacy' in *Dissemination* (1981). Writing, in the Derridean sense, would also include not only speech, but non-verbal 'inscription' of all kinds, for example the 'language' of film, music, sculpture, dance and military strategy (e.g. Derrida 1976: 9).

3 Compare Woodhead's antipathy towards academic writing with this complaint by Condillac about the writing crimes of philosophers in eighteenth-century France: 'Regarding writing as below them, they have long made it their business to be unintelligible [. . .] That is why their works have produced so many frivolous disputes and contributed so little to the progress of the art of reasoning' (quoted in Derrida 1980: 126).

4 However, as Barbara Johnson (1995) notes, the 'privilege' accorded speech has never been unambiguous. She reminds us that writing was central in colonial domination, ensuring that 'European civilization functioned with great effectiveness by remote control' (p. 47). She also points to the notorious history of social repression through the denial of access to writing to subordinate groups, such as American slaves and women. The negative status of writing as 'dead letter' can also switch to a 'positive' charge in the speech/writing dichotomy when the *permanence* of records is at issue. Harry Torrance (personal communication) points to the tradition in some cultures of tattooing one's lineage on the body: a permanent yet transportable record, in contrast to the ephemeral (and retractable) status of spoken claims. These observations about the 'covert privilege' of writing (Johnson 1995: 47) underline the logic of *différance* at work in the speech/writing opposition; indeed, they demonstrate the propensity of *différance* to destabilize *both* sides of binary distinctions.

5 This quotation was discussed briefly in Chapter 1. The reference to boats is part of an extended nautical metaphor, in which Hammersley argues the need to preserve the structural integrity of the 'boat' of ethnography, even though it will be necessary to replace some individual planks over time.

Chapter 7

1 See, for example, Butt *et al.* (1992): 'The notion of the teacher's voice is important in that it carries the tone, the language, the quality, the feelings that are conveyed in the way a teacher speaks or writes. In a political sense the notion of the teacher voice addresses the right to speak and be represented' (p. 57).

2 'Implication' is itself one of the words in the web of fabric-words with which this chapter plays, with etymological links to French and Latin words for 'fold'.

3 Woods (1993: 453) invokes the distinction between the enduring 'substantial' self and the 'situationist' selves – that is, the 'guises' that the individual adopts in particular situations.

4 I have selected an article by Peter Woods partly because he has been one of the leading developers of qualitative research methodology in education from the mid-1970s and can, therefore, be regarded as exemplary in his approach to issues. The article that is the subject of this chapter is not, therefore, offered as unusual or extreme in its metaphorical structure. On the contrary, many of the metaphors used by Woods are, as noted, commonplace in research writing.

5 Derrida (1998) associates 'chemistry' with those sciences, social as well as natural, which search for the 'simple and the ordinary'. He is keen to dissociate deconstruction from chemistry, despite their seemingly common projects of 'desedimenting' and 'undoing': 'Nothing is further from deconstruction, despite certain appearances, nothing is more foreign to it than chemistry, that science of simples' (p. 27).

6 The quoted phrase comes from Spivak's discussion of the concept of the 'engineer' in Derrida's work (Spivak 1976: xix). Derrida, after Levi-Strauss, contrasts the *engineer* and the *bricoleur* as knowledge seekers in the human and natural sciences. In contrast to the *bricoleur*, a kind of DIY expert who makes do and mends with whatever comes to hand, the engineer seeks means–ends solutions via technical mastery of a universe, which is, in principle at least, knowable. Spivak and Derrida argue, however, that the opposition between *bricoleur* and engineer is unstable, in that all knowledge is ultimately *bricolage*, since absolute certainty is, in principle, impossible.

7 This is the title of a chapter in Derrida's (1976) *Of Grammatology*. The phrase is taken from Rousseau. See Barbara Johnson's translator's note in Derrida (1981: 110, fn. 16).

8 See the Liddell-Scott-Jones lexicon of Classical Greek, online at http://www.rocq.inria.fr/~kloukina/proselhnos.html.

9 Bass (1978), discussing Derrida's chaining of text–tissue–weaving, notes: 'the word *texte* is derived from the Latin *textus*, meaning cloth (*tissu*), and from *texere*, to weave' (p. xiii).

10 Rambo Ronai uses the metaphor of sketching, rather than weaving, in her notion of the 'layered text'.

11 'I take the self out of itself and clothe it in a sequined négligé [*sic*] (a négligé as impenetrable as steel) to insinuate that psychological, sociological and philosophical works of self on self are too heavy for everyday life, like the

suits of deep-sea divers. No doubt this will raise the eyebrows of pinstriped selves everywhere' (Travers 1993: 128).

Chapter 8

1 This chapter is based on a paper presented to an invitational conference on 'Feminism and Educational Research' held at Manchester Metropolitan University, UK, May 1999.

2 I don't mean by this that women have been physically prevented from putting pen to paper, although it may be the case that women often find it harder than men to find and protect a 'space' for writing in their domestic arrangements.

3 The titles of this and the following sub-sections ('Writing lesson 1, 2', etc.) carry a trace of the writings of two very powerful male 'ancestors' – Jacques Derrida and Claude Levi-Strauss (see Derrida 1976: 101–40) – as does this chapter and the book as a whole. One of the ironies that this chapter enacts is that its identification of the dilemmas facing women writing under the sign of male theory is itself indebted to such theory, in the form of Derrida's path-breaking work on writing. 'Writing lesson 4' discusses this issue further.

4 This is, of course, an authoritative and singular story that could have been told otherwise. Moreover, it draws on Ruth Behar's account, which she herself acknowledges represents *Writing Culture* as a 'monolithic text' (Behar 1995: 24, fn. 8). Behar notes that not all the chapters in the collection fit neatly within Clifford's textualist rubric. She argues that the book nevertheless came to figure as a 'programmatic treatise', 'read through the filter of Clifford's introduction'. It is certainly the case that the book is still widely cited and not just in anthropological circles.

5 Clifford's justification was prompted by Barbara Babcock's critical review of the manuscript (see Babcock 1993: 64, fn. 2). The one woman contributor was Mary Louise Pratt, whose contribution was discussed at some length in Chapter 5 of this book.

6 Women anthropologists who had attempted textual innovations, wrote Clifford (1986a), 'had not done so on feminist grounds', while those who wrote as feminists had not produced 'either unconventional forms of writing or a developed reflection on ethnographic textuality as such' (pp. 21–2).

7 Which is not to say that the 'erasure' of women's writing, or the adoption of a male-theoretic voice, is only practised by male academics: as Babcock notes, feminist academics may also be practitioners. I would also have to con-clude, reviewing my own work, that there is a lot of the male-theoretic voice in it, especially in its uncritical championing of 'play' without recognizing the differential positioning of men and women as 'playful' subjects.

8 These can be found in the anthology edited by Ruth Behar and Deborah Gordon, *Women Writing Culture* (1995), an explicit rejoinder to Clifford and Marcus, as the title indicates.

9 It could, however, be argued that the feminist readings engage more closely, and in more detail, with the specifics of these writings as *texts*.

10 This term was used by Elaine Showalter (1987).

11 See also Elam (1994) and the anthology edited by Feder *et al.* (1997).

12 Braidotti finds Foucault and Deleuze to have less toxic implications for feminism, however, because of their greater emphasis on transgression and disper-
sion as the enduring 'conditions' of power and subjectivity.

13 Braidotti is referring to the film *Tootsie*, directed by Sidney Pollack (1982), in
which Dustin Hoffman played an actor who impersonates a woman to advance his career, but who 'learns' the much deeper lesson of how wonderful
women are. I hated it.

14 You probably shouldn't make a joke if you have to explain it, but I couldn't
resist. So for those whose age or nationality makes the allusion meaningless,
Gregory's Girl is a film directed by Bill Forsyth (1980), in which the awkward
teenage hero, Gregory, admires and desires the beautiful and confident girl
who outshines all the boys on the school football (soccer) team. Gregory
doesn't get that girl; his real girl turns out to be the friend who was under his
nose all along. I really liked it.

Chapter 9

1 This chapter should have seen the reproduction of the pictures that are
(mimetically) rendered here in words. But the technicalities, the cost and the
time involved in gaining permissions to reproduce them from museums and
publishers proved too much for this author. I have, where possible, provided
directions to internet websites where the images can be viewed.

2 An example is the *Cubiculum* (bedroom) from the villa at Boscoreale,
near Pompeii, installed at the Metropolitan Museum, New York. This can
be viewed electronically in the museum's online collection. Go to http://
www.metmuseum.org/collections/ and follow the link to the 'Greek and
Roman Art' collection.

3 This appetite for mimesis, parody, artifice and simulation, says Bryson, was
an expression and exploration of *excess*. Excess in the sphere of representation mirrored the socio-economic excess of Imperial Rome, where colossal
accumulation had taken the affluent consumer well beyond the satisfaction
of basic needs. Wealth and representation were intimately related, in a time
and culture that had outstripped necessity and constraint. Both had 'the
capacity for exceeding the real and for creating a fictional expansion that
transcends the limitations of appetite, the parameters of space, and the ontology of the actual world, (Bryson 1990: 51–2).

4 This mimetic art goes back even further in time. Commentators often mention
the Roman mosaic entitled *The Unswept Dining Room* from the second century
BC (e.g. Battersby 1974: 9), which depicts the detritus of a meal scattered
where it has apparently fallen on the floor, each scrap casting its illusionistic
shadow. Moreover, the Roman pavement is *itself* a copy of a 'lost' Greek
original. We are back with copies and doubles again – and copies that are,
moreover, more real than their originals (which were themselves simulations),
since the copy endures while the 'original' is irretrievable. An even older
example, albeit one that only endures in *written* accounts, is the much-quoted
account by Pliny the Elder, of the grapes painted by the ancient Greek artist

Zeuxis, which were so realistic that birds tried to eat them. Zeuxis' triumph was short-lived, however; when he asked for the curtain over the painting by his rival Parhassios to be drawn back, he discovered that the curtain was itself a painted illusion. Bryson (1990: 32) argues that most commentators have overlooked the multiple levels of reality invoked in (Pliny's description of) the paintings, which apparently took part on a stage, so that the paintings were actually backdrops in an already illusionistic (theatrical) space. So Parhassios' fake curtain was also a 'real' curtain. And the 'real' birds which flew in to peck Zeuxis' fake grapes must have traversed several boundaries, from 'pre-cultural' (natural) to cultural space, to the stage, to the illusions embedded within that fictional space.

5 The bible is held by Corpus Christi College (MS CCC 1 f.215v). The image can be viewed in the Bridgman Art Library, Item 95500, accessible via Grove Art: http://www.groveart.com/index.html.

6 Cornelis Gijsbrecht's *The Reverse of a Framed Painting*, 1670/72, oil on canvas, 66.6 × 87.0 cm, Statens Museum for Kunst, Copenhagen. An electronic version can be viewed online at http://www.oxygen.force9.co.uk/archive/issue2/temp/gijsbrechts.htm.

7 One of Gijsbrechts' letter rack paintings can be seen online at http://www.oxygen.force9.co.uk/archive/issue2/temp/gijsbrechts.htm (*Trompe l'oeil of a Letter Rack with Christian V's Proclamation*, 1671, oil on canvas, 138.5 × 181.5 cm, Statens Museum for Kunst, Copenhagen). Other typical subjects for *trompe l'oeil* across the centuries include violins, pipes, random objects on shelves and in niches, painters' accoutrements and paper money.

8 The shock, as Bryson and Baudrillard both intimate, is something to do with death too. And no doubt with orgasm. Indeed, the 'sudden laugh from nowhere' is Georges Bataille's phrase, quoted by Michael Taussig (see immediately below), and invokes Bataille's famous description of orgasm as 'dying laughing and laughing [at] dying' (quoted by Derrida 1993: 201). Derrida's wholly un-summarizable work, 'The Double Session,' from which this quote comes, is an extended play with notions of mimesis, illusion, copies without originals and the (im)possibility of reference – all elaborated from a reading of a short piece by Mallarmé on the death of Pierrot as performed by a mime artist. You can see death, orgasm and the sudden laugh in this sentence: 'Pierrot then mimes all the way to the "supreme spasm" the rising of ecstatic hilarity' (Derrida 1993: 201). Derrida refers to the 'false bottoms', 'abysses' and *trompe l'oeil* of Mallarmé's piece (p. 202).

9 I found several websites advertising 'traditional' molas for sale. Taussig (1993) notes the (mimetic) conjuncture of colonialism, capitalism and patriarchy in this commodification of the molas: 'Since US-mediated goods have passed into Cuna purview by means of Cuna men working in the Canal Zone since the 1930s, thanks to their convivial relationship with the United States, the chests (and backs) of the women have formed a species of trade catalog' (p. 228). Interestingly, I found several embroidery websites offering mola patterns, alongside other categories such as 'traditional' American quilts, etc. So now we have, presumably, Western women mimicking the traditional craft work of the Cuna women. And, as Taussig also notes, although the molas have become *the* signifier of Cuna 'tradition', this tradition probably goes back

only to the nineteenth century, and has always depended on traded goods from 'outside' (scissors, cloth, needles, etc.). Once again, therefore, the narrative of tradition and origins turns out to be considerably less than 'pure'.

10 Taussig (1993) discusses (and deconstructs) the notion of 'first contact' in detail, referring among other instances to Darwin's account of his arrival in Tierra del Fuego (pp. 73–9).

11 Even where methodology claims postmodern allegiance to notions of multiple selves, I suspect that there is often a tacit assumption that these must be, somehow, 'real' multiple selves – not selves assumed and discarded in a spirit of mimicry and emulation.

12 I am indebted to Karl Nunkoosing for helping me to 'see' the mimesis in research.

13 Interestingly, Bal is drawing on literary theory here to explore the notion of quotation in *painting*.

14 The term 'profane illumination', used by Taussig (1993) as one of several phrases to describe the effect of mimesis, comes originally from Walter Benjamin (1978). See Cohen (1993) for a discussion of the significance of this notion in Benjamin's 'Gothic Marxism', and its debt to the Surrealist project of releasing 'the energies of intoxication for the revolution' (Benjamin, quoted in Cohen 1993: 9).

Chapter 10

1 See Stronach and MacLure (1997: 1–13) for a discussion of the significance of 'opening' in deconstruction.

2 This, it will be recalled, is the title of Slavoj Zizek's (1991) book on Lacan. Zizek introduces key elements of Lacan's thought, including the principle of 'looking awry' itself, by 'looking awry' at Lacan through popular film (especially Hitchcock) and fiction.

3 Recall the discussion in Chapter 6 of Rorty's (1978) version of the philosopher's fantasy, of injecting knowledge straight into the brain.

4 *Buffy the Vampire Slayer* television series, Warner Bros, Series 3, Episode 18, 'Earshot'.

5 There is also a 'gynophobic' interpretation of the Medusa story, which Calvino does not mention – that it is a myth about the threat of the *femme fatale* and the dangers of looking (cf. Bal 1999: 135).

6 See, for example, Derrida (1990) and Stronach and MacLure (1997, 'Opening') for a discussion of this issue.

7 For some examples of educational research texts that play, intentionally, with alternative genres and formats, see Lather and Smithies (1997), the final chapter in Stronach and MacLure (1997), Clough (2000), McCoy (2000) and Rambo Ronai (1998).

8 The 'lucky find' (in French, *le trouvaille*) is a keyword in the surrealism of André Breton and his circle, as is the notion of the 'fascination' of the lucky find. The discussion in this final section is informed by Breton's surrealism, as relayed by Margaret Cohen (1993), and carries the traces of a surrealist vocabulary.

9 Krauss was referring specifically to structuralist theory in the early decades of the twentieth century and its 'love of the diagrammatic', but her comments are applicable to the impulse towards abstraction in Enlightenment thought in general.

10 Krauss takes the word *déjouer* from Barthes' discussion of a story by Georges Bataille.

Appendix I

1 Some idea of the different conceptual 'maps' available can be seen in two recent overviews. Wetherell *et al.* (2001: 6) propose 'six, more or less distinct, discourse traditions': 'conversation analysis and ethnomethodology; interactional sociolinguistics and the ethnography of communication; discursive psychology; critical discourse analysis and critical linguistics; Bakhtinian research; Foucauldian research'. Cameron (2001: 48) identifies five 'approaches' to (spoken) discourse analysis: ethnography of speaking, pragmatics, conversation analysis, interactional sociolinguistics and critical discourse analysis.

2 Contestation over terms and allegiances abounds. For example, some of the big names associated with poststructuralism were formerly held to be exponents of structuralism, including Barthes, Lacan and Foucault (see Culler 1983: 25). 'Poststructuralism' is also tangled up with 'postmodernism' – terms that are often used interchangeably, but which, for some authors, have distinct meanings. I have chosen to stick with poststructuralism, since for me it is more closely linked with issues of *textuality*. I have included deconstruction, which informs all aspects of the present book, under the broad umbrella of poststructuralism, whereas others would want to keep the terms apart (e.g. Culler 1983).

3 See Kirby (1997: ch. 1) for an extended discussion of the nature and limits of Saussure's structuralism and its relation to poststructuralism/deconstruction. Culler (1983) explores the relationships among these terms with specific reference to literary theory.

4 'A dominant class isn't a mere abstraction, but neither is it a pre-given entity. For a class to become a dominant class, for it to ensure its domination and for that domination to reproduce itself is certainly the effect of a number of actual pre-meditated tactics operating within the grand strategies that ensure this domination. But between the strategy which fixes, reproduces, multiplies and accentuates existing relations of forces, and the class which thereby finds itself in a ruling position, there is a reciprocal relation of production. One can say that the strategy of moralising the working class is that of the bourgeoisie. One can even say that it's the strategy which allows the bourgeois class to be the bourgeois class and to exercise its domination. But what I don't think one can say is that it's the bourgeois class on the level of its ideology or its economic project which, as a sort of at once real and fictive subject, invented and forcibly imposed this strategy on the working class' (Foucault 1980: 202).

5 Feminist critiques of poststructuralism/postmodernism include Mascia-Lees *et al.* (1989). The limitations – as well as the strengths – of poststructuralism

for black feminism are argued by Patricia Hill Collins (2000). Teresa Ebert (1996) presents a Marxist feminine critique. An ill-informed Marxist critique of postmodernism in educational thinking is offered by Rikowski and McLaren (1999). The simplistic nature of this polemic is highlighted when contrasted with the sophisticated (and no less critical) engagements of Marxist theory with deconstruction in the collection edited by Michael Sprinkler (1999).

6 Poststructural orientations in education have been brought to bear on policy analysis and evaluation (e.g. Ball 1990a; Stronach 1999), curriculum and pedagogy (e.g. Gilbert 1989; Luke and Gore 1992; Davies 1994; Green 1998), teacher education (Britzman 1991), gender (e.g. Walkerdine 1990; Lather 1991; Luke and Gore 1992), queer theory (Britzman 1995; Tierney 1999) and critical race theory (Parker 1998). Works with a specifically methodological slant include St Pierre and Pillow (2000), Stronach and MacLure (1997), Scheurich (1997), Brown and Jones (2001) and Poynton and Lee (2000). Two edited collections of Foucauldian analyses are Ball (1990) and Popkewitz and Brennan (1997). Henriques *et al.* (1998), first published in 1984, remains an outstanding exploration of the significance of Foucault's work for psychology and education.

7 'Working the hyphens' is a phrase coined by Michelle Fine (1994) to invoke a poststructuralist ethic of undecidability in relations between 'self' and 'other' in research. 'Disappointment' and resistance to 'closure' are discussed by Stronach and MacLure (1997: 4–5) as part of a postmodern orientation to research.

8 Books surveying the field of discourse analysis from a linguistic point of view include Shiffrin (1994), Georgakopoulou and Goutsos (1997), Van Dijk (1997) and Cameron (2001). Although the primary orientation in these books is linguistic, the authors also reference other discursive traditions, such as poststructuralism, Bakhtin and the ethnography of communication. This is further evidence of the blurring of the boundaries between disciplines. Wetherell *et al.* (2001) provide a selection of articles exemplifying an even wider range of approaches, although the focus remains predominantly upon empirical analysis of language data.

9 Like Saussure, Searle forms part of the common 'ancestry' that paradoxically *divides* linguists and poststructuralists. Austin's speech act theory was the subject of a deconstructive critique by Derrida, provoking an acerbic exchange with John Searle (see Derrida 1988). Derrida argued that Austin's/Searle's project of formalizing the 'sincerity conditions' for carrying out speech acts was ultimately untenable, since it was always necessary to provide exemption clauses for 'supplementary' cases where speech acts were done 'insincerely' (e.g. on the stage, in jokes, as textbook examples). The boundary between serious and frivolous, sincerity and insincerity, could never, therefore, be permanently fixed through the appliance of science. Derrida's critique of Austin/Searle is worth reading as an exemplary instance of deconstruction, as it shows how 'supplementary' logic always leads to the unsettling of binary oppositions. Later chapters of this book deal with other instances of such supplementary logic.

10 Consider, for instance, Hammersley's (1977) concluding remarks in a study of the 'cultural resources' needed by a class of secondary school students to

answer a teacher's question: 'The methods the pupils must use if they are to answer the teacher's question sustain his claim to legitimately control classroom events. [. . .] The socio-cultural forces operating on this teacher and on others in similar social structural locations need to be explored. It is in this complex of forces that the explanation will lie, though whether these forces can simply be traced back to the nature of capitalism or industrialism remains to be seen' (pp. 83–4).

11 The first, 1989 version of the UK National Curriculum for English similarly reflected the opening up of the language curriculum to the new discursive complexity envisaged for the 'post-Fordist', post-industrial workforce, in its expansive range of speaking and listening attainment targets. The examples of oral language activities invoked a population of young service workers, middle managers, advertising executives and market researchers – flourishing slides, overhead transparencies, diagrams and databases, as they chaired meetings, designed ad campaigns, conducted surveys, presented scientific reports and interviewed potential employees for mini-companies (see MacLure 1994b).

12 One could, of course, only 'say' this from the perspective of *one particular 'side'* in the opposition – that is, from the 'side' occupied by poststructuralism.

13 Other linguists whose work has been described as critical discourse analysis (CDA), or which has affinities with it, include Ruth Wodak, Jay Lemke, James Gee, Colin Lankshear, Malcolm Coulthard and Carmen Caldas-Coulthard. The work of many, though not all, of those linguists associated with CDA is represented in a four-volume edited collection entitled *Critical Discourse Analysis* (Toolan 2002), which brings together publications previously scattered across journals and book chapters, together with key texts by theoretical 'precursors'.

14 Widdowson (1995) questions the validity of critical discourse analysis from within the discipline of applied linguistics, suggesting that analysts often impose their own interpretations on data, in line with their political investments. Hammersley (1997) makes a similar charge.

15 Further studies of educational issues from a conversation analysis/ethnomethodological perspective include Cuff and Hustler (1981), Heap (1985), Cicourel *et al.* (1974), Payne and Cuff (1982), French and MacLure (1981) and Baker (2000).

16 Watson is citing Baker and Freebody here, who were in turn citing an earlier author.

17 Consider, for instance, Watson's (1992) summary of Sacks' analytic practice as: 'rigorous, exhaustive, repeated and reduplicable analytical inspection which in turn could sustain systematically demonstrated statements that were amenable to "checking out" by others' (p. 262).

18 The phrase 'jump clear' comes from Malcolm Bowie (1991), writing of Lacan's notion of theory: 'The analyst who tries to jump clear of his own language as he uses it – or tries to build within that language a permanent conceptual home – is a charlatan or a fool' (p. 12).

References

Agard, J. (1985) *Mangoes and Bullets: Selected and New Poems, 1972–84*. London: Pluto Press.

Atkinson, P. (1990) *The Ethnographic Imagination: Textual Constructions of Reality*. London: Routledge.

Attridge, D. (1996) Expecting the unexpected in Coetzee's 'Master of Petersburg' and Derrida's recent writings, in J. Brannigan, R. Robins and J. Wolfreys (eds) *Applying: To Derrida*. London: Macmillan.

Austin, J.L. (1962) *How to Do Things with Words*. Oxford: Clarendon Press.

Babcock, B. (1993) Feminisms/pretexts: fragments, questions and reflections, *Anthropological Quarterly*, 66(2): 59–66.

Babcock, B. (1995) 'Not in the absolute singular': re-reading Ruth Benedict, in R. Behar and D. Gordon (eds) *Women Writing Culture*. Berkeley, CA: UCLA Press.

Baker, C. (1984) The 'search for adultness': membership work in adolescent-adult talk, *Human Studies*, 7(3/4): 301–23.

Baker, C. (2000) Locating culture in action: membership categorisation in texts and talk, in A. Lee and C. Poynton (eds) *Culture and Text: Discourse and Methodology in Social Research and Cultural Studies*. Lanham, MD: Rowman & Littlefield.

Baker, C. and Freebody, P. (1987) Constituting the child in beginning school reading books, *British Journal of Sociology of Education*, 8(1): 55–76.

Baker, C. and Keogh, J. (1995) Accounting for achievement in parent–teacher interviews, *Human Studies*, 18(2/3): 263–300.

Bakhtin, M. (1981) *The Dialogic Imagination* (edited by M. Holquist). Austin, TX: University of Texas Press.

Bal, M. (1999) *Quoting Caravaggio: Contemporary Art, Preposterous History*. Chicago, IL: University of Chicago Press.

Ball, S.J. (1981) *Beachside Comprehensive: A Case Study of Secondary Schooling*. Cambridge: Cambridge University Press.

Ball, S.J. (ed.) (1990a) *Foucault and Education: Disciplines and Knowledge*. London: Routledge.

Ball, S.J. (1990b) *Politics and Policymaking in Education: Explorations in Policy Sociology*. London: Routledge.

Ball, S.J. (1993) Education policy, power relations and teachers' work, *British Journal of Educational Studies*, 41(2): 106–21.

Ball, S.J., Kenny, A. and Gardiner, D. (1990) Literacy, politics and the teaching of English, in I. Goodson and P. Medway (eds) *Bringing English to Order: The History and Politics of a School Subject*. Lewes: Falmer Press.

Barnes, D. (1976) *From Communication to Curriculum*. Harmondsworth: Penguin.

Barthes, R. (1967) *Writing Degree Zero* (translated by A. Laver and C. Smith). London: Cape.

Barthes, R. (1968) L'effet du réel, *Communications*, 4: 84–9.

Barthes, R. (1990) *The Pleasure of the Text* (translated by R. Miller). Oxford: Blackwell.

Bass, A. (1978) Introduction, in J. Derrida, *Writing and Difference* (translated by A. Bass). London: Routledge.

Bassey, M. (1993) Some FRIPPERIES and FLAWS of research papers, *Research Intelligence*, 48: 21.

Bates, I. (1998) The 'empowerment' dimension in the GNVQ: a critical exploration of discourse, pedagogic apparatus and school implementation, *Evaluation and Research in Education*, 12(1): 7–22.

Battersby, M. (1974) *Trompe L'Oeil. The Eye Deceived*. London: Academy Editions.

Baudrillard, J. (1996) *The Perfect Crime* (translated by C. Turner). London: Verso.

Baudrillard, J. (1998) The trompe-l'oeil, in N. Bryson (ed.) *Calligram: Essays in New Art History from France*. Cambridge: Cambridge University Press.

Baynham, M. (1995) *Literacy Practices: Investigating Literacy in Social Context*. London: Longman.

Behar, R. (1995) Introduction: out of exile, in R. Behar and D. Gordon (eds) *Women Writing Culture*. Berkeley, CA: UCLA Press.

Behar, R. and Gordon, D. (eds) (1995) *Women Writing Culture*. Berkeley, CA: UCLA Press.

Belsey, C. (1980) *Critical Practice*. London: Methuen.

Benjamin, W. (1978) *Reflections* (edited by P. Demetz and translated by E. Jephcott). New York: Harcourt Brace Jovanovich.

Benjamin, W. (1979) *One Way Street and Other Writings* (translated by E. Jephcott and K. Shorter). London: New Left Books.

BERA (British Educational Research Association) (1999) *Good Practice in Educational Research Writing*. Southwell, Notts: BERA.

Bernstein, B. (1971) *Class, Codes and Control*, Vol. 1. London: Routledge & Kegan Paul.

Bhabha, H. (1994) *The Location of Culture*. London: Routledge.

Bowie, M. (1991) *Lacan*. London: Fontana.

Braidotti, R. (1991) *Patterns of Dissonance*. London: Polity Press.

Breton, A. (1986) *Manifestos of Surrealism* (translated by R. Seaver and H.R. Lane). Ann Arbor, MI: University of Michigan Press.

Brice Heath, S. (1983) *Ways with Words: Language, Life and Work in Communities and Classrooms*. Cambridge: Cambridge University Press.

Britzman, D. (1991) *Practice Makes Practice: A Critical Study of Learning to Teach*. Albany, NY: SUNY Press.

Britzman, D. (1995) Is there a queer pedagogy? Or, stop reading straight, *Educational Theory*, 45(2): 151–65.

Britzman, D. (1998) *Lost Subjects, Contested Objects: Toward a Psychoanalytic Inquiry of Learning*. Albany, NY: SUNY Press.

Britzman, D. (2000) 'The question of belief': writing poststructural ethnography, in E.A. St. Pierre and W. Pillow (eds) *Working the Ruins: Feminist Poststructural Theory and Methods in Education*. New York: Routledge.

Brown, T. and Jones, L. (2001) *Action Research & Postmodernism: Congruence & Critique*. Buckingham: Open University Press.

Bryson, N. (1990) *Looking at the Overlooked: Four Essays on Still Life Painting*. London: Reaktion Books.

Butler, J. (1993) *Bodies that Matter: On the Discursive Limits of 'Sex'*. London: Routledge.

Butler, J. (1997) *Excitable Speech: A Politics of the Performative*. New York: Routledge.

Butler, J. and Scott, J. (eds) (1992) *Feminists Theorize the Political*. London: Routledge.

Butt, R., Raymond, D., McCue, G. and Yamagishi, L. (1992) Collaborative autobiography and the teacher's voice, in I. Goodson (ed.) *Studying Teachers' Lives*. London: Routledge.

Button, G. (1991) Conversation in a series, in D. Boden and D.W. Zimmerman (eds) *Talk and Social Structure: Studies in Ethnomethodology and Conversation Analysis*. Cambridge: Polity Press.

Calvino, I. (1994) *Cosmicomics*. London: Picador.

Calvino, I. (1996) *Six Memos for the Next Millennium*. London: Vintage.

Cameron, D. (1992) *Feminism and Linguistic Theory*, 2nd edn. London: Macmillan.

Cameron, D. (2001) *Working with Spoken Discourse*. London: Sage.

Cameron, D. and Bourne, J. (1989) No common ground: Kingman, grammar and the nation, *Language and Education*, 2(1): 147–60.

Casey, K. (1990) Teaching as mother: curriculum theorizing in the life histories of contemporary women teachers, *Cambridge Journal of Education*, 20(3): 301–20.

Chomsky, N. (1965) *Aspects of the Theory of Syntax*. Cambridge, MA: MIT Press.

Cicourel, A., Jennings, K.W., Jennings, S.H.M. *et al.* (eds) (1974) *Language Use and School Performance*. New York: Academic Press.

Clandinin, D.J. and Connelly, F.M. (2000) *Narrative Inquiry: Experience and Story in Qualitative Research*. New York: Jossey-Bass.

Clark, A. and Power, S. (1998) *Could Do Better. School Reports and Parents Evenings: A Study of Secondary School Practice*. London: RISE.

Clifford, J. (1986a) Introduction, in J. Clifford and G. Marcus (eds) *Writing Culture: The Poetics and Politics of Ethnography*. Berkeley, CA: UCLA Press.

Clifford, J. (1986b) On ethnographic allegory, in J. Clifford and G. Marcus (eds) *Writing Culture: The Poetics and Politics of Ethnography*. Berkeley, CA: UCLA Press.

Clifford, J. (1990) Notes on field(notes), in R. Sanjek (ed.) *Fieldnotes: The Makings of Anthropology*. Ithaca, NY: Cornell University Press.

Clifford, J. and Marcus, G. (eds) (1986) *Writing Culture: The Poetics and Politics of Ethnography*. Berkeley, CA: UCLA Press.

Clough, P.T. (2000) *Autoaffection: Unconscious Thought in the Age of Teletechnology*. Minneapolis, MI: University of Minnesota Press.

Cohen, M. (1993) *Profane Illumination: Walter Benjamin and the Paris of Surrealist Revolution*. Berkeley, CA: University of California Press.

Collins, P.H. (2000) What's going on? Black feminist thought and the politics of postmodernism, in E.A. St Pierre and W. Pillow (eds) *Working the Ruins: Feminist Poststructuralist Theory and Methods in Education.* New York: Routledge.

Crapanzano, V. (1986) Hermes' dilemma: the masking of subversion in ethnographic description, in J. Clifford and G. Marcus (eds) *Writing Culture: The Poetics and Politics of Ethnography.* Berkeley, CA: UCLA Press.

Crowley, T. (1989) *Standard English and the Politics of Language.* Urbana, IL: University of Illinois Press.

Crowley, T. (1996) *Language in History: Theories and Texts.* London: Routledge.

Crozier, G. (1998) Parents and schools: partnership or surveillance?, *Journal of Education Policy,* 13(1): 125–36.

Cuff, E.C. and Hustler, D.E. (1981) Stories and story time in an infant classroom, in P. French and M. MacLure (eds) *Adult Child Conversation at Home and at School.* London: Croom Helm.

Culler, J. (1983) *On Deconstruction: Theory and Criticism after Structuralism.* London: Routledge.

David, M. (1993) *Parents, Gender and Education Reform.* Cambridge: Polity Press.

Davies, B. (1993) *Shards of Glass: Children Reading and Writing Beyond Gendered Identities.* Sydney, NSW: Allen & Unwin.

Davies, B. (1994) *Poststructuralist Theory and Classroom Practice.* Geelong, VIC: Deakin University Press.

DeCastell, S.C., Luke, A. and Luke, C. (eds) (1989) *Language, Authority and Criticism: Readings on the School Textbook.* London: Falmer Press.

Delamont, S., Coffee, A. and Atkinson, P. (2000) The twilight years? Educational ethnography and the five moments model, *International Journal of Qualitative Studies in Education,* 13(1): 223–38.

De Lillo, D. (1998) *Underworld.* London: Picador.

Derrida, J. (1973) *Speech and Phenomena and Other Essays on Husserl's Theory of Signs.* Evanston, IL: Northwestern University Press.

Derrida, J. (1976) *Of Grammatology* (translated by G.C. Spivak). Baltimore, MD: Johns Hopkins University Press.

Derrida, J. (1978a) *Spurs: Nietzsche's Styles* (translated by B. Harlow). Chicago, IL: University of Chicago Press.

Derrida, J. (1978b) *Writing and Difference* (translated by A. Bass). London: Routledge.

Derrida, J. (1980) *The Archaeology of the Frivolous: Reading Condillac.* Pittsburgh, PA: Duquesne University Press.

Derrida, J. (1981) *Dissemination* (translated by B. Johnson). London: Athlone Press.

Derrida, J. (1982) *On the Margins of Philosophy* (translated by A. Bass). Brighton: Harvester.

Derrida, J. (1987) *The Truth in Painting* (translated by G. Bennington and I. McLeod). Chicago, IL: University of Chicago Press.

Derrida, J. (1988) *Limited Inc.* Evanston, IL: Northwestern University Press.

Derrida, J. (1990) Some statements and truisms about neologisms, postisms, parasitisms and other small seisisms, in D. Carroll (ed.) *The States of 'Theory': History, Art and Critical Discourse.* New York: Columbia University Press.

Derrida, J. (1996) *As if* I were dead: an interview with Jacques Derrida, in J. Brannigan, R. Robbins and J. Wolfreys (eds) *Applying: To Derrida.* London: Macmillan.

Derrida, J. (1998) *Resistances of Psychoanalysis* (translated by P. Kamuf, P.-A. Briault and M. Naas). Stanford, CA: Stanford University Press.

DES (Department of Education and Science) (1988) *English for Ages 5–11*. London: HMSO.

DES (Department of Education and Science) (1989) *English for Ages 5–16* (The 'Cox Report'). London: HMSO.

DfE (Department for Education) (1993) *English for Ages 5–16*. London: HMSO.

DfE (Department for Education) (1995) *English in the National Curriculum*. London: HMSO.

DfEE (Department for Education and Employment) (1999) *Teachers*, Issue 1, Spring.

DfEE (Department for Education and Employment) (2000) *National Literacy Strategy: Glossary of Terms*, http://www.standards.dfee.gov.uk/literacy/

Douglas, M. (1970) *Purity and Danger: An Analysis of Concepts of Pollution and Taboo*. Harmondsworth: Penguin.

Drew, P. and Heritage, J. (eds) (1992) *Talk at Work: Interaction in Institutional Settings*. Cambridge: Cambridge University Press.

Ebert, T. (1996) *Ludic Feminism and After*. Ann Arbor, MI: University of Michigan Press.

Edwards, A.D. and Furlong, V.J. (1978) *The Language of Teaching*. London: Heinemann.

Edwards, D. (1996) *Discourse and Cognition*. London: Sage.

Edwards, D. and Mercer, N. (1987) *Common Knowledge: The Development of Understanding in the Classroom*. London: Routledge.

Elam, D. (1994) *Feminism and Deconstruction: Ms en Abyme*. London: Routledge.

Elbaz, F. (1983) *Teacher Thinking: A Study of Practical Knowledge*. London: Croom Helm.

Eliot, G. (1994) *Middlemarch*. Harmondsworth: Penguin.

Elliott, J. (1991) *Action Research for Educational Change*. Buckingham: Open University Press.

Esty, J.D. (1999) Excremental postcolonialism, *Contemporary Literature*, 40: 22–59.

Fabian, J. (1983) *Time and the Other: How Anthropology Makes its Object*. New York: Columbia University Press.

Fairclough, N. (1992) *Discourse and Social Change*. Cambridge: Polity Press.

Fairclough, N. (1995) *Critical Discourse Analysis: The Critical Study of Language*. London: Longman.

Fairclough, N. (2000) *New Labour, New Language?* London: Routledge.

Fanon, F. (1986) *Black Skin, White Masks*. London: Pluto.

Feder, E.K., Rawlinson, M.C. and Zakin, E. (eds) (1997) *Derrida and Feminism: Recasting the Question of Woman*. London: Routledge.

Fine, M. (1994) Working the hyphens: reinventing self and other in qualitative research, in N.K. Denzin and Y.S. Lincoln (eds) *Handbook of Qualitative Research*. Thousand Oaks, CA: Sage.

Foucault, M. (1972) *The Archaeology of Knowledge*. London: Tavistock.

Foucault, M. (1979) *Discipline and Punish: The Birth of the Prison* (translated by A. Sheridan). Harmondsworth: Penguin.

Foucault, M. (1980) *Power/Knowledge: Selected Interviews and Other Writings 1972–77 by Michel Foucault* (edited by C. Gordon). London: Harvester Wheatsheaf.

French, P. and MacLure, M. (eds) (1981) *Adult–Child Conversation at Home and at School*. London: Croom Helm.

Fuller, G. (2000) The textual politics of good intentions: critical theory and semiotics, in A. Lee and C. Poynton (eds) *Culture and Text: Discourse and Methodology in Social Research and Cultural Studies*. Lanham, MD: Rowman & Littlefield.

Galton, M. (1998) Review of Sanger 'The Compleat Observer', *Educational Research*, 40(1): 111–14.

Garfinkel, H. (1967) *Studies in Ethnomethodology*. Englewood Cliffs, NJ: Prentice-Hall.

Gates, H.L. (1988) *Signifying Monkey: A Theory of African–American Literacy Criticism*. New York: Oxford University Press.

Gee, J.P. (1992) *The Social Mind: Language, Ideology and Social Practice*. New York: Bergin & Garvey.

Gee, J.P. (1999) *An Introduction to Discourse Analysis*. London: Routledge.

Geertz, C. (1983) *Local Knowledge: Further Essays in Interpretive Anthropology*. New York: Basic Books.

Geertz, C. (1988) *Works and Lives: The Anthropologist as Author*. Cambridge: Polity Press.

Georgakopoulou, A. and Goutsos, D. (1997) *Discourse Analysis: An Introduction*. Edinburgh: Edinburgh University Press.

Gilbert, P. (1989) *Writing, Schooling and Deconstruction: From Voice to Text in the Classroom*. London: Routledge.

Giroux, H. (1992) Language, difference and curriculum theory: beyond the politics of clarity, *Theory into Practice*, 31: 219–27.

Goodson, I. (1995) The story so far: personal knowledge and the political, in J.A. Hatch and R. Wisniewsky (eds) *Life History and Narrative*. London: Falmer Press.

Goodson, I. and Medway, P. (1990) Bringing English to order: introduction, in I. Goodson and P. Medway (eds) *Bringing English to Order: The History and Politics of a School Subject*. Lewes: Falmer Press.

Goodson, I. and Sikes, P. (2000) *Life History Research in Educational Settings*. Buckingham: Open University Press.

Goodson, I. and Walker, R. (1991) *Biography, Identity and Schooling: Episodes in Educational Research*. London: Falmer Press.

Green, B. (1994) Editorial, *Australian Educational Researcher*, 21(3): i–iv.

Green, B. (1998) Born again teaching? Governmentality, 'grammar', and public schooling, in T.S. Popkewitz and M. Brennan (eds) *Foucault's Challenge: Discourse, Knowledge, and Power in Education*. New York: Teachers College Press.

Grice, H.P. (1975) Logic and conversation, in P. Cole and J.L. Morgan (eds) *Syntax and Semantics*. New York: Academic Press.

Gurevtich, Z. (1999) The tongue's break dance: theory, poetry, and the critical body, *Sociological Quarterly*, 40(3): 525–40.

Habermas, J. (1986) *The Theory of Communicative Action, Vol. 1: Reason and the Rationalization of Society*. Cambridge: Polity Press.

Hammersley, M. (1977) School learning: on the cultural resources required by pupils to answer a teacher's question, in P. Woods and M. Hammersley (eds) *School Knowledge: Explorations in the Sociology of Education*. London: Croom Helm.

Hammersley, M. (1997) On the foundations of critical discourse analysis, *Language and Communication*, 17(3): 237–48.

Hammersley, M. (1999) Not bricolage but boatbuilding: exploring two metaphors for thinking about ethnography, *Journal of Contemporary Ethnography*, 28: 574–85.

Haraway, D. (1992) Ecce homo, ain't (ar'n't) I a woman, and inappropriate/d others: the human in a post-humanist landscape, in J. Butler and J. Scott (eds) *Feminists Theorize the Political*. London: Routledge.

Haraway, D. (1995) Writing, literacy, and technology: toward a cyborg writing, in G. Olson and E. Hirsch (eds) *Women Writing Culture*. New York: SUNY Press.

Hargreaves, A. (1994) *Changing Teachers, Changing Times*. London: Cassell.

Hargreaves, D. (1967) *Social Relations in a Secondary School*. London: Routledge & Kegan Paul.

Heap, J. (1985) Ethnomethodology and education: possibilities, *Journal of Educational Thought* (Forum Section).

Heath, C. (1992) The delivery and reception of diagnosis in the general-practice consultation, in P. Drew and J. Heritage (eds) *Talk at Work: Interaction in Institutional Settings*. Cambridge: Cambridge University Press.

Henriques, J., Hollway, W., Urwin, C., Venn, C. and Walkerdine, V. (1998) *Changing the Subject: Psychology, Subjectivity and Social Regulation*, 2nd edn. London, Routledge.

Heritage, J. (1984) *Garfinkel and Ethnomethodology*. Cambridge: Polity Press.

Hernandez, G. (1995) Multiple subjectivities and strategic positionalities: Zora Neale Hurston's experimental ethnographies, in R. Behar and D. Gordon (eds) *Women Writing Culture*. Berkeley, CA: UCLA Press.

Hillage, J., Pearson, R., Anderson, A. and Tamkin, P. (1998) *Excellence in Research on Schools*, DfEE Publications. London: HMSO.

Honey, J. (1983) *The Language Trap: Race, Class and the Standard English Issue in British Schools*. London: National Council for Educational Standards.

Huberman, A.M. (1993) *The Lives of Teachers*. New York: Teachers College Press.

Hurston, Z.N. (1978a) *Mules and Men*. Bloomington, IN: Indiana University Press.

Hurston, Z.N. (1978b) *Their Eyes were Watching God*. Bloomington, IN: Indiana University Press.

Hutchby, I. and Wooffitt, R. (1998) *Conversation Analysis: An Introduction*. Cambridge: Polity Press.

Hymes, D. (1972) On communicative competence, in J.B. Pride and J. Holmes (eds) *Sociolinguistics*. Harmondsworth: Penguin.

Jayyusi, L. (1984) *Categorisation and the Moral Order*. London: Routledge.

Johnson, B. (1987) *A World of Difference*. Baltimore, MD: Johns Hopkins University Press.

Johnson, B. (1995) Writing, in F. Lentricchia and T. McLaughlin (eds) *Critical Terms for Literary Study*, 2nd edn. Chicago, IL: University of Chicago Press.

Johnson, B. (1998) *The Feminist Difference*. Cambridge, MA: Harvard University Press.

Kavanagh, J. (1995) Ideology, in F. Lentricchia and T. McLaughlin (eds) *Critical Terms for Literary Study*, 2nd edn. Chicago, IL: University of Chicago Press.

Kelman, J. (1995) *How Late It Was, How Late*.

Keogh, J. (1992) Identity, ideology and power: a study of parent–teacher interviews, unpublished M.Ed. dissertation. Victoria: University of Wellington.

Kipling, R. ([1902] 1994) *Just So Stories*. London: Puffin.

Kirby, V. (1997) *Telling Flesh: The Substance of the Corporeal*. London: Routledge.

Krauss, R. (1993) *The Optical Unconscious*. Cambridge, MA: MIT Press.

Kress, G. (1990) Critical discourse analysis, *Annual Review of Applied Linguistics*, 11: 84–99.

Kress, G. (1985) *Linguistic Processes in Sociocultural Practice*. Geelong, VIC: Deakin University Press.

Kristeva, J. (1982) *Powers of Horror: An Essay on Abjection*. New York: Columbia University Press.

Kushner, S. (1985) *Working Dreams: Innovation in a Conservatoire*. Norwich: Centre for Applied Research in Education.

Kvale, S. (1996) *Interviews: An Introduction to Qualitative Research Interviewing*. London: Sage.

Lacan, J. (1977) *Ecrits: A Selection* (trans. A. Sheridan). New York: Norton.

Lacey, C. (1970) *Hightown Grammar: The School as a Social System*. Manchester: Manchester University Press.

Lakoff, G. and Johnson, M. (1980) *Metaphors We Live By*. Chicago, IL: University of Chicago Press.

Lankshear, C. (1987) *Literacy, Schooling and Revolution*. London: Falmer Press.

Lather, P. (1991) *Getting Smart: Feminist Research and Pedagogy with/in the Postmodern*. London: Routledge.

Lather, P. (1996a) Troubling clarity: the politics of accessible language, *Harvard Educational Review*, 66(3): 525–54.

Lather, P. (1996b) Methodology as subversive repetition: practices towards a feminist double science. Paper presented to the *Annual Meeting of the American Educational Research Association*, New York, April.

Lather, P. and Smithies, C. (1997) *Troubling the Angels: Women Living With HIV/ AIDS*. Boulder, CO: Westview Press.

Latour, B. (1986) Writing science – fact and fiction, in M. Callon, J. Law and A. Rip (eds) *Mapping the Dynamics of Science and Technology*. London: Macmillan.

Latour, B. and Woolgar, S. (1979) *Laboratory Life: The Construction of Scientific Facts*. Beverley Hills, CA: Sage.

Lee, A. and Poynton, C. (eds) (2000) *Culture and Text: Discourse and Methodology in Social Research and Cultural Studies*. Lanham, MD: Rowman & Littlefield.

Lemke, J. (1995) *Textual Politics*. London: Taylor & Francis.

Lepore, J. (2001) Wigwam words, *American Scholar*, Winter, pp. 97–108.

Levine, C. (1998) Seductive reflexivity: Ruskin's dreaded *trompe l'oeil, Journal of Aesthetics and Art Criticism*, 56(4): 366–75.

Lewis, B. (1992) *ESRC-InTER Programme: Dissemination Seminars 1992*. Lancaster: University of Lancaster, mimeo.

Lofland, J. (1974) Styles of reporting qualitative field research, *American Sociologist*, 9: 101–11.

Luke, A. (1995) Text and discourse in education: an introduction to critical discourse analysis, *Review of Research in Education*, 21: 3–47.

Luke, A. and Gilbert, P. (eds) (1993) *Literacy in Contexts: Australian Perspectives and Issues*. Sydney, NSW: Allen & Unwin.

Luke, C. and Gore, J. (eds) (1992) *Feminisms and Critical Pedagogy*. New York: Routledge.

Lupton, D. (1995) Postmodernism and critical discourse, *Discourse and Society*, 6(2): 302–4.

Lutz, C. (1995) The gender of theory, in R. Behar and D. Gordon (eds) *Women Writing Culture*. Berkeley, CA: UCLA Press.

Macbeth, A. (1989) *Involving Parents*. Oxford: Heinemann.

Macdonell, D. (1986) *Theories of Discourse: An Introduction.* Oxford: Blackwell.

MacLure, M. (1993) *The Groupwork with Computers Programme: A Case Study.* Report to ESRC as part of the Independent Evaluation of the ESRC InTer Initiative. Norwich: Centre for Applied Research in Education, mimeo.

MacLure, M. (1994a) The embrace of uncertainty: language and discourse (Review Essay), *British Journal of Sociology of Education,* 15(2): 283–300.

MacLure, M. (1994b) Language at home and at school, in *Encyclopedia of Language and Linguistics.* London: Pergamon Press.

MacLure, M. (1994c) Talking in class: rationales for the rise of oracy in the UK, in J. Maybin and B. Stierer (eds) *Language, Literacy and Learning in Educational Practice.* Clevedon: Multilingual Matters.

MacLure, M. and Pettigrew, M. (1996) *The Press, Public Knowledge and Education.* End of Award Report to the Economic and Social Research Council. Norwich: Centre for Applied Research in Education, mimeo.

MacLure, M. and Stronach, I. (1993) Great accidents in history: vocationalist innovations, the National Curriculum and pupil identity, in J. Wellington (ed.) *The Work-Related Curriculum.* London: Kogan Page.

MacLure, M. and Walker, B. (1999) *Secondary School Parents Evenings: A Qualitative Study.* End of Award Report to the Economic and Social Research Council. Norwich: Centre for Applied Research in Education (available at http://www.uea.ac.uk/care/research/parents.html).

Mascia-Lees, F., Sharpe, P. and Cohen, C. (1989) The postmodernist turn in anthropology: a feminist perspective, *Signs,* 15: 7–33.

Maybin, J. (2001) Language, struggle and voice: the Bakhtin/Volosinov writings, in M. Wetherell, S. Taylor and S.J. Yates (eds) *Discourse Theory and Practice: A Reader.* London: Sage.

McCoy, K. (2000) White noise – the sound of epidemic: reading/writing a climate of intelligibility around the 'crisis' of difference, in E.A. St. Pierre and W. Pillow (eds) *Working the Ruins: Feminist Poststructural Theory and Methods in Education.* New York: Routledge.

McHoul, A.W. (1978) The organization of formal talk in the classroom, *Language in Society,* 7: 183–213.

McHoul, A.W. and Luke, A. (1989) Discourse as language and politics: an introduction to the philology of political culture in Australia, *Journal of Pragmatics,* 13: 323–32.

McKernan, J. (1991) *Curriculum Action Research: A Handbook of Methods and Resources for the Reflective Practitioner.* London: Kogan Page.

McWilliam, E. (1993) 'Post' haste: plodding research and galloping theory, *British Journal of Sociology of Education,* 14: 199–205.

Michaels, S. (1981) 'Sharing time': children's narrative styles and differential access to literacy, *Language in Society,* 10: 423–42.

Mills, S. (1997) *Discourse.* London: Routledge.

Morley, L. and Rassool, N. (1999) *School Effectiveness: Fracturing the Discourse.* London: Falmer Press.

NCC (National Curriculum Council) (1992) *National Curriculum English: The Case for Revising the Order.* York: National Curriculum Council.

Nespor, J. and Barber, L. (1991) The rhetorical construction of the teacher, *Harvard Educational Review,* 61(4): 417–85.

Nias, J. (1981) Highstones: mirror images and reflections, in *Case Studies in School Accountability*, Vol. II. Cambridge: Cambridge Accountability Project, mimeo.

Parker, L. (1998) Race is . . . race ain't: an exploration of the utility of critical race theory in qualitative research in education, *International Journal of Qualitative Studies in Education*, 11: 43–57.

Payne, C. and Cuff, E. (eds) (1982) *Doing Teaching: The Practical Management of Classrooms*. London: Batsford.

Pennycook, A. (1994) Incommensurable discourses?, *Applied Linguistics*, 15(2): 115–37.

Pettigrew, M. and MacLure, M. (1997) The press, public knowledge and grant-maintained schools, *British Journal of Educational Studies*, 45(4): 392–405.

Pigiaki, P. (1995) The disorientation of David Hargreaves' proposals for educational reform: a critique, *Educational Review*, 47(3): 289–97.

Popkewitz, T.S. and Brennan, M. (eds) (1997) *Foucault's Challenge: Discourse, Knowledge, and Power in Education*. New York: Teacher's College Press.

Poulson, L. (1996) Accountability: a key-word in the discourse of educational reform, *Journal of Education Policy*, 11: 580–92.

Poynton, C. (2000) Linguistics and discourse analysis, in A. Lee and C. Poynton (eds) *Culture and Text: Discourse and Methodology in Social Research and Cultural Studies*. Lanham, MD: Rowman & Littlefield.

Pratt, M.L. (1986) Fieldwork in common places, in J. Clifford and G.E. Marcus (eds) *Writing Culture*. Berkeley, CA: University of California Press.

Poynton, C. and Lee, A. (2000) Culture and text: an introduction, in A. Lee and C. Poynton (eds) *Culture and Text: Discourse and Methodology in Social Research and Cultural Studies*. Lanham, MD: Rowman & Littlefield.

Rambo Ronai, C. (1998) Sketching with Derrida: an ethnography of a researcher/ erotic dancer, *Qualitative Inquiry*, 4(3): 405–21.

Rambo Ronai, C. (1999) The next night 'sous rature': wrestling with Derrida's mimesis, *Qualitative Inquiry*, 5(1): 114–29.

Rikowski, G. and McLaren, P. (1999) Postmodernism and educational theory, in D. Hill, P. McLaren, M. Cole and G. Rikowski (eds) *Postmodernism in Educational Theory*. London: Tufnell Press.

Rorty, R. (1978) Philosophy as a kind of writing: an essay on Derrida, *New Literary History*, 10(1): 141–60.

Sacks, H. (1974) On the analyzability of stories by children, in R. Turner (ed.) *Ethnomethodology: Selected Readings*. Harmondsworth: Penguin.

Sacks, H. (1984) On doing 'being ordinary', in J.M. Atkinson and J. Heritage (eds) *Structures of Social Action*. Cambridge: Cambridge University Press.

Sacks, H. (1992) *Lectures on Conversation*, Vols 1 and 2 (edited by G. Jefferson). Oxford: Blackwell.

Sacks, H., Schegloff, E.A. and Jefferson, G. (1974) A simplest systematics for the organization of turn-taking for conversation, *Language*, 50(4): 696–735.

Sampson, G. (1925) *English for the English: A Chapter on National Education*. Cambridge: Cambridge University Press.

Sanjek, R. (1990) *Fieldnotes: The Making of Anthropology*. Ithaca, NY: Cornell University Press.

SCAA (Schools Curriculum and Assessment Authority) (1994) *English in the National Curriculum: Draft Proposals* (The 'Dearing Review'). London: HMSO.

Scheurich, J.J. (1997) *Research Method in the Postmodern*. London: Falmer Press.

Scheurich, J.J. (2000) A RoUGH, ramBling, strAnGe, muDDy, CONfusing, elLIPtical Kut: from an archaeology of plain talk, *Qualitative Inquiry*, 6(3): 337–48.

Shapiro, M. (2001) Textualizing global politics, in M. Wetherell, S. Taylor and S.J. Yates (eds) *Discourse Theory and Practice: A Reader*. London: Sage.

Shiffrin, D. (1994) *Approaches to Discourse*. Oxford: Blackwell.

Shostak, M. (1981) *Nisa: The Life and words of a !Kung Woman*. New York: Random House.

Showalter, E. (1987) Critical cross-dressing: male feminism and the woman of the year, in A. Jardine and P. Smith (eds) *Men in Feminism*. New York: Methuen.

Sikes, P. (1997) *Parents Who Teach: Stories from Home and from School*. London: Cassells.

Sikes, P., Measor, L. and Woods, P. (1985) *Teacher Careers: Crises and Continuities*. Lewes: Falmer Press.

Silverman, D. (1987) *Communication and Medical Practice*. London: Sage.

Sinclair, J.M. and Coulthard, M. (1975) *Towards an Analysis of Discourse: The English Used by Teachers and Pupils*. London: Oxford University Press.

Smith, R. (1995) *Derrida and Autobiography*. Cambridge: Cambridge University Press.

Spivak, G.C. (1976) Preface, in J. Derrida, *Of Grammatology* (translated by G.C. Spivak). Baltimore, MD: Johns Hopkins University Press.

Spivak, G.C. (1993) *Outside in the Teaching Machine*. London: Routledge.

Sprinkler, M. (ed.) (1999) *Ghostly Demarcations. A Symposium on Jacques Derrida's Specters of Marx*. London: Verso.

St Pierre, E.A. and Pillow, W. (eds) (2000) *Working the Ruins: Feminist Poststructural Theory and Methods in Education*. New York: Routledge.

Stanley, L. and Wise, S. (1990) *Feminist Praxis: Research, Theory and Epistemology in Feminist Sociology*. London: New York.

Steedman, C. (1986) *Landscape for a Good Woman*. London: Virago.

Stenhouse, L. (1975) *An Introduction to Curriculum Development and Research*. London: Heinemann.

Stubbs, M. (1989) *Language and Literacy: The Sociolinguistics of Reading and Writing*. London: Routledge.

Strathern, M. (2000) The tyranny of transparency, *British Educational Research Journal*, 26(3): 309–21.

Stronach, I. (1988) Vocationalism and economic recovery: the case against witch-craft, in S. Brown and R. Wake (eds) *Education in Transition*. Edinburgh: Scottish Council for Reseach in Education.

Stronach, I. (1999) Shouting theatre in a crowded fire: 'educational effectiveness' as cultural performance, *Evaluation*, 5(2): 173–93.

Stronach, I. and Macdonald, B. (1991) *Faces and Futures: The Second Interim Report of the InTER Evaluation*. Norwich: Centre for Applied Research in Education, mimeo.

Stronach, I. and MacLure, M. (1997) *Educational Research Undone: The Postmodern Embrace*. Buckingham: Open University Press.

Swain, H. and Williams, L. (2000) David Hargreaves, *Times Higher Education Supplement*, 28 April, p. 8.

Taussig, M. (1993) *Mimesis and Alterity: A Particular History of the Senses*. London: Routledge.

Ten Have, P. (1991) Talk and institution: a reconsideration of the 'asymmetry' of doctor–patient interaction, in D. Boden and D. Zimmerman (eds) *Talk and Social Structure: Studies in Ethnomethodology and Conversation Analysis*. Cambridge: Cambridge University Press.

Thomas, D. (1993) Empirical authors, liminal texts and model readers: a response to 'Managing marginality', *British Educational Research Journal*, 19(5): 467–74.

Threadgold, T. (2000) Poststructuralism and discourse analysis, in A. Lee and C. Poynton (eds) *Culture and Text: Discourse and Methodology in Social Research and Cultural Studies*. Lanham, MD: Rowman & Littlefield.

Tierney, W. (ed.) (1999) Queer frontiers: qualitative research and queer theory. Special issue of *Qualitative Studies in Education*, 12(5).

Toolan, M. (ed.) (2002) *Critical Discourse Analysis*. London: Routledge.

Torrance, H. and Pryor, J. (1998) *Investigating Formative Assessment: Teaching, Learning and Assessment in the Classroom*. Buckingham: Open University Press.

Tough, J. (1977) *The Development of Meaning*. London: George Allen & Unwin.

Travers, A. (1991) From 'normal appearances' to 'simulation' in interaction, *Journal for the Theory of Social Behaviour*, 21(3): 297–338.

Travers, A. (1993) An essay on self and camp, *Theory, Culture & Society*, 10(1): 127–43.

Trinh, T. Minh-ha (1989) *Woman, Native, Other*. Bloomington, IN: Indiana University Press.

Van Dijk, T. (1997) *Discourse Studies: A Multidisciplinary Introduction*. Thousand Oaks, CA: Sage.

Van Dijk, T. (2001) Principles of critical discourse analysis, in M. Wetherell, S. Taylor and S.J. Yates (eds) *Discourse Theory and Practice: A Reader*. London: Sage.

Walker, B. (1998) Meetings without communication: a study of parents' evenings in secondary schools, *British Educational Research Journal*, 24(2): 163–78.

Walkerdine, V. (1988) *The Mastery of Reason: Cognitive Development and the Production of Rationality*. London: Routledge.

Walkerdine, V. (1990) *Schoolgirl Fictions*. London: Verso.

Watson, R. (1992) Ethnomethodology, conversation analysis and education: an overview, *International Review of Education*, 38(3): 257–74.

Wells, C.G. (ed.) (1981) *Learning Through Interaction*. Cambridge: Cambridge University Press.

Wetherell, M., Taylor, S. and Yates, S.J. (eds) (2001) *Discourse Theory and Practice: A Reader*. London: Sage.

Widdowson, H. (1995) Review of N. Fairclough 'Discourse and Social Change', *Applied Linguistics*, 16(4): 510–16.

Woodhead, C. (1998) Academia gone to seed, *New Statesman*, 20 March, pp. 51–2.

Woods, P. (1985) Conversations with teachers: some aspects of life history method, *British Educational Research Journal*, 11(1): 13–26.

Woods, P. (1993a) Managing marginality: teacher development through grounded life history, *British Educational Research Journal*, 19(5): 447–65.

Woods. P.J. (1993b) Keys to the past – and to the future: the empirical author replies, *British Educational Research Journal*, 19(5): 475–88.

Zeller, N. and Farmer, F.M. (1999) 'Catchy, clever titles are not acceptable': style, APA, and qualitative reporting, *International Journal of Qualitative Studies in Education*, 12(1): 3–20.

Zizek, S. (1991) *Looking Awry: An Introduction to Jacques Lacan through Popular Culture*. Cambridge, MA: MIT Press.

Zorbaugh, H.W. (1929) *The Gold Coast and the Slum*. Chicago, IL: University of Chicago Press.

Index

abject, 40–3
accent, 36–8, 40–1
action research, 4, 12, 15, 16, 100, 101–2, 114
Agard, J., 46–7
analysis, 43–4, 110–20, 127–8, 159
arrival narratives, 87, 95–6, 156
'asymmetrical talk', 50, 64
Atkinson, P., 81, 84, 87, 89
Attridge, D., 102
Austin, J.L., 182
authenticity, 114–15, 119–21, 127, 143, 157, 165

Babcock, B., 137, 141–2
Baker, C., 48, 49, 54, 58, 68, 189
Bakhtin, M., 16, 20, 34
Bal, M., 153, 159, 172, 190
Ball, S.J., 11, 14, 24, 25, 74, 75, 78, 178, 179, 185
Barnes, D., 184
Barthes, R., 81, 117, 128, 159, 174
Bassey, M., 107, 109
Bates, I., 179
Baudrillard, J., 151, 153, 154, 167, 180
Behar, R., 137, 141
'being there', 84–5
Belsey, C., 90, 93
Benedict, R., 137
Benjamin, W., 21, 155, 156, 172–3

Bernstein, B., 4, 37
Bhabha, H., 96–7, 146
bias, 72, 73, 74, 79, 81, 120–1
binary oppositions, 9–11, 12, 15, 27, 42, 66, 67, 73–7, 79, 103, 105–6, 122, 126, 131, 144, 151, 160, 165, 172, 178, 179, 181, 186, 190, 204
biographical research, see life history research
body, 40–3
boundaries
    blurring of, 4, 7, 8, 42–3, 87–8, 95, 112–13, 131, 137–8, 149–50, 157, 172, 191
    maintenance of, 27, 42–3, 64, 67–8, 83, 91–2, 113
Bowie, M., 106
Braidotti, R., 135, 142–3
Brice Heath, S., 177, 184
British Educational Research Association (BERA), 108
Britzman, D., 170, 174
Bryson, N., 150, 154, 156
Buffy the Vampire Slayer, 167
Butler, J., 41, 42, 45, 46, 133
Butt, R., 115, 120–1, 132
Button, G., 56

Calvino, I., 1–3, 167
    Mrs. Ph(i)Nk$_0$, 1–3, 13, 17, 96, 106

Cameron, D., 17, 36, 182
camp self, 132, 157, 161, 171
'child', discursive construction of, 4,
    17–20
Clandinin, J., 100
clarity, 27, 37, 40, 44, 114, 116–18,
    146, 168, 169–70, 171
classroom, discursive construction of,
    13–17, 173
'cleverness', 7, 110–11
    see also frivolity
Clifford, J., 85, 90, 91, 136–7, 141,
    146
Clough, P., 94
Cohen, M., 173
colloquial language, 115
colonialism, 34, 36, 45, 96–9, 103,
    104, 114, 117, 146
    see also postcoloniality
conversation analysis, 48–9, 68,
    188–90
Cox Report, 23, 24, 26, 27, 28, 36, 37
Crapanzano, V., 84
'crisis of representation', 4, 150
critical discourse analysis (CDA), 102,
    186–7
cross-dressing (theoretical), 136,
    141–4, 147–8
Crowley, T., 24, 31, 34, 39
Crozier, G., 65, 179
Culler, J., 110, 113, 180, 181
culture
    Roman, 150
    textual construction of, 91–2, 99

Davies, B., 187
De Lauretis, T., 94
De Lillo, D., 140, 157, 158
DeCastell, S.C., 187
deconstruction, 21, 77, 82, 118,
    124–6, 134, 135, 142, 143, 148,
    150, 163, 168–73, 179–80, 202
déjouer, 163, 172–3
Derrida, J., 3, 7, 10, 13, 17, 43–4, 81,
    99, 101–2, 103, 106, 109–10,
    111–12, 113, 115, 117, 124–9,
    142, 143, 153, 165–6, 168, 174,
    179, 189

Desbordes-Valmore, M., 139
DfEE (Department for Education and
    Employment), 7
dialects, non-standard, 25–31, 117
différance, 3–4, 10, 115, 135, 142,
    169, 170, 179
difference, 3, 7, 10, 17–18, 27, 28,
    38, 96–9, 106, 112–13, 116,
    138, 156, 158, 164–6, 170, 172,
    175–6
    see also writing, différance
discipline, 176
disconcertion, 156
discourse
    Anglo-American vs European
        traditions, 174, 187, 189, 190
    definitions, 175
    'discourse of derision', 11, 12
    'discourse of disgust', 22, 33–6,
        40–3, 44, 45
    and reality, see language and reality
discourse analysis, 6, 10, 23, 68, 79,
    134
    and classroom research, 183–4
    linguistic discourse analysis, 182–7
    see also critical discourse analysis,
        Foucault
discourse-based orientation to
    research, 9, 12, 20, 68
discourse communities, 116–17
discursive literacy, 5–9, 79
dissemination, 103, 142
double binds, 58, 64–6, 126–7, 136,
    137, 141, 146
doubles, 150, 151, 161, 165
Drew, P., 49, 50

Edwards, A.D., 184
Edwards, D., 4, 184
Elbaz, F., 100
Elliott, J., 100
Enlightenment, 17, 41, 90, 172, 174,
    179, 187
entanglement, 5, 7, 42, 127, 153,
    156, 168, 95
'eternal feminine', 139, 140
ethnographic guilt, 97
ethnographic present, 90–1

ethnomethodology, 188
experience, discursive construction of, 18–19

Fabian, J., 90
fabrication, 5, 9, 23, 43–4, 73, 80, 81, 83, 85, 88, 101, 104, 110, 119–20, 127–8, 131–2, 172, 176, 190
Fairclough, N., 25, 29, 33, 37, 77, 102, 179, 186
feminist discourses, 46, 94
feminist methodology and theory, 94, 98, 99–100, 114, 133–47, 181
fictional (in opposition to real), 79, 110
field, discursive construction of, 84–5
Fine, M., 4, 99
Foucault, M., 20, 49, 66, 68, 174, 175, 176–9, 185
framing, 90, 91–2, 95, 103, 147
frivolity, 73, 74, 110–13, 114, 117, 152–3, 154
Fuller, G., 98

Garfinkel, H., 188
Gee, J., 175, 176–7, 187
Geertz, C., 84, 86, 87–8, 111, 137, 180
Ghisbrechts, C., 151–2
Giroux, H., 117
Goodson, I., 39, 100, 114, 148
Green, B., 14, 38–9, 134
Grice, P., 183
Gurevitch, Z., 40, 41, 45–6

Habermas, J., 115, 187
Hammersley, M., 7, 112, 187
Haraway, D., 117, 120, 145
Hargreaves, A., 148
Hargreaves, D., 72, 73, 74, 75, 78, 88–92, 161
Heath, C., 55
Heritage, J., 49, 189
Hernandez, G., 137, 138, 139
home–school relations, 48, 67
Huberman, M., 121

humanism, 145
Hurston, Z.N., 137, 138–9
hymen, 142
Hymes, D., 183

identity, 3, 8–9, 11, 17–19, 49, 54–5, 62, 66, 67, 85, 120, 128–32, 157, 162
in colonial/postcolonial contexts, 96–9
and gender, 17, 137
national identity, 23, 24, 45
innocence, critique of, 12, 80, 85, 88, 94, 95, 103–4, 116, 145–6, 169, 181
inside/outside, 15–17, 42, 86, 90, 99–104, 113, 126, 137
institutional talk, 48, 50, 56
institutions and discourse, 5, 16, 49, 68, 176, 178
interpellation (Althusser), 93
intertextuality, 6, 23, 72, 73, 79, 83, 92–5, 104
interviews, 115, 119–21, 156–7

jargon, 7, 74, 75, 107, 108, 111, 114, 117
Jayyusi, L., 55–7, 188
Johnson, B., 82, 106, 133, 138–41, 144–6, 148, 171, 180

Kavanagh, J., 94–5
Keogh, J., 40
Kirby, V., 42, 175, 179
Krauss, R., 163, 172, 173
Kress, G., 91, 186
Kristeva, J., 42–3, 45, 174
Kvale, S., 115, 119

L'Ecole des Femmes, 144
Lacan, J., 17, 136, 165
Lacey, C., 78
Lakoff, G., 120
language
and class, 37–9, 117, 176–7
of New Labour, 6, 12, 77
'plain language', 4, 108, 114, 116–18, 152

and reality, 3, 4, 5, 12, 33, 80–1,
83, 85, 88, 93, 150–1
transparency of, 12, 107, 180
and truth, 163–5
Lankshear, C., 187
Lather, P., 4, 117, 145
Latour, B., 81
Lee, A., 174
Lemke, J., 84, 102
Levine, C., 151–2
Levi-Strauss, C., 102, 174
Lewis, B., 15, 101
life history research, 100, 114,
110–20, 121–4, 126, 127,
132
'linguistic turn', 4, 17, 134
Listen Mr Oxford Don, 46
logocentrism, 10
Luke, A., 5, 8, 18, 176, 182, 185,
186, 187
Lupton, D., 187
Lutz, C., 134, 141

Macdonell, D., 176
MacLure, M., 11, 24, 29, 111, 178,
184, 185
McHoul, A.W., 174, 189
McWilliam, E., 111
Marxism, 181
Mascia-Lees, F., 134
masks, (un)masking, 121, 132, 150,
157
mastery, dilemmas of, 119, 120, 124,
125, 127–8, 131, 146, 153, 154,
168, 182
membership categorization, 54–5,
188, 189
metaphor, 26, 28–9, 40, 108, 119,
120, 121–4, 126, 127–8, 129,
131–2
metaphorization of 'woman', 142
Michaels, S., 177
Mills, S., 178
mimesis, 149, 151, 154–62, 172
mimicry, 144, 171
in postcolonial contexts, 97, 146,
154–6
see also mimesis

modernity, 150, 158
Morley, L., 179

National Curriculum, 4, 22–6, 183
nausea, 152, 171
New Right, 25, 38, 179

Ofsted (Office for Standards in
Education), 72
oracy, 184
'Other', 'Otherness', 3, 23, 27, 31,
33–6, 41–2, 44, 67, 74, 90, 91,
96–7, 99, 113, 136, 156, 158,
170–1

Pennycook, A., 174, 178, 182, 185,
187, 190
pharmakon, 106, 125–6, 165
pharmakos, 113
Plato, 109, 126, 168
play, 134, 144, 146, 148, 150–1, 173
postcoloniality, 45, 96–9, 154–5, 158
postmodernism, 77, 106, 111, 112,
134–5, 136, 150, 151
appropriation of the feminine,
133–5, 141–4, 147–8
'postmodern turn', 134, 150
postmodernity, 150
poststructuralism, 17, 21, 111,
134–5, 142, 143, 174–81, 182,
185–6
Poulson, L., 179
power
and discourse, 9, 37, 45, 49, 55–6,
66, 68, 82, 171, 176, 178, 187
in research relationships, 95–9,
100–4, 114–15, 116–17, 120,
124, 127
see also Foucault
Poynton, C., 40, 68, 174, 182, 186,
187, 190
Pratt, M.L., 87, 91, 95, 96, 97, 98,
113
presence, 3, 4, 13, 101, 106, 115,
123, 124, 127, 150, 164, 166–8,
169
'profane illumination', 21, 160,
172–3

progressive education, discourses of, 15, 19, 23, 24–5, 27, 29, 37, 38, 185
'puritan' methodology, 114, 116

racist discourse, 34, 45, 46
Rambo Ronai, C., 129–31
readers, 81, 91, 92
realism, 84, 89, 92–5, 151, 161
'reality effect', 159
reality, textual nature of, 4, 5, 7–11, 151–3, 159, 164, 180
  the 'appeal to the real', 12, 79, 107
researcher–subject relationships, 4, 95–9, 111, 123–4, 127, 128–31, 156–7, 170–1
'reverse citation', 45
  see also Butler, J.
Rorty, R., 109
Ruskin, J., 152

Sacks, H., 188–9
Sanjek, R., 159
Saussure, F., 20, 174, 175
Scheurich, J., 37, 116
Searle, J., 182
self, self-hood, *see* identity, subjectivity
Shapiro, M., 179
shock, 154, 173
Shostak, M., 88–92, 95–9, 103
Sikes, P., 12, 67
Silverman, D., 64
Simpsons, The, 5
simulation, 150, 157, 158, 164
Sinclair, J., 182
Smith, R., 108, 154, 163
speech acts, 182
Spivak, G.C., 123, 143, 146, 147, 164, 165
St Pierre, E., 181
standard English
  and economic prosperity, 22, 24, 30, 39
  and literary values, 22
  and moral values, 22–3
  in the National Curriculum, 22–6
  and national identity, 22, 24, 39
  and social order, 22, 31, 117

Stanley, L., 135
Stenhouse, L., 100
Strathern, M., 169, 171
Stronach, I., 7, 13, 39, 81, 83, 134
structuralism, 175–6, 189
subject position, 2, 17–18
subjectivity, discursive constitution of, 17–19, 34, 41–3, 45, 49, 67, 68, 136, 139–40, 143, 145, 176–7, 180
supplement, 124–6
surrealism, 172–3

Taussig, M., 154–6, 158, 160, 163, 170, 171
textual authority, 82, 84–5, 86, 87
textuality, 5, 8, 43–4, 80, 81, 104, 111, 117, 179
  etymology ('textile', texture', 'tissue' etc.), 43, 120, 127–8
Threadgold, T., 20, 178, 185
Toolan, M., 187
trace, 142, 191
transparency, *see* clarity
Travers, A., 131–2, 157, 171
trickster, as a postmodern figure, 138
Trinh, T., 146
trompe l'oeil, 149, 151–2, 153–4, 156, 157, 158, 160
truth, 4, 19, 49, 80, 93, 108, 111, 115, 116, 119, 126, 134, 135, 142, 143, 148, 152–3, 177–8
TTA (Teacher Training Agency), 13, 14, 15
turn taking, 51, 188–9

uncanny (Freud), 180, 181
'undecidables', 142

validity, 123
Van Dijk, T., 186
vernacular accounts, 100
'vernacular' methodology, 114–15
vertigo, 152, 154, 171
'visualism', 91–2
voice, 86, 99–101, 114–15, 119–21, 123, 129, 147–8

Walker, B., 50, 66, 67
Walkerdine, V., 15, 19
Watson, R., 188, 189
weave (of discourse), *see* fabrication
Wells, C.G., 184
women's writing, dismissal of, 133, 135, 136–47
Woodhead, C., 11–12, Chapter 4, 106, 108, 114, 161
Woods, P., 115, 119, 121–3, 124, 125, 161–2
Woods, P.J., 162
Wright, R., 138
Writing Culture, 136–7, 141
writing
  confessional writing, 138, 145
  and deconstruction, 106
  and difference, 165–6
  ethnographic writing, 86, 87, 88–94, 95–9
  instrumental view of writing, 105–6, 169
  'literal' writing, 133, 135, 138, 140–1, 144–6, 172
  and mimesis, 158–9
  and philosophy, 109–11, 113
  proper and improper writing, 107–8, 113–15
  and 'reality', 73, 79, 80–1, 85, 88, 109–10, 115, 116, 153
  and research, 73, 81–2, 86–7, 99–101, 106, 110, 113–15, 165–7
  and speech, 106, 109, 110, 113, 115, 124, 126
  see also supplement, *différance*, *pharmakon*, *pharmakos*, women's writing

Zeller, N., 108, 152
Zorbaugh, H.W., 88–92

NARRATIVES AND FICTIONS IN EDUCATIONAL RESEARCH

Peter Clough

In this bold and very important work, Peter Clough shows how the truths about educational issues can be told using fictional devices. This work legitimates the narrative turn in the human disciplines. He shows educational researchers how narrative inquiry can be used for progressive moral and political purposes.

Norman K. Denzin, University of Illinois at Urbana-Champaign

This compelling book takes a fresh approach to educational research, considering the role and use of literary and ethnographic approaches. There is growing interest in the use of narrative and fictional methods and this book sets out to:

- locate narrative and fictional methods within the traditions of education research;
- exemplify the use of narrative in studies of educational and social settings;
- explain the processes of composing narrative and fictional research.

A distinctive feature of the book is the inclusion of five 'fictional' stories which demonstrate the use of narrative in reporting research. Detailed discussion of these five stories shows how they were created from actual events and the varied role of the author in their creation. The methodological implications of such an approach are considered along with its potential merits and difficulties and its possible uses.

Contents

Preface – The man with the blue guitar – Stories from educational research: an introduction – The map is not the terrain – Klaus – Molly – Rob – Bev – Lolly (the final word) – Hard to tell: the readings of the stories – Narratives of educational practice – To the things themselves – References – Index.

128pp   0 335 20791 X (Paperback)   0 335 20792 8 (Hardback)

UNDERSTANDING, DESIGNING AND CONDUCTING QUALITATIVE RESEARCH IN EDUCATION
FRAMING THE PROJECT

John F. Schostak

- How do I get my research off the ground and ensure that it is 'new', 'novel' and 'important'?
- How do I make sense of data, build theories and write a compelling thesis?
- How can my research bring about change?

This book is more than an introduction to doing research – it aims to help readers identify what is new and important about their project, how their research relates to previous work and how it may be used to bring about change at individual, community, national or even international levels. A total strategy is offered focussing on the notion of the 'project' as an organizing framework that ensures that the methods chosen are appropriate to the subject and aim of the study. The intention throughout is to help readers move from being able to apply methods to being able to interrogate the theoretical underpinnings of particular perspectives so that they can feel confident about the particular kinds of knowledge claim they are making. The book will be important reading for students at Masters and doctoral level and will be particularly helpful for professionals from education, health, social work, criminal justice and business who carry out research in their workplace and who need to reflect upon the consequences and possibilities for action and change.

Contents
Introduction – Finding bearings – Subjects: choices and consequences – The other: its objects and objectivity – Handling complexity and uncertainty – Sense and nonsense – Braving the postmodern, broaching the novel – Being shy of the truth – Framing texts and evidence: con/texts, intertextuality and rhetoric – Framing ethics and political issues – Framing ethical actions – Writing it – Conclusion – Notes – References – Index.

256pp   0 335 20509 7 (Paperback)   0 335 20510 0 (Hardback)

ACTION RESEARCH AND POSTMODERNISM
CONGRUENCE AND CRITIQUE

Tony Brown and Liz Jones

Make something new, Derrida says, that is how deconstruction happens. This book exemplifies such a move in the way it addresses the stuck places of practitioner oriented research with its rational, intentional agents seeking to empower both teacher self and students. An example of putting postmodernism to work in educational research, the book asks hard questions about necessary complicities . . . grounded in nursery teaching and math education, it attempts to develop a better language toward a more complicated understanding of what knowledge means . . . without reverting to the quick and narrow scientism of the past.

Patti Lather, Ohio State University

- How can we move forward from or develop traditional approaches to action research which have dominated teacher research for many years now?
- How can teachers work at improving their teaching when there are so many different understandings of what education is trying to achieve?
- In what ways can post-structuralism, which has had such a major impact in other disciplines, offer practical support to teachers developing their own professional practices?

A premise of much teacher research is that reflection on practice can lead to a development of that practice. Such reflection, it is purported, enables the practitioner in organizing the complexity of the teaching situation, with a particular emphasis on how 'monitoring of change' can be converted to 'control of change'. This book questions the notion of construing developing practice as 'aiming for an ideal' and suggests that such a pursuit has a questionable track record. The very desire for control, and the difficulties encountered in trying to document it, can cloud our vision from the very complexities we seek to capture. The book offers detailed discussion of teacher research enquiries carried out in the context of masters and doctoral degrees. It focuses in particular on how the reflective writing generated by the teacher might build towards an assertion of professional identity through which professional demands are mediated.

Contents

Introduction – Emancipation and postmodernism – Research and the development of practice – Part 1 The hermeneutic backdrop: narrating the researcher – Creating data in practitioner research – Transitions: issues of temporality and practitioner research – On identity – Part 2 The postmodern turn – Deconstructing the nursery classroom – From emancipation to postmodernism: a nursery study – A tale of disturbance – Identity, power and resistance – Deconstructing the nursery classroom: that will undo nicely, but so what? – Transgressive agents: an optimistic possibility? – Conclusion – Critical pedagogy in a postmodern world – Bibliography – Index.

210pp   0 335 20761 8 (Paperback)   0 335 20762 6 (Hardback)